ARCHITECTURAL GRAPHICS
TRADITIONAL AND DIGITAL COMMUNICATION

WITHDRAWN

Glenn Goldman
New Jersey Institute of Technology

Prentice Hall

Upper Saddle River, New Jersey   *Columbus, Ohio*

Library of Congress Cataloging-in-Publication Data

Goldman, Glenn.
    Architectural graphics : traditional and digital communication /
Glenn Goldman.
        p.   cm.
    Includes bibliographical references and index.
    ISBN 0-13-341967-3
    1. Architectural drawing—Technique.
    2. Architectural drawing—Data processing.
    3. Architectural rendering—Technique.
    4. Architectural rendering—Data processing.
    5. Communication in architectural design.
    I. Title.
NA2708.G65   1997
720′.28′4—dc20   96-22585
                                                          CIP

Cover art: Amado Batour
Editor: Ed Francis
Production Editor: Stephen C. Robb
Design Coordinator: Jill E. Bonar
Text Designer: Carlisle Publishers Services
Cover Designer: Brian Deep
Production Manager: Deidra M. Schwartz
Marketing Manager: Danny Hoyt
Production and Editing Coordination: Carlisle Publishers Services

This book was set in Univers and Garamond by Carlisle Communications, Ltd., and was printed and bound by Courier/Kendallville, Inc. The cover was printed by Phoenix Color Corp.

© 1997 by Prentice-Hall, Inc.
Simon & Schuster Company/A Viacom Company
Upper Saddle River, New Jersey 07458

The author and publisher of this book make neither warrantees nor representations of any kind, expressed or implied, with regard to the methods, means, techniques, equipment, software programs (including their effectiveness), or computer hardware mentioned in this book. The author and publisher shall not be liable in any event for incidental or consequential damages in connection with, or arising out of, the use or performance (or lack thereof) of any and all methods, programs, and/or equipment mentioned or described in this book.

Illustration Credits: Top left, page 280. Tung Ch'i-ch'ang (1555–1636), *Landscape after a Poem by Tu Fu "The Rock Cliff Reveals, After the Clouds Passing by, Its Face of Brocade and Embroidery."* Series: *Landscapes in the Style of the Old Masters* (1621–24).THE NELSON-ATKINS MUSEUM OF ART, KANSAS CITY, MISSOURI. (Purchase: acquired through the generosity of the Hall Family Foundation and the exchange of other Trust properties.) Bottom left, page 280. *The Arrival of the Normandy Train at the Gare Saint-Lazarre* (1877) by Claude Monet. THE ART INSTITUTE OF CHICAGO.

Printed in the United States of America

10 9 8 7 6 5 4 3 2 1

ISBN: 0-13-341967-3

Prentice-Hall International (UK) Limited, *London*
Prentice-Hall of Australia Pty. Limited, *Sydney*
Prentice-Hall Canada, Inc., *Toronto*
Prentice-Hall Hispanoamericana, S. A., *Mexico*
Prentice-Hall of India Private Limited, *New Delhi*
Prentice-Hall of Japan, Inc., *Tokyo*
Simon & Schuster Asia Pte. Ltd., *Singapore*
Editora Prentice-Hall do Brasil, Ltda., *Rio de Janeiro*

CONTENTS

5. RENDERING

6. IMAGE PROCESSING AND PRESENTATION

PREFACE

The field of graphics is in transition. Both what we create and the way we create are changing.

Some of the drawings created in the field of architecture look no different from comparable ones produced years ago. On the other hand, some are quite different. New media have the power to alter the way we make images and perceive proposals. We can look at projects that do not yet exist in a serial, time-dependent manner. We can explore the formal implications of complex abstractions that would be time-consuming or difficult to draw with traditional media. Our understanding of architecture through graphics has been expanded.

It would be naive to state that there are no differences between media. The speed with which an image can be created varies with both level of skill and the particular drawing type and medium selected. Methods of drawing, image reproduction, and dissemination vary. The tools with which images are created are also media dependent.

The new graphic opportunities that exist, however, are *in addition to,* and not instead of, existing ones. Design professionals have abandoned neither the conventions nor the media that have long been part of the architectural and engineering vocabulary. The abstractions associated with plans, sections, and paraline drawings continue to help us understand what we are doing. They help us design. They help inform about the nature of our designs.

Traditional and digital graphics have much in common—especially the need for care and a professional attitude toward drawing. Regardless of medium, every drawing and image has a purpose. Architects, landscape architects, engineers, and designers are all trying to communicate something to themselves, to colleagues, to critics, and so on. If there is an idea, there is usually a variety of methods by which to create images expressing it.

The relationship between the mind, eye, and hand is a fundamental part of the design and presentation processes. One must be able to see clearly in order to draw well. This principle is applicable to any medium used. The sense of craft one brings to a project also transcends any particular medium. The person who spends time to create a crisp corner in an ink presentation drawing is the same person who will make the effort to carefully adjust focus, color balance, and brightness levels when fine-tuning a rendering that was created with electronically automated processes. Issues of format and composition are also medium independent. Elegance, coherence, and clarity are a function of *what* is created, not how. Beauty and quality can be found with any medium—and do not necessarily know boundaries.

There is a comfort level associated with any way of creating drawings or images. There is also a considerable investment in developing expertise, as well as obtaining equipment and supplies. One will, however, find that there are too many opportunities missed if the possibilities of using multiple media for architectural design are ignored. Professionals need to feel comfortable moving back and forth between media—using each one for what it can contribute.

It is important to note that the decision to use one medium rather than another may also be a function of the purpose of the images or drawings—and the situation in which one may be operating. When learning how to draw, productivity is not often a primary concern. Rather, an understanding of various media, tools, and skills—and the development of craft—are critical. There are times, however, when a professional is called upon to perform work rapidly and the speed of drawing or image creation and the ability to transmit the information to another party become a priority. Different media have varying strengths and weaknesses in the creation and modification of design documents depending on the image type, and its purpose(s), and the time frame involved.

The images in this book were created with a variety of media. Some were created exclusively with digital media and some were created using only traditional tools. Many, however, started out in one medium and were worked over in others. Traditionally created drawings were scanned, digitized, and edited electronically. Drawings initially created on computer were printed and modified with pen or pencil. To have removed any tool would have hindered the production of this effort. Although the process is not necessarily "pure," one can, if necessary, mimic one medium with another. At some point, however, architects must feel comfortable with the variety of graphic possibilities available.

If one accepts the assumption that both traditional and digital media are important, the sequence of topics for discussion in this book becomes a difficult subject. There are some sequences that make more sense for one medium than for another. Where instances existed in which a decision on sequencing had to be made, the order selected was based on which sequence would, overall, make the most sense and be easiest to understand. (For example, in traditional media, shades and shadows are often taught together. However, they *are* distinct. Whereas one deals with expression of surfaces without direct light, the other deals with the impact the shaded surfaces have on other surfaces. In digital media the distinction is reinforced by the fact that shading is often found as a quick visualization tool within modeling programs and shadow casting is usually found in rendering programs [or rendering components of programs]. Whenever a sequencing choice was taken in the organization of this text, a "bias" would be evident. Because digital media are, in some ways, newer and the body of collective experience is less, this sequence was arranged to facilitate the understanding of CAD/graphics.)

Readers inevitably will come to this book with different backgrounds. As an introductory text, it emphasizes design and presentation drawings. Some readers may be familiar with one set of tools and some readers with another. Sections that are not needed, or that are merely review, can be lightly skimmed. However, in the interest of being inclusive (at least in an introductory sense), material was included even when needed for the discussion of only one medium. It is easier to see how tools and media compare when information about both traditional and digital media is presented. Only by looking at the media in relation to one another can one become familiar with their relative attributes.

It must be understood that this text is *not* software specific. The different software *types* are explained: painting, drawing, modeling, rendering, and image processing. Any installation really needs to accommodate all of these types and have software applications that permit the transfer of files between them. (There are a number of application packages that have more than one function bundled together.) Neither are the issues in the text platform specific (although, for reasons of production, the illustrations generally are from a single platform). There are very few popularly used software packages that are not available on more than one platform. Many are available on both the personal computer (with its various operating systems) and workstation platforms. To as great an extent as possible, general principles and ways of creating digital images and models are discussed. When relevant, the merits of—and reasons for—using various media or techniques are included. Not all possibilities are available in all application packages. Various commands and ways of doing things are common to many applications. In some instances, different programs have different names for the same function. Idiosyncrasies within each program, of course, vary. Furthermore, the programs themselves change *very* frequently. This book is meant to be a beginning text and an introduction to the world of architectural graphics that should be supplemented, where necessary, with software-specific manuals and tutorials.

Finally, it is important to state that, although this book is written from the point of view of today's architect, most of the principles discussed are applicable to a wider range of design professionals. As the distinctions and separation of roles between professionals become blurred, and as complex projects require efforts of more than one professional, it is important that all have a common language of graphic communication. Furthermore, the processes and tools used by the various professions are the same. The unique and one-off nature of architectural projects make them excellent examples for the study of graphic communication and expression. Graphic tools and conventions are introduced in a manner that should be relevant to all individuals in the building delivery process: architects and landscape architects, engineers, interior designers, planners—and those people who work with them.

ACKNOWLEDGMENTS

The creation of this book would have been impossible without the assistance of many people. I consider myself extremely fortunate to have had such enormous support.

My wife, Beth, an interior designer and professional member of the American Society of Interior Designers, assisted in the editing, review, and layout of the project. Many of the diagrams were drawn by her. I am grateful for her assistance, perseverance, and patience.

Prof. Michael Stephen Zdepski at the New Jersey Institute of Technology (NJIT) has been working with me since we established electronic design studios at the NJIT together in 1985 with a grant from the New Jersey Department of Higher Education. Many of the images in this book are from his students. No faculty member at any institution could wish for a better colleague and friend.

It was my good luck that the original and experimental work that preceded this project was performed at the New Jersey Institute of Technology, a computing-intensive environment that fosters the growth of new ideas and experimentation.

Dr. Gary Thomas, Vice President for Academic Affairs and Provost at the New Jersey Institute of Technology, has been extraordinarily supportive of my efforts over the years. NJIT would not be as innovative and progressive as it is without his influence.

Urs P. Gauchat, Dean of the School of Architecture at NJIT (and former teacher of mine at Harvard), has provided support, encouragement, and images for this text.

Prof. Sanford Greenfield, former Dean of the School of Architecture at NJIT, provided the initial encouragement to become involved with computers in an architectural context.

Michael Hoon, my graduate assistant throughout the preparation of this book, has been invaluable. He created many of the diagrams in the text and assisted in the prepress formatting. As the network manager of the Imaging Laboratory at NJIT, he also served as a reviewer and technical resource for this text.

Various professional images have been contributed by many people, including Prof. William Bricken of the University of Michigan, Prof. Jeffrey Hildner of the University of Virginia, and Profs. Frank Arvan, Alastair Standing, Michael Mostoller, and the late Fred Travisano of the New Jersey Institute of Technology. Professional work was also received from Nelson Chen of Wong Chen Associates in Hong Kong; Jung/Brannen Associates of Boston; the New York City office of Resolution: 4 Architecture (Joseph Tanney, Gary Shoemaker, and Robert Luntz, partners); and Keyes Condon Florance Architects of Washington, D.C. Stuart Feldman, Vice President of Lightscape Technologies, Inc., contributed a number of professional digital renderings.

Three former teachers of mine at Columbia need to be acknowledged as well: J. Woodson Rainey, who taught me how to draw; Robert A. M. Stern, who taught me that quality and craft take effort but are always worthwhile; and the late Eugene Santomasso, who exposed me to the art of architecture and convinced me to follow its path.

The Association for Computer-Aided Design in Architecture (ACADIA) has been a fertile ground for the exploration of ideas. I have found ACADIA and its members to be an excellent forum to test new concepts, and I am grateful for my opportunities within the organization.

Dean Edward Baum of the School of Architecture at the University of Texas at Arlington has graciously made available student work for publication. A number of teachers at various schools of architecture have assisted me by providing samples of their students' work, including Bill Boswell, Todd Hamilton, George Gintole, Deborah Natsios, and Carlos Jimenez of the University of Texas at Arlington; Branko Kolarevic and Erick Valle of the University of Miami; William Bricken of the University of Michigan; Bill Fox of Temple University; and Vojislav Ristic of NJIT.

Chris Yessios of auto•des•sys, Inc. (form•Z), Don Peterson of MegaCADD (MegaMODEL), Lee Anderson of SketchTech (upFRONT), and Gary Yost and Bill Tryon of Autodesk (3D Studio and AutoCAD) have made their software manuals available as resources for images and ideas. I am grateful for their help and generosity.

Various corporations have been gracious in supplying photographic material and are recognized within the body of the text.

I would like to thank Ed Francis, Senior Editor, and the rest of the Prentice Hall publishing staff, as well as Cindy Trickel of Carlisle Publishers Services and the staff of Carlisle Communications for their efforts and assistance in this work.

Finally, I must thank the many architecture students at the New Jersey Institute of Technology. This book stands as a testimony to their continued high level of achievement.

WHY ARCHITECTS AND DESIGNERS USE GRAPHICS

Architects, engineers, and designers draw and create images, in part, because *the act of creation itself is enjoyable*. There is yet additional pleasure to be gained from looking at one's accomplishment when a drawing takes on a life of its own on paper or screen.

Beyond providing the creator with pleasure, however, the act of drawing serves other purposes. Ideas need to be communicated: to clients, builders, friends, critics, teachers, and consultants, as well as to oneself. Vitruvius, in his *Ten Books on Architecture* written more than two thousand years ago, declared that an architect "must have a knowledge of drawing so that he can readily make sketches to show the appearance of the work which he proposes."[1] The ideas that any designer has must be

[1]*Vitruvius. 1960.* Ten books on architecture. *New York: Dover Publications (originally published by Harvard University Press, 1914, and edited by Morris Hicky Morgan).*

transferred from the designer's mind into some viewable medium for others to see. Although words can usually begin to describe ideas that ultimately must take on a physical form, graphics frequently can do it better and faster. Furthermore, ideas often can be developed more quickly using graphics.

The media used to create architectural drawings are varied. Basic principles for drawing all types, however, from two-dimensional orthographic projections (plans, elevations, etc.) to perspectives and axonometrics, are media independent. Whereas "what the images are" may be constant, the way in which they are created and modified is, at times, media dependent and therefore variable. Because we can only modify what we create, the media employed can affect an image's or drawing's future uses and possibilities. Any individual contemplating entry into one of the building design professions must be comfortable with a variety of media—and must be able to move actively between them.

COMMUNICATION WITH ONESELF

During the design process, an architect's, engineer's, planner's, interior designer's, or landscape architect's mind fills with ideas and images. These images, in order to be remembered and used, must be recorded in some manner. History is filled with examples of artists and inventors creating logs that document their design explorations. Leonardo da Vinci went so far as to write backwards in his notebook while looking in a mirror so that his personal code would not be read by casual observers. The keeping of a sketchbook, which is a graphic archive of a designer's ideas, has been referred to by twentieth-century architect and visionary Paolo Soleri as "the procedure of a bookkeeping of the mind."[2] Sketches and notes are tools that have long been used for communicating with oneself.

Design drawings (for any purpose) vary, from preliminary pencil sketches and electronic conceptual collages to precise measured drawings that can explore the relationships between materials on a building facade, the intricacies of the connections between a column and a beam, or the details of a piece of custom-designed furniture. At the early stage of a project, a designer can create rough sketches with sufficient ambiguity that they serve as catalysts for continued design development. Both the act of drawing and the drawings themselves can be viewed as forms of graphic brainstorming. As we look at the images we create, we can work over them, change them, trace them, modify them, and so on. Design issues are tested and studied diagrammatically with graphics.

We can be our own design critic as we check to see if the ideas in our mind still work when we force the discipline of measured drawings upon them. These ideas must be tested against the realities of the architectural program, site constraints, budgets, structural necessities, and design intent, as well as against principles of form, order, and perception. In order to aid the designer in the visualization of these ideas, drawings are created. When a drawing or sketch is created, a designer can look at the work and change it.

[2]Soleri, Paolo. 1971. Sketchbooks of Paolo Soleri. Cambridge, Mass.: MIT Press.

COMMUNICATION WITHIN A DESIGN TEAM

Graphics are also used as a means to exchange ideas and facilitate communication among members of a design team. With the building delivery process becoming increasingly complex, the practice of architecture is evolving, under some circumstances, into what Walter Gropius (director of the Bauhaus in Germany during the 1920s and, later, founder of the firm The Architects Collaborative in Massachusetts) called a team activity. Frequently, more than one architect or engineer will work on a project—sometimes in distant locations. There are assistants within the architectural and engineering offices who contribute to the process. In fact, a variety of professionals often participate in the design and development process. Sketches, diagrams, and marked-up drawings are used at the beginning stages of the project to work back and forth between individual contributors. Drawings created by one professional can become the base for design development by others. All of these people work together and need to share information and ideas.

COMMUNICATION TO CLIENTS AND THE PUBLIC

Descriptive drawings that explain how a building works, and what it is like, are needed not only for internal discussion among design team members, but also for owners and the general public in order for them to previsualize the nature of any proposed environment. The descriptive drawings (often called **presentation draw-**

ings) are one tool a designer can use to show the intent of a project. (Physical models, video or screen animations, and written reports are additional tools used by design professionals to explain architectural projects.) Well-crafted, clear illustrations of a design, understandable to the nonprofessional, can aid communication between the client and designer and increase the likelihood that what is built is what is desired. Descriptive images are also valuable in discussion with regulatory agencies (planning boards, boards of adjustment, historic preservation commissions, etc.) in explaining the impact of a design project.

COMMUNICATION TO CONTRACTORS

The documents used to explain design proposals to builders and manufacturers are yet another component of the building delivery process. Graphics (including their associated text) are used to explain precisely what a building or space should look like, the dimensions of the various components, the materials included, the structure, the finishes, and so on. It is from the construction documents that the cost of a project can be determined by those people entrusted to undertake the work. The production of these documents is a significant aspect of one's professional practice. The importance of the drawings and images contained in the construction documents and the influence they have on the final project are enormous. Errors in the drawings can easily be translated into errors in a building. Yet, when potential problems and details are worked out graphically—before construction—the quality of the project is likely to be enhanced. Quality can be improved when architects "prebuild" projects graphically.

CRAFT AND QUALITY

A sense of craft and caring should be brought to the creation of drawings and images. Any work a professional creates should be made with the highest possible standards in mind. It is important to remember that, in most instances, the drawings we create are *not* the end product: they are a means to an end. They help us create buildings and places that, we hope, will improve the built environment. Nevertheless, although we do not (necessarily) physically build projects for our clients, a sense of craft in image creation can serve as an indication of the care and thoroughness we bring to the design of the project itself. Care, precision, thoughtfulness, and excellence are all qualities in drawing and image creation worthy of pursuit.

1 GRAPHICS TOOLS

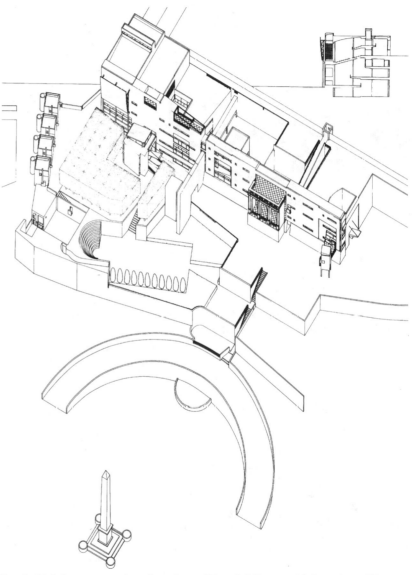

1.1 TRADITIONAL DRAWING TOOLS

1.1.1 Leaving Your Mark

Architects and designers must use a medium to draw. Lead (graphite), ink (Fig. 1–1), and charcoal have been among the media most commonly used for years. The drawing tool is viewed as an extension of the hand with which the designer makes marks on a surface capable of receiving the points, lines, shapes, and tones. The mark is the result of the residue left by the drawing implement on the drawing surface. The nature of the mark depends on the medium being used, the type of receiving surface (material, texture, color), and, of course, the individual creator. Depending on the purpose of the drawing, media may be mixed in order to clearly communicate the intent of the designer.

Fig. 1–1 Ink presentation drawing (*Randal Brown, University of Texas at Arlington*)

Sketch Pencils and Charcoal

At the beginning of any design process, architects frequently create rough concept drawings with broad strokes. The broad stroke and thickness of the lines help the designer focus on large conceptual issues of the project and its visual form while making it more difficult to get wrapped up in small, fine details too soon, thereby making this problem less likely (Fig. 1–2). Initial sketches also, of necessity, have a degree of ambiguity in their lack of precision that can serve as a catalyst for the designer to try new ideas without getting locked into a specific solution (Fig. 1–3).

Initial design sketches—as well as freehand modifications or enhancements to drafted or printed images—can be made with sketch pencils or charcoal. Some sketch pencils have soft graphite cores of large diameter for broad, free-flowing strokes. Sticks made of natural charcoal, either held by hand or in charcoal holders, can also be used for rough sketches. The nature of the materials is such that the creation of thin, precise lines is difficult. Although suitable for sketching, charcoal and soft sketch pencils are not generally used for technical drafting.

Pencils and Lead Types

Lead holders and mechanical pencils are used by the designer to create pencil drawings. The wide range of mark types that can be made with pencils makes

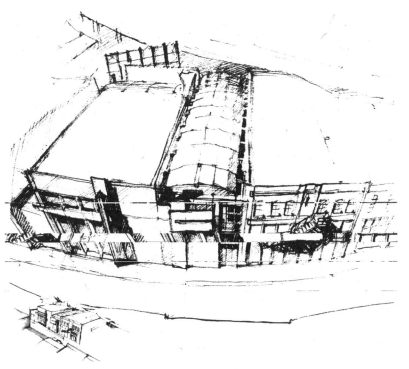

Fig. 1–2 Freehand sketches of building design (*Michael Patrick and John Taylor, University of Texas at Arlington*)

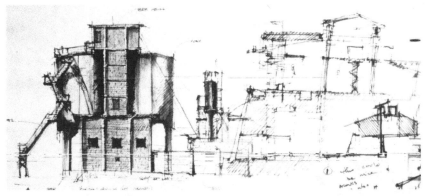

Fig. 1–3 Schematic freehand sketches (*Gordon Gill, University of Texas at Arlington*)

them useful tools to create drawings of both a schematic and a finished nature. The degree of hardness or softness of the lead is selectable and can be changed at the discretion of the person drawing. (See Box 1–A.)

Given equal hand pressure, the harder and denser the lead, the thinner the marks. Soft leads create darker and wider lines. Thickness of marks varies with the intent of the line. Although thin marks may provide an opportunity for greater accuracy, they may be very light and difficult to read or reproduce. When 6H lead is used on paper to create darker lines, heavy pressure must be applied and erasure is difficult. *Any lead, when applied with great pressure, may be difficult to erase from paper.* "Engraving" with too heavy pressure can leave permanent imprints in many drawing surfaces that make clean changes virtually impossible. It is important to note that some reproduction processes pick up and print even the ghosts of erased lines that were applied too heavily.

Varying the pressure on any lead will cause the darkness or intensity of the line to vary. Furthermore, as the point gets dull, the line width will vary. To minimize line variation, the pencil should be rotated, or twirled, as long lines are drawn. Leads should be kept relatively sharp.

Hard leads may be applied with minimal pressure for guidelines that remain light on a drawing and are not meant to be part of a final reproduced image. 4H leads are often used for grid or construction lines. Soft leads

---

Box 1–A

PENCIL LEAD WEIGHTS

6H	Thin, hard line
4H	Used for construction line; lightweight
2H	General drafting
H, HB, F, B	Soft leads; darker and wider lines; hand lettering
2B, 4B, 6B	Soft leads used to create texture or tone
Nonphoto and nonprint	Guidelines that do not reproduce

Box 1–B

PLASTIC AND COMPOSITE LEADS

Lead Types and/or Nomenclature and/or Manufacturers' Designations

N0	N1	N2	N3	N4	N5	(Plastic lead)
E0	E1	E2	E3	E4	E5	(Plastic lead)
	FTR11	FTR22	FTR33	FTR44	FTR55	(Composite lead)
Softest		$\rightarrow$	$\rightarrow$	$\rightarrow$		Hardest

In addition to traditional leads used on paper, there are film and reproduction leads that contain plastic (and break more easily) for use on other media. N, K, and E leads at any degree of hardness or softness are all very hard when drawing on paper but are appropriate for drafting film where they do not smear to an excessive degree. FTR leads are a compromise between the plastic and graphite leads. They are less brittle than N or E leads and do not smear as much as the H or B leads.

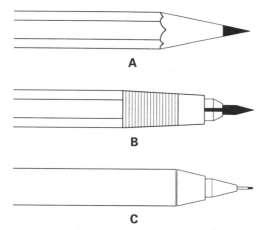

Fig. 1–4 Pencils and lead holders. *A,* Wood-encased pencil. Requires sharpening with traditional hand-held, crank, or electric sharpener. *B,* Clutch-type lead holder. Requires sharpening with lead pointer. Point length is adjustable by user and may be varied based on hardness of lead, other drawing implements used, and personal preference. *C,* Lead holder or mechanical pencil with very thin leads. No sharpening is required. As point wears down, the user simply extends the lead by pushing a button at the end or on the side of the holder. Very thin leads may break more easily than thicker leads.

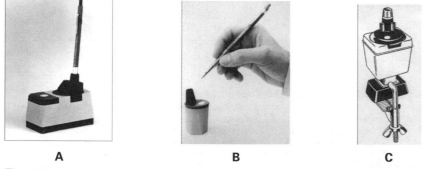

Fig. 1–5 Lead pointers (A *and* B, *Sanford-Berol;* C, *Koh-I-Noor, Inc.*)

are used to create texture or tone and for hand lettering. Note that softer leads will smear more easily than will hard leads.

Paper type and roughness impact the apparent line weights of leads. Tracing paper, which is thin in order to be semitransparent, tears easily with sharp or hard leads. One can use harder leads on rough, thick paper or poster board, which require the use of these leads to make precise, thin drafted lines. Other drawing surfaces require different lead types. (See Box 1–B.)

Finally, there are leads that are used solely for laying out a drawing or to produce guidelines because they do not reproduce in either photographs or the commonly used blue, black, and brown line prints. **Nonphoto blue** leads (which will not reproduce with conventional photography) and **nonprint** leads (which will not reproduce on prints created with the diazo reproduction process that is described later) are used on both paper and film.

Although traditional wood-encased pencils can be used for drafting, the wood can get in the way of using other drafting equipment. When the point is extended by shaving the wood back so that supplemental equipment can be used, the point breaks more easily. **Lead holders** (Fig. 1–4) afford one the opportunity to adjust the length of the point based on convenience, and the lead is easily sharpened with the use of lead pointers (Fig. 1–5) in order to maintain a fine edge (necessary for thin and consistent line weights). Inevitably, each person develops a preference for a type of pencil or holder, and high-quality work can be created with any choice.

Pens

Drafting or **technical pens** (Fig. 1–6) can be used for crisp hard-line drawings that are used by designers to communicate their ideas to clients and critics. Line thickness is determined by the point size. Pen point sizes vary from the extremely fine 000000, or 6 × 0, (.13 mm = .005") to the very wide 7 (2 mm = .079") (Fig. 1–7). **Brush pens** are also available for use when large areas must be filled solid with ink. Sizes in the United States are most commonly listed by pen number, whereas European designations are by precise line widths. Pressure, unlike that used when drawing with lead, should be light and, when applied properly, does not impact on the line weight. Occasionally, line weight will vary according to the consistency of speed with which the line is drawn (Fig. 1–8). Larger widths can be built up with multiple passes of smaller-sized pens—which also produce crisper and more square ends than do the rounded edges of larger-sized pens (Fig. 1–9). Very thin pens, like 6 × 0, tend to be more fragile and less tolerant of dirt or foreign substances on the drawing surfaces than do thick pens.

Like leads, pen point materials may vary depending on the surface on which one expects to draw. Typical stainless steel points (the least expensive) may be appropriate for vellum or bond paper but clog and wear out against drafting film. Jewel tips or tungsten tips

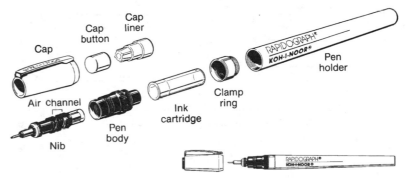

Fig. 1–6 Technical pen (*Koh-I-Noor, Inc.*)

Most common pen widths— suitable for most drawings.

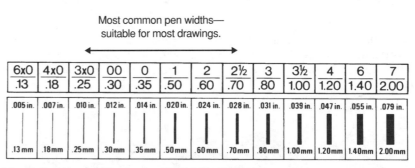

6x0	4x0	3x0	00	0	1	2	2½	3	3½	4	6	7
.13	.18	.25	.30	.35	.50	.60	.70	.80	1.00	1.20	1.40	2.00
.005 in.	.007 in.	.010 in.	.012 in.	.014 in.	.020 in.	.024 in.	.028 in.	.031 in.	.039 in.	.047 in.	.055 in.	.079 in.
.13 mm	.18 mm	.25 mm	.30 mm	.35 mm	.50 mm	.60 mm	.70 mm	.80 mm	1.00 mm	1.20 mm	1.40 mm	2.00 mm

Fig. 1–7 Pen width chart (*Koh-I-Noor, Inc.*)

Fig. 1–8 Magnification of ink line illustrating the end of a segment drawn quickly. When the hand slows down to stop, the ink flows out of the point and the line enlarges. The enlargement is most noticeable with thicker pen points and single lines. If objectionable, the enlargement effect can be reduced by a steady hand speed and by building up thick line segments with multiple passes of thin lines (Fig. 1–9).

vs.

Fig. 1–9 Multiple passes of small pen widths provide crisper corners or ends than do larger pen widths because technical pen nibs are usually round in shape.

A   B

Fig. 1–10 Traditional pens that require a great deal of practice and care for effective use. *A,* Dip pen. As pressure is applied, the flexible point bends and wider ink lines are created. *B,* Thumbscrew controls the width of the line.

Fig. 1–11 Felt tip marker drawing. Schematic design presentation of single family residence. Note that background strokes are all vertical. (*Urs P. Gauchat, Gauchat Architects*)

are needed when drawing on film and can also be used on paper. (Although the purchase is more expensive initially, the cost of the proper pen tip is usually less than the total cost of the replacement points needed when using stainless steel tips on drafting film.)

Technical pens use ink as the medium for placing marks. Because the ink in the pens can dry out and points can get clogged, the pens should be cleaned after each use to maximize their life expectancy. Keeping lids on ink bottles and caps on pens also assists in preventing too-rapid drying. Pens can sometimes be shaken a little to get ink flowing, but it is not a good idea to shake ink bottles because this may introduce air bubbles into the ink that can then clog pens.

Although not used as frequently as in the past, there are other instruments used for placing ink onto a drawing. Fountain pens and pens that must be dipped into an inkwell are still available (Fig. 1–10). These tools tend to require greater hand control (and practice) than do technical pens in order to be used as effective drafting tools. However, because they provide such a direct relationship between the hand (both movement and pressure) and line, some artists and delineators use these for artistic, graphic, and calligraphic purposes.

Markers

Like other media, **felt tip markers** (Graphic Markers, Design Markers, Art Markers, Magic Markers, etc.) are used for a variety of drawing types, from freehand sketching to final presentation drawings (Fig. 1–11). They are frequently mixed with other media in drawings and are available in varying colors, tip or nib shapes (Figs. 1–12, 1–13), and dye types.

Marker tips come in a range of widths from "very fine point" (narrow lines) all the way up to "broad point" (wide lines) for different effects on a drawing. Dye types may be water soluble or waterproof depending on their ingredients (water-, oil-, and alcohol-based dyes are most common), with each type having a different purpose. (See Box 1–C.)

Markers may be used to add color to drawings whose outlines are created with pen or pencil. Markers are also used to add color to prints of drawings (blue, black, or brown line and sepia), but some papers can cause marker colors to bleed and become muddy. (Note: It is advisable to test the markers being used on the same type of paper or board as the intended drawing surface in order to facilitate marker selection and to avoid unwelcome surprises.) Areas of line drawings may be selectively colored for emphasis in a particular image. Because the stroke of a marker is visible on the page after its application, an image colored in marker may look neatest with all of the strokes going carefully in one direction.

Very thin markers may be used in lieu of pens or pencils for drawing and are frequently used to trace over pencil guidelines to give a drawing an informal, or freehand, look. Drafted hard-line drawings can sometimes give an impression that the project

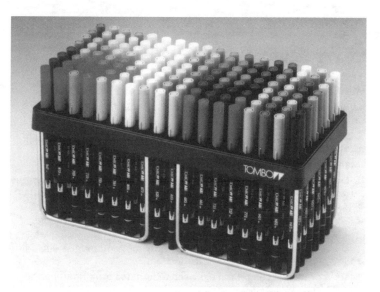

Fig. 1–12   Felt tip markers are available for individual purchase, in large assorted groups, and in "color groups." Color groups include yellow/green; red/pink; orange/brown; and warm/cool gray. (*American Tombow, Inc.*)

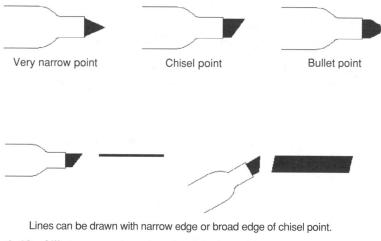

Very narrow point   Chisel point   Bullet point

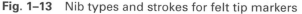

Lines can be drawn with narrow edge or broad edge of chisel point.

Fig. 1–13   Nib types and strokes for felt tip markers

FELT TIP MARKERS

Attributes

- Wide variety of colors and shades of warm and cool gray are available.
- Manufacturing consistency allows for re-creation of palettes for different drawings.
- Markers are low-maintenance tools.
- Different tips, or nibs, available for different types of lines. Some tips allow for different lines by use of different sides or edges. Rotating tip during drawing provides additional calligraphic variety.
- Markers can be used effectively in conjunction with other media.
- The type of paper, or surface, on which the marker is applied affects the drawing. (Markers can bleed or spread on some materials—including many papers used for diazo reproduction.)
- Marker drawings can fade if exposed to light for prolonged periods.
- Marker strokes are visible on a drawing. The buildup of one marker stroke over another emphasizes the stroke.
- Markers that are drying out provide a different look than saturated markers.
- Combinations of shades or colors are best to give a sense of depth to materials.
- Marker drawings can be either loose and sketchlike or very polished.

Impacts of solvents

- Water-soluble and non-water-soluble solvents are available.
- When applying markers over ink drawings, a solvent should be selected that does not mix with the ink and cause it to run.
- If using markers to blend colors by successive strokes, succeeding layers should be able to dissolve and mix with earlier ones.
- When adding colors over others for various effects (like transparency), the second solvent should not be able to dissolve the first.
- Marker colors can be diluted by dipping the tip in a cup of solvent.

represented is developed to an advanced stage. When presented to a critic or client, these drawings may invite reaction to details that have not yet been resolved and divert attention from other issues and from the fact that the design is still fluid in the designer's mind. If the lines are less precise, or give the appearance that they were drawn freehand, the drawing is less likely to be considered as "final." Yet, in order to portray ideas precisely, and because drafting can be fast, it may make sense to create an image in pencil that can be traced (either on the same paper or on an overlay) with a very fine point felt tip marker.

Airbrush

Airbrush is a tool that allows one to do very fine, precise spray painting for finished drawings or on physical models. A compressor is connected to a nozzle that is activated or opened by a hand-held trigger that pulls a needle back from the opening. The needle and nozzle combination can change the spray patterns from narrow to wide. Very precise work can be accomplished with an airbrush, which can be used to build up subtle colors and tones. Careful application can be used to create smooth gradations.

A summary of the attributes of various media, including airbrush, can be found in Box 1–D.

Box 1–D

ATTRIBUTES OF TRADITIONAL MEDIA

Charcoal

- Available in compressed sticks for mechanical clutch holders, in natural sticks of charred wood, and in traditional wood pencils.
- Varying degrees of hardness available.
- Good for freehand sketching and application of tone.
- Charcoal is excellent for preliminary design explorations because the comparatively thick marks prevent one from becoming too involved in, or worrying too much about, small details. The inability to make thin marks, however, makes charcoal unsuitable for precision drafting.

Conté crayon

- Similar to charcoal but somewhat harder. Available as stick or wood-encased pencil.
- Broad marks make it suitable for freehand drawing and sketching but not suitable for precise drafting.
- Suitable for renderings with limited palettes. Limited color selection includes sepia, black, and white.

Grease pencil

- Thick, "waxy" type of lead capable of marking on glass or photographic film or slides. Works well for live presentations with overhead projectors because it is suitable for making marks on transparencies.
- Generally not used on paper because the medium is too thick for precision drafting and too sticky for loose freehand sketching.
- Instead of sharpening, additional material can be exposed by pulling string downwards and tearing the layer of spirally wrapped paper to be removed.

Pencil

- Available in traditional wood-encased form, as well as in manufactured leads for clutch holders.
- Variety of lead types and colors available suitable for different drawing surfaces.
- Variety of hardness available. (Given the same hand pressure, harder leads leave thinner and lighter lines than do soft leads.)
- Soft pencils generally more suitable for sketching than hard leads. Hard leads require more precision in hand control and tend to make finer lines required for measured drawings.
- Color pencils are suitable for rendering on paper or film. Color pencils (traditionally red pencils) are widely used to mark existing drawings that need editing.

Pen

- Available as refillable technical drawing pens or as dip, fountain-type pens (in many varieties).
- Inks of various types are available. Clog-resistant inks have been formulated for use in technical drafting pens. Most inks may be diluted with water, which may change the color. Special ink is available that will etch the surface of plastic for permanent adhesion but that may damage normal drafting tools and, in general, would not be used for drawing on paper or drafting film.
- Dip pens can control line width either with pressure on a flexible point or with a thumbscrew control regulating the flow of ink (Fig. 1–10).
- Technical drafting pens are available in different point sizes, each of which is capable of producing a different line width.
- Materials used for the points of technical pens vary with the intended drawing surface. Stainless steel points are the least expensive and are suitable for vellum, but tungsten or jewel tip points are more wear resistant and are better for use on polyester drafting film.

Felt tip marker

- Available in an assortment of colors, nib (or tip) styles, and solvent types.
- Used for sketching and to add color to line drawings.
- Thin markers suitable for freehand line drawing.
- Fine-point rolling ball markers used in pen plotters to print copies of line drawings created on computer.

Airbrush

- Compressor used to spray paint onto paper, board, or film through nozzle.
- Color is applied to exposed areas. Areas not to be colored should be masked with paper, cardboard, masking adhesive film, or other suitable material.
- The variety of tone that can be applied is suitable for renderings of presentation drawings. Less frequently, airbrush is used to apply a tone or visual texture to physical models. The time-consuming nature of the process makes it less than used for interim schematic work and, consequently, not often considered for spontaneous design work.

ERASER TYPES AND CHARACTERISTICS

Kneaded, kneaded rubber
- Effective for charcoal.
- Used to create intentional smudges and soften the look of the drawing.

Pink pencil (Pink Pearl)
- Soft and pliable.
- Works well for removal of pencil on paper.
- May mar drafting film and is capable of marking some papers and illustration boards.

Gum
- Soft but has increased abrasiveness to clean deeper into paper surface.
- Wears itself away and forms disposable "strings" that are brushed away.

White plastic
- Low in abrasiveness and relatively "safe."
- Good first solution but does not always erase darkest lines on paper.

White vinyl (Magic Rub)
- Excellent for use on drafting film and paper.
- Effective in eliminating lines while protecting drawing surface.
- Erases ink from drafting film when eraser is wetted slightly.

Erasers soaked with erasing fluid
- Effective at erasing ink on film but can leave a residue on the drawing surface that must be cleaned prior to redrawing.

Gray ink
- Very abrasive—must be used with care.
- May remove portions of drawing surface.
- Can be used for ink on paper when erasure marks on a surface may be less noticeable than marks made in error. (Note: If the drawing is to be reproduced by photographic means, the damage may not show up, whereas the errant ink line[s] might.)

Erasers and Shields

Not all drawings are created by putting the correct line in the correct place the first time. Mistakes *are* made, and if a drawing is to be a working document, changes *will* be made.

Different materials used for erasers are suitable for different purposes (Box 1–E). *An eraser should be selected that does not discolor or mar the drawing surface while eliminating the marks intended for erasure.* Erasers are either manual (hand held) or electric (Fig. 1–14).

The least abrasive eraser that works should be used. If unsure of the ability of an eraser to remove marks, one can try a variety of erasers, starting with non-abrasive vinyl or plastic. Beware of old erasers—they can dry out and mark the drawing surface! Be warned also that grinding away with an eraser too long in a single spot can wear away the drawing surface.

If necessary, ink lines can be "cleaned up" very carefully by using a very sharp graphic arts blade (X-ACTO blade) and scraping away the mistake. This works best for small errors that would be difficult to erase neatly. The scraping technique is most commonly used to remove ink from vellum where the scrape would not be noticed and to remove minor crosses or overruns at the intersections of lines in order to give the appearance of great precision. Care should be taken not to cut or tear the paper.

Erasing shields are thin metal (usually stainless steel) plates with holes of varying sizes that are used as "stencils" to expose portions of drawings that are to be erased while protecting the rest (Fig. 1–15). Erasing shields increase the level of precision available when making changes to a drawing (Box 1–F). Just as care must be taken in putting pencil or pen to paper, so too must care be taken in removing the marks made.

1.1.2 Helping the Hand

T Squares and Parallel Rules

Architects frequently have to draw lines that are orthogonal and parallel to one of the edges of the paper. **T squares** and **parallel rules** are straightedges that facilitate the manual drawing of horizontal straight lines parallel to the top or bottom of the paper. The rule serves as a straight guide against which the pen or pencil can be held while drawing the line. The long edge of the rule should be clear plastic in order to facilitate visibility while drawing the line.

The advantages of a T square are its relatively low cost and portability. It has a fixed head held tightly in place against the side of the drawing board or table with a wood and plastic or metal and plastic blade (Fig. 1–16). It can be carried from place to place if drawing tables are available. However, it may wobble and one hand (and/or part of an arm) must continuously apply pressure on it in order to prevent unwanted movement.

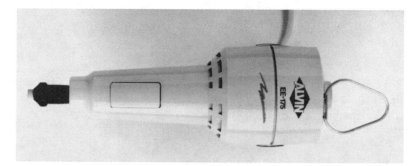

Fig. 1–14   Electric eraser   (*Art provided by Alvin & Company, Inc.*)

Fig. 1–15   Erasing shields (black shapes represent openings in the shield) (*Charrette Corporation*)

Box 1–F

ERASING SHIELDS

- The eraser (either manual or electric) is rubbed over the opening. The shield protects lines that are expected to remain from being erased and allows for greater precision.

- Holes with square corners are good for maintaining crisp edges.

- Long, thin cutouts are useful for erasing single lines that are in close proximity to other lines.

- Erasing shields are particularly useful with electric erasers to prevent the eraser from "getting away" from the user and erasing too large an area.

- When using a shield with a wet vinyl eraser to erase ink from film, it is possible that water may get under the shield and affect other areas of the drawing. The minimum amount of water or wetness should be used. Any overspill should be blotted immediately with a tissue, and the affected areas should be redrawn or touched up as necessary.

- By erasing over equally spaced dots on the shield, one can create dashed lines with even spacing and even-sized segments.

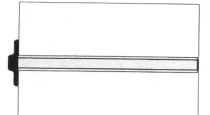

Fig. 1–16 T square. One edge held tightly against side of board. One side is free.

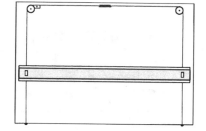

Fig. 1–17 Parallel rule. Held to board with guide wires. Both sides are fixed (which reduces wobble). Parallel rules available that move on rollers. Most common sizes: 42″, 48″, 52″, 60″.

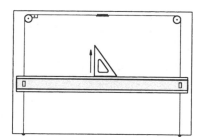

Fig. 1–18 Any two lines can be drawn perpendicular to one another with a right triangle and parallel rule.

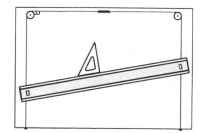

Fig. 1–19 Thumbscrew in upper left corner can be used to adjust angle of parallel rule (must be kept tight or parallel lines can become skewed).

The longer the T square, the more likely is the edge remote from the head to wobble or move. T squares should, in most cases, be limited to 42″ in length. Because drawing with a T square can be time-consuming, they are rarely used in architectural offices except on a temporary basis when more permanent drafting stations are occupied. Because they are not affixed to a desk or table, however, they can be useful tools for laying out straight lines when constructing cardboard models.

The parallel rule (Fig. 1–17), although more expensive and less portable than the T square, facilitates both greater speed and accuracy in drafting. As with the T square, it is necessary to hold the parallel rule in place while drawing, but the task is less cumbersome because the tool is attached to the drawing board itself. And, because both sides are held in place, there is no wobble. Although parallel rules can be detached from the drawing board, it is not practical to do this repeatedly. It is possible to purchase small (up to 24″ × 36″) portable drawing boards with parallel rules attached, but these can be awkward to carry on a regular basis.

Neither the T square nor the parallel rule should be longer than the drawing surface. To keep drawings clean, the edges and bottoms of T square and parallel rule should be cleaned of dirt and graphite regularly.

Triangles

Triangles used for drawing are three-sided closed geometric shapes, usually made of plastic, that act as rules for vertical and angled lines. Fixed-size triangles used are right triangles (90°) with the other two angles either 45°, or 30° and 60° (Box 1–G). When a triangle is used for drawing vertical lines, the right angle is held snugly against the T square or parallel rule in order to create a guide exactly perpendicular to the line formed by the horizontal rule (Figs. 1–18, 1–19). It is usually easiest to start the vertical line on the side closest to the horizontal rule and draw in a direction away from the parallel rule. Care must be taken, and the nondrawing hand must be placed, to hold both the parallel rule and the triangle in place. Larger triangles should be used for long vertical lines. If the vertical line is longer than the triangle, the parallel rule can be slid up (or down) the drawing and the triangle repositioned.

Adjustable triangles have a moveable leg that can serve as a guide for lines of any angle with the horizontal (or vertical) (Fig. 1–20). Held by a thumbscrew, the angle can be repeated for ease of drawing any sloped line. Also, because there is a protractor-like scale on the triangle itself, it can be used to measure any angle on the drawing for repetition in another portion of the image. (These two traits are particularly useful for drawing views of sloped roofs or angled walls in buildings.) Standard triangles may also be combined to create different angles with the horizontal (Fig. 1–21).

Box 1–G

TRIANGLE SIZES AND THEIR ATTRIBUTES AND USES

Triangle sizes are based on the length of the longer leg of the two sides making the right triangle (not the hypotenuse, or leg opposite the right angle).

>14"
- Long vertical lines.
- Straightedge to connect distant points (useful in traditional perspective creation).

10"–14"
- Common sizes for architectural drawings.
- Usually valuable to have a variety of sizes (for convenience and comfort). Most often, the 30°-60° triangle will be one size and the 45°-45° triangle will be another.

4"–6"
- Convenient for small (8 ½" × 11") drawings or when the lines being drawn are confined to a small area.
- Hand lettering guides.
- Many closely spaced, parallel, angled lines.

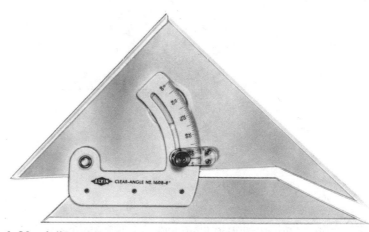

Fig. 1–20 Adjustable triangle *(Art provided by Alvin & Company, Inc.)*

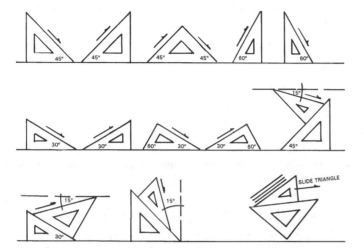

Fig. 1–21 Guides for angled lines are created by holding one of the acute angles against the horizontal rule. The two types of triangles (45°-45° and 60°-30°) can be used in combination, one held against the other to form angles in increments of 15°. (*From Muller, E. and J. Fausett. 1993. Architectural drawing and light construction. Englewood Cliffs, N.J.: Prentice Hall, p. 7. Adapted with permission.*)

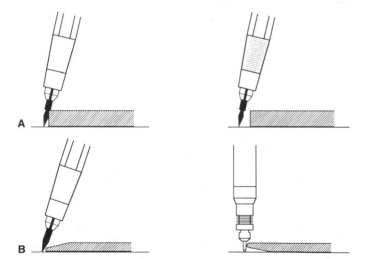

Fig. 1–22 Edges and drawing implements. *A,* Square edges and damaged lead (exaggerated in image). *B,* Beveled edge for pencil and raised edge for pen.

Triangles and other drawing aids are available with a variety of edge types to be used with different drafting implements: beveled edges are more appropriate for pencils so that a sharp corner does not chew into the lead point causing excessive breaking; raised edges work well with technical pens so that ink does not bleed under the triangle (allows pen to be held relatively straight for smooth ink flow); and so on (Fig. 1–22).

Drafting Machines

Drafting machines combine an adjustable triangle and short moveable parallel rule into one drawing tool (Fig. 1–23). Designed for efficiency when used in production drafting, the angle adjustment knob can be controlled with one hand while lines are drawn with the other. Among the characteristics that make the drafting machine a preferred tool among engineers is that it provides the ability to draw straight lines quickly at irregular or nonstandard angles—an important trait when designing or drawing objects and components of objects in great detail (from machine parts, to bolts with threads at various angles, to plumbing systems with pitched pipes, to the subtle camber and slope of a beam). Furthermore, the comparatively short legs on the drafting machine are generally of sufficient length to draw discrete objects, yet not so long as to get in the way. Architects, on the other hand, more commonly use parallel rules because they tend to draw buildings at scales which do not require the frequent depiction of very slight angles and they need the ability to draw the long lines typically associated with large sites and orthogonal buildings.

Compasses

The **compass** is an instrument used for drawing circles and parts of circles with either pencil or pen. Small circles are drawn with a bow compass. Circles with radii just beyond the limits of the bow compass may be drawn with an extension arm attached to the compass. A circle with a very large radius is drawn with a beam compass (Fig. 1–24). When using pencil, lead points in the compass must be kept sharp in order to prevent too great a change in line width as the circle is drawn. Also, the degree of hardness should be selected with care: very soft leads may wear down and create thicker marks by the end of a large circle, whereas very hard ones may leave too light a mark. (It is difficult to apply great pressure to lead when drawing with a compass.)

When drawing an arc, or portion of a circle, that is connected to another line, one should try to draw the arc first and then start the line at the point of connection in order to get a smooth transition from the straight to the curved line. (Starting at the other end, and trying to connect to the straight line, is considerably more difficult and depends on the angle of the hand, exact position of the compass, etc.)

Templates

Templates are stencils of predetermined shapes or objects that can be used by the architect or artist to add the selected element to a drawing. This can be

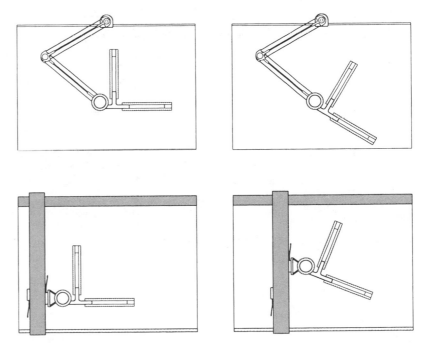

Fig. 1–23 Drafting machines. Arm- and track-style drafting machines work well for efficient drafting where short lines and many angles are required.

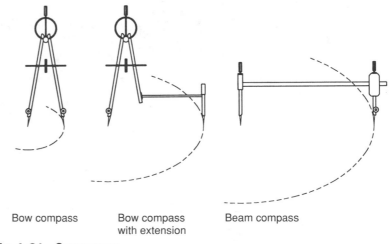

Bow compass   Bow compass with extension   Beam compass

Fig. 1–24 Compasses

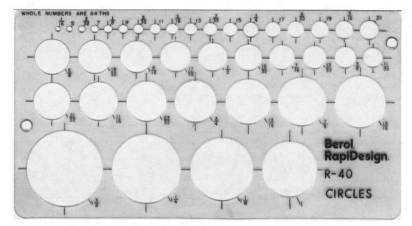

Fig. 1–25   Circle template   (*Sanford-Berol*)

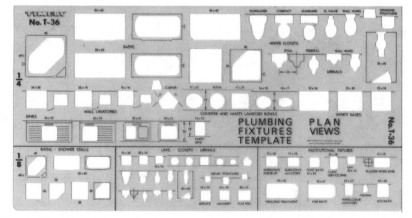

Fig. 1–26   Plumbing or bathroom template   (*Timely Products Co., Inc.*)

done with the hand by literally tracing with pen or pencil the hole(s) cut out in plastic or heavy cardboard. *When using templates, the exact size and scale needed for the drawing must be selected.* (This explains the need for "circle templates" containing many different sizes of circles [Fig. 1–25].) The primary purpose of templates is to save drawing time by preventing the need for measuring and construction of repetitive or complex shapes built up of multiple simpler shapes. Templates also save time and promote uniformity in drawing repeated elements.

Templates can be obtained for shapes (circles, ellipses, squares, triangles, etc.) or for unique elements that are frequently used in drawings. Furniture templates have symbols for desks, chairs, tables, and other common elements. Bathroom templates have plumbing fixtures (tubs, toilets, sinks, showers) of different sizes (Fig. 1–26). There are also templates for other specialized elements, including lettering, as well as electrical and structural symbols.

Templates (like T squares, parallel rules, and triangles) should be cleaned regularly to avoid smearing dirt or graphite on the drawing. In order to prevent ink from running under the template during its use, the template may be raised above the drawing surface by taping a few coins to the bottom of the template.

French Curves and Flexible Rules

French curves are guides for irregular curves, usually made of plastic or metal (Fig. 1–27). **Flexible rules** are rules, usually made of metal (with or without a rubber coating), that can be shaped into a variety of curvilinear forms to be used as drawing guides (Fig. 1–28). The french curve may have to be moved a number of times to create a smooth curve connecting position-critical points; and great precision may be required for smooth transitions. As was the case with arcs drawn with compasses, it is helpful whenever possible to start the curve at the intersection of another line rather than trying to meet a line already drawn. When the curve is connected by straight lines or regular geometric curves, it is sometimes helpful to draw the irregular curves first. Because of the comparative frequency of orthogonal conditions and regular curves in building, french curves and flexible rules are used with less frequency than the other tools previously mentioned.

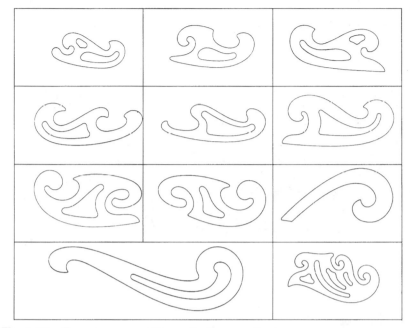

Fig. 1–27 French curves (*Charrette Corporation*)

Scales

The word *scale*, in describing architecture, refers to how big something is (or seems to be) in relation to something else. The scale of a drawing is the relation of the size of the object as drawn (fraction or increment) to full size. Architects frequently draw representations of buildings or parts of buildings that are smaller than full size in order to fit the image on a standard sheet of paper. Some complex small details may be drawn larger

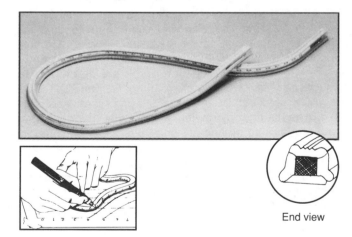

End view

Fig. 1–28 Flexible rule with inking diagram (*Art provided by Alvin & Company, Inc.*)

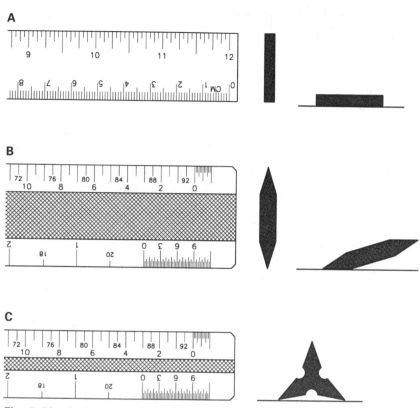

Fig. 1–29 Architectural scales. Scales above are smaller than actual size. Not shown are two-sided beveled scales (flat and opposite). *A,* Square edge rulers. Graduations sit above the paper. Precise reading and measuring of lines are difficult. *B,* Four-bevel scale. The scale can be pressed down at any edge so that graduation marks are placed flat against the drawing surface to facilitate accurate reading. *C,* Triangular scale. Perhaps the most widely used architectural scale, it has six marked edges, two of which always lie flat on the drawing surface. The triangular shape makes the operation of picking up and moving the scale easy. To improve drafting speed and productivity, many triangular scales have the concave center stripes color coded to facilitate scale identification and reduce the need to check the graduations each time the scale is used. Typical triangular architectural scales have eleven scales on six sides: (1) ¼" and ⅛"; (2) 1" and ½"; (3) 1½" and 3"; (4) ⅜" and ¾"; (5) ³⁄₁₆" and ³⁄₃₂"; and (6) 16 graduations per inch.

than full size in order to study the precise way materials are to be connected. The scale at which an image is drawn or printed can vary depending on its intended use and the amount of information it contains. *The larger the scale of a drawing, the more information one expects to see on that drawing.*

Typical architectural scales are expressed in inches to feet but may be more easily understood when expressed in consistent units (like inches to inches). For example, ¼" = 1'0" (which is the same as ¼" = 12") is actually $\frac{1}{48}$ full size, since 1" = 48". Similarly, ⅛" = 1'0" (or ⅛" scale) is $\frac{1}{96}$" full size, and 3" = 1' is ¼ full size. (See Box 1–H.)

Scale, when describing a drawing *tool,* refers to an instrument marked with precise graduations used for proportional representation.

Scales are used to help measure or create a line on a drawing that represents a line of a different length in the building or object itself. Scales are available in varying sizes and shapes (Fig. 1–29). Drawings or images created in which the representation is the same size as the object are said to be "full or actual size" or "full or actual scale." (Many other nations and international organizations use the metric *Système International d'Unités* [often abbreviated as SI metric] established in 1960 rather than the English system.) **Engineering scales** (different from metric scales) are usually expressed in decimal proportion and include 1 to 10 (1' = 10', written 1:10), 1:20, 1:30, 1:40, 1:50, and 1:60.

Box 1–H

SCALES IN ARCHITECTURE AND DESIGN

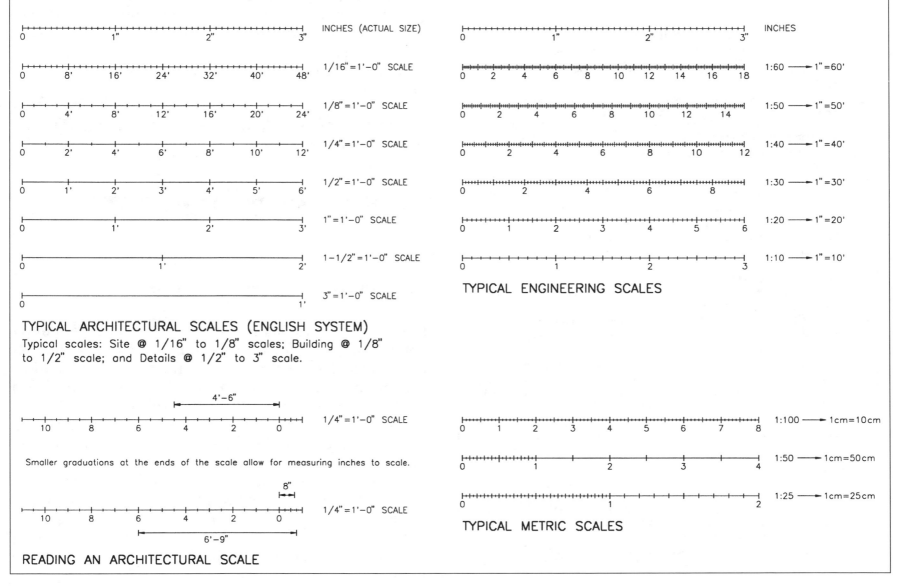

INCHES (ACTUAL SIZE)

1/16"=1'-0" SCALE

1/8"=1'-0" SCALE

1/4"=1'-0" SCALE

1/2"=1'-0" SCALE

1"=1'-0" SCALE

1-1/2"=1'-0" SCALE

3"=1'-0" SCALE

TYPICAL ARCHITECTURAL SCALES (ENGLISH SYSTEM)
Typical scales: Site @ 1/16" to 1/8" scales; Building @ 1/8" to 1/2" scale; and Details @ 1/2" to 3" scale.

4'-6"

1/4"=1'-0" SCALE

Smaller graduations at the ends of the scale allow for measuring inches to scale.

8"

1/4"=1'-0" SCALE

6'-9"

READING AN ARCHITECTURAL SCALE

INCHES

1:60 ⟶ 1"=60'

1:50 ⟶ 1"=50'

1:40 ⟶ 1"=40'

1:30 ⟶ 1"=30'

1:20 ⟶ 1"=20'

1:10 ⟶ 1"=10'

TYPICAL ENGINEERING SCALES

1:100 ⟶ 1cm=10cm

1:50 ⟶ 1cm=50cm

1:25 ⟶ 1cm=25cm

TYPICAL METRIC SCALES

With practice, architects have traditionally learned to think and see in typical scales. As will be seen later, one of the greatest differences between drawing and modeling buildings on computer and by hand is the reduced reliance on proportional scales. The model and drawing can be created in the computer in full scale and just viewed on the computer screen (usually) as a smaller or larger representation.

A summary of drafting tips for use with traditional media is given in Box 1–I.

1.2 DIGITAL DRAWING TOOLS

1.2.1 Putting Images on Screen

Design professionals involved in graphics frequently create images with the assistance of digital media. Images can be created in their entirety as digital information, or there can be a mix of digital (computer) and analog (hand-drawn and/or photographed) information—mixed media. Like the pen and pencil, the mouse and stylus can be seen as extensions of the hand, creating lines and areas of color that can be seen on a computer screen and stored as digital, electronic information. Although there are some common characteristics noticeable in digital imagery, the computer can nevertheless assist the designer in creating unique images or it can simulate aspects of traditional media.

Computers and Monitors

Computers (Figs. 1–30, 1–31) are useful machines for architectural design in part because they can process numeric digital information rapidly and can represent it graphically. (The graphic files one sees displayed on a computer screen are, in fact, created and stored digitally.) The generic components of significance to those who wish to use the computer as a graphic tool are the processor(s) (central processing unit [CPU], chips made with silicon wafers), storage devices for keeping files of the drawings made and to store the graphic programs used in drawing (hard disk, tape, floppy or portable disks of various types, etc.), the memory used by the computer while it is working (random access memory [RAM]), a method of displaying information (monitor, graphics card, display device and driver), and a way to put data into the computer (mouse, stylus, keyboard, etc.). (See Box 1–J.)

The **central processor**, in part, determines the capabilities and speed of the computer. It is the "main brain" of the machine. When one selects computers to work on, or moves from one to another, it is important to determine if the processor will be able to (efficiently) run a particular application. The type, speed, and number of processors establish a number of the working parameters for the computer.

Storage space is always at a premium for graphics. Although a typical compact disc with read-only memory (CD-ROM) may be able to contain an entire encyclopedia with thousands of pages of text (and still have room

Fig. 1–30 CAD/graphics workstation. Computer (tower case), monitor, keyboard, and mouse. (*Digital Equipment Corporation*)

Fig. 1–31 Students working in a digital design studio. Computer hardware with a variety of application packages is available for use. (*New Jersey Institute of Technology*)

Box 1–J

COMPUTER COMPONENTS AND ATTRIBUTES

Central processor

- Partly responsible for determining the capabilities of the computer. Manufactured by different companies (Intel, Motorola, Cyrix, AMD, DEC, etc.), the central processor type determines which set(s) of software will run on the computer and, to some extent, how fast it can run.

- Responsible for much of the sorting of instructions and calculations (the "computing") in a computer.

- Because graphics is very processor intensive, slow processors can result in long delays for creating and redrawing images.

- Manipulating images requires so much memory and computer power (much more than typical analytical engineering applications) that it almost always makes sense to use the most powerful and fastest computer processor available.

- Computers are available with more than one processor, which allows instructions to be divided among them and worked on at the same time ("parallel processing").

Random access memory

- Short-term operating storage for running computer software.

- When the computer is turned on, RAM is memory that is active and available for use. When the computer is turned off, the information in RAM disappears.

- The amount of RAM available for active use depends on how much is installed in the computer and the amount being used to operate the system itself.

- RAM is both temporary storage and active working space. While the computer is on, the program (or portions of the program) is loaded into RAM in order to work more efficiently. The size of RAM limits the type of program one can run. *Insufficient RAM can prevent the operation of various graphic programs.*

- The amount of RAM can limit the file size for the drawing or electronic model that one creates. Various CAD/graphics programs require that the active file—or drawing information—be loaded into RAM in order to work. *Note: In many instances, the active drawing file is required to be loaded into RAM in order to be modified. If there is insufficient RAM, the file cannot be opened. A file created on a computer with a certain amount of RAM may not be able to be transferred to, and worked on in, a machine with smaller amounts of RAM.*

- In those instances where a program allows operation even if it cannot be accommodated by installed RAM, intermittent and slow referring (or "paging") to the permanent storage on the fixed hard disk is usually needed. *Insufficient RAM can slow down the operation of the computer.*

"Permanent" storage

- File-cabinet-like storage for both programs and drawings or models.

- Once saved, the files placed in storage reside on the medium until erased or destroyed. Note: Overwriting a file (saving with the same file name) is equivalent to erasing and destroying the older version. The information remains intact when the computer is turned off.

- Hard disks (either mounted within the computer or externally connected), floppy disks, tape, CD-ROM, magneto-optical disks, and floptical disks as well as proprietary solutions, are among the common storage devices and are available in various capacities.

- Large amounts of storage are needed for both graphics programs and graphics files. *(One two-dimensional bit-mapped image [true color at 800×600 resolution] easily fills a portable high-density 1.44 MB floppy disk. Three-dimensional models frequently exceed the capacity of most "consumer-sized" floppy disks and need to be transferred from one machine to another over a network [hard-wired connection] or modem*

Cont'd

COMPUTER COMPONENTS AND ATTRIBUTES, CONT'D

[telephone link used to transmit data between otherwise unconnected computers]).

- Portable or external hard disks, tape, floptical disks, and optical disks can be used to transfer and store large files.

Monitor

- The screen used for visible display of work, which, together with the display driver, determines what one actually sees.
- Screen sizes vary, with 17" to 21" the preferable sizes. Monitor sizes below 15" are not viable for graphics work. If one is limited by the size of the monitor, it may be difficult to see—and therefore create—large portions of images with detail. Since many architects and designers may spend a great deal of time designing and drawing in front of a computer screen, large monitors can help to reduce fatigue and usually become a good investment in productivity.
- Monitor size and clarity have no impact on the drawing file itself.
- Antiglare coating on screens can help reduce veiling reflections present under poor room lighting conditions.
- Dot pitch, the size of the individual elements displayed by the monitor, affects the clarity of the image. The smaller the dot pitch, the finer the image. For graphics work, dot pitches of .28 mm and below are helpful.
- Screens are available with varying degrees of flatness. All other factors being equal, monitors that are described as flattened, or flat in the vertical dimension, show less distortion.
- Brightness and contrast controls are available on almost all monitors. The ability to rotate slightly skewed images or to adjust pincushioning distortion (bulging or constriction along the horizontal centerline) are helpful features available on some monitors used for CAD/graphics.

to spare), it would be able to contain fewer than four hundred mid- to high-resolution two-dimensional images without compressing the files. (Compressing a file uses mathematical formulae for reducing the amount of space the program file takes on its storage device, which, at times, can result in loss of portions of the data.) Three-dimensional digital files can take up even more space. The programs used for graphics creation and manipulation are larger still. As computers become more powerful graphic tools, demands for storage capacity increase.

When one creates a drawing on the computer, some programs and operating systems require the storage of temporary information on the hard disk, thereby taking up room that one would otherwise think is available. It is, therefore, often important to keep room available for work.

A wide variety of media is available for transferring or storing files and programs. In general, the more storage space available, the longer one will be able to use a particular computer. It is important to remember that graphics takes up so much file space that the workstations used by architects and designers usually require extensive storage capacity—considerably beyond that of the typical business user. The smallest unit of storage in a computer is a **bit,** which refers to binary information: 1 or 0, on or off, presence or lack of presence of a signal. A **byte** is a storage unit of 8 bits. A "simple" ten-minute animation or walk-through of an architectural project needs digital storage that exceeds 1 gigabyte (GB). Internal hard disks (nonremovable, inside the box of the computer) used for CAD/graphics are commonly measured in gigabytes. Externally connected storage devices are available in varying capacities (Fig. 1–32).

The monitor and display driver determine what one actually sees while working. Although final output does not necessarily depend on what one sees, the process of image creation does. The screen is made up of **pixels** (picture elements), which are individual dots of color (Fig. 1–33). Resolution of the screen varies. When personal computers were introduced in the early 1980s the common resolution was 320 pixels wide by 200 pixels high. Resolutions for graphics continue to increase, with 1280 × 1024 pixels, 1600 × 1200 pixels, and higher readily available. Higher resolutions produce clearer pictures that allow for greater precision in image creation (Box 1–K). (*A very important note: A pixel-based image of a specific resolution requires the same storage capacity as another image of the same resolution—regardless of the number of lines or shapes! The higher the resolution, the larger the image file and the greater the need for large amounts of digital storage.*) In addition to the resolution of the screen, the dot pitch (how large the individual pixels look on the monitor) also affects the apparent clarity of the image. For graphics work, dot pitches of .28 mm and below should be used. (In general, the smaller the dot pitch, the finer the image. However, some monitor tube types, like Trinitron, measure "lines" rather than dots. Apparent clarity may be equivalent at *slightly* higher numbers.) *The dot pitch does not affect file size or hard-copy output—only the appearance on*

Fig. 1–32 Disk array. External disks may be grouped and connected to desktop computers or servers to provide gigabytes of additional storage. (*Raidion Disk Array by Micropolis Corporation*)

Fig. 1–33 Pixels are individual picture elements that exist as dots of color. The number of pixels available on the screen is dependent on the monitor and graphics device driver.

screen. Screen brightness and the lighting in the room in which the monitor is placed also impact the apparent clarity.

Monitor size, like dot pitch, affects only what one sees on the screen and has no impact on the file itself. However, if one is limited in size by the monitor, it may be difficult to see—and therefore create—large portions of images with detail. (Constant zooming in or out, and moving of an image to see portions of it clearly, can slow down the designer, which may inhibit the creation process and prevent the designer from being able to evaluate relationships between areas of a drawing.) In general, monitors to be used for CAD/graphics for extended periods of time should be at least 17" if working with 1024 × 768 resolution. Higher resolutions show enough information to warrant larger monitors.

Input Devices

A computer can only process and display information that has been put into it. An **input device** is a piece of equipment used by a person to give a computer information. Input devices often need cleaning or maintenance. Broken or improperly operating devices can greatly reduce the efficiency of CAD/graphics operations and result in enormous frustration on the part of the user.

A number of different input devices are used by the architect and designer when working with a computer

Box 1–K

SAMPLE IMAGE RESOLUTIONS AND FILE SIZES

Resolution (pixels)	Grayscale (8 bit) (256 shades)	True Color (24 bit)	True Color (32 bit)
320 × 200	64 KB	187 KB	250 KB
512 × 482	241 KB	723 KB	964 KB
640 × 400	250 KB	750 KB	1.0 MB
640 × 480	300 KB	900 KB	1.2 MB
800 × 600	468 KB	1.406 MB	1.875 MB
1024 × 768	768 KB	2.304 MB	3.072 MB
1152 × 870	978 KB	2.936 MB	3.915 MB
1280 × 1024	1.28 MB	3.84 MB	5.12 MB
1600 × 1200	1.875 MB	5.625 MB	7.5 MB

Increase in either the number of pixels in an image or the color information (color "depth") results in an increase in file size for the image. The larger the file size, the greater the need for storage.

The resolutions in pixels shown above represent common "platforms" or maximums available with different systems. Images can be sized to be less than the maximum within paint and image processing programs.

Note: In the chart above, *KB* represents kilobytes (1024 bytes) and *MB* represents megabytes (1024 kilobytes). File sizes are uncompressed and represent TGA (Truevision Targa) files.

Fig. 1–34 Drawing tablets. Small tablets may be used for input with puck or stylus. The stylus is held in the same way one would hold a pen. (*DrawingSlate II, photograph courtesy of CalComp*)

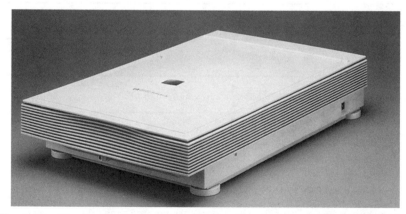

Fig. 1–35 Desktop color scanner. Flat-bed scanners capable of accepting work from 8½″ × 14″ to 11″ × 17″ are relatively inexpensive and good for incorporating photographs, site information, and other artwork into schematic design activities or in the preparation of electronic documents and presentation images. Together with optical character recognition (OCR) software for scanning printed text into a word processing program, a scanner is part of most desktop publishing facilities. (*Hewlett-Packard*)

(Box 1–L). The **keyboard** and **mouse** are two of the most ubiquitous devices, but the **trackball, stylus** or **pressure pen, digitizing tablet** (Fig. 1–34), and **scanner** are also used.

Care must be taken when using the mouse and keyboard to avoid repetitive stress injury. Wrist pads and braces, as well as specially designed keyboards, have been created with the intention of increasing comfort and reducing the likelihood of injury. The constant and rapid clicking of a mouse button with the same finger (usually the index finger) must also be controlled. Occasional rest and exercise are often important when using these devices.

Scanners are in a somewhat different category of input devices because they have more in common with office photocopy machines than they do with other input mechanisms (Figs. 1–35, 1–36). Scanners take electronic pictures of items—which is a direct method for taking analog information (printed or drawn images on paper or transparencies) and copying it into the computer, converting it into two-dimensional images on a pixel-by-pixel basis.

Typical flat-bed scanned images contain only dot-by-dot information and do not contain information associated with lines, shapes, or three-dimensional form. The computer must process line drawings through a set of complex instructions and tests in order to make an initial attempt to convert the dots to line data if desired. Because of the imperfection of initial drawings being scanned (including skips and jagged edges), and

Box 1–L

INPUT DEVICES AND ATTRIBUTES

Keyboard

- An alphanumeric console (sometimes called **QWERTY keyboard**, because these are the first six letters at the top left of the board) used to enter character-based information or commands (text and numeric values) for CAD/graphics applications.
- Used to enter dimensional information (lengths of lines, sizes of shapes, distance between objects, etc.).
- Using the keyboard is frequently the fastest method of entering commands or information into the computer. Although frequently less intuitive than graphic-based commands, keyboard "shortcuts" can speed up operation for a variety of applications.
- Common to virtually every computer used by design professionals for CAD/graphics work.

Mouse

- Central component of a graphic (sometimes referred to as "graphical") user interface (GUI) and used in some way by virtually every graphics application program.
- Controls the cursor (pointer) on the screen.
- A line drawn with a mouse into the computer is analogous to a line drawn with pen or pencil on paper.
- Depending on the particular program being used, different buttons on the mouse and the number of "clicks" of the button execute different commands.
- Used as a selection device to choose commands from a list on the screen (menu) rather than typing the commands in on a keyboard.
- Mice may be mechanical, optical, or a combination of the two. Mechanical mice require periodic cleaning of the rolling ball and contacts.
- A mouse pad helps protect the mouse and makes motion smoother.

Trackball

- Comparable to an "inverted" mouse with the ball moved directly with the hand.
- Oils and dirt from the user's hand are easily transferred to the trackball, causing skipping and other symptoms of improper operation.
- Although it is suitable for business applications, many people find it difficult to use with precision as compared to using a mouse.

Stylus/pressure pen

- Looks and feels like a ballpoint pen and is used in conjunction with a dedicated tablet (6″ × 9″ minimum).
- Pressure-sensitive, or pressure-sensing stylus and tablet combinations available, which, with certain programs, allow one to create correspondingly darker or lighter and thicker or thinner lines depending on the pressure applied.
- Useful for electronic freehand sketching and when using the computer to simulate pressure-sensitive traditional media (felt tip marker, oil, etc.)
- Feels most like a "traditional" tool.
- May be physically connected to the computer or may be wireless.

Digitizing tablet

- Used most commonly with electronic drafting programs to increase efficiency by acting as a means to shortcut keyboard commands.
- The tablet is a pad connected to the computer that is configured, according to its particular set of instructions, so that contacts at particular points on the tablet correspond to instructions and/or places on screen. It is used to transfer screen menus (icons or pictures, or text) or command line activity to selection points on the tablet.
- Particularly useful when working with landscape or geographic information systems (GIS) as a means to transfer data about landform into digital format. Because points on a tablet correspond to points in the image, one can "trace" with the puck (a mouse-type device associated with a digitizing tablet) information on the tablet and convert it into a drawing on screen—and in the computer. (This type of "manual" tracing can be applied to other image types as well.)

because of the ambiguity of certain graphic conventions and lines, the conversion processes can be inadequate and require additional input (and work) by the user from within the drafting program.

Scanned photographic images may need modification by the user to improve color, brightness, contrast, and clarity (focus or sharpness). Nevertheless, in a modified design process that utilizes the potential of electronic media, scanners become a critical component and important input device. They are particularly useful in placing images, like photographs of building sites or furniture that will be used in a new project, into the computer for electronic modification.

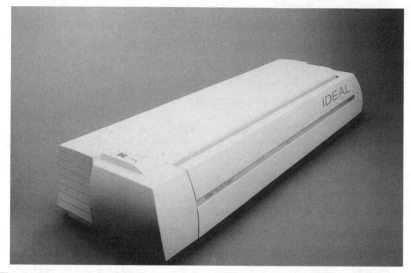

Fig. 1–36 Large-format scanner. Scanners that can accept large (up to 48" wide) drawings are most widely used in commercial applications for converting existing traditional line drawings to digital vector drawings for storage and manipulation. Conversion to digital format allows for their use in facilities management applications and renovation of existing buildings, and, increasingly, for rapid transmission of graphic information to emergency personnel (fire department and police) in case of disaster. (*Ideal Scanners and Systems*)

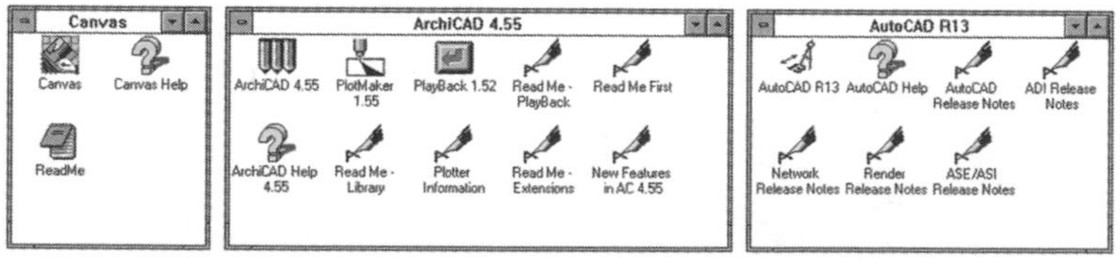

1.2.2 Helping the Hand and Machine— Computer Software

Computer software consists of the list of instructions, in order, given to a computer to execute a program. **CAD** (sometimes written CADD or CAAD) software ambiguously refers to programs that involve either computer-aided drafting or computer-assisted design. The acronym CADD actually refers to computer-aided drafting and design software, whereas CAAD more specifically refers to computer-aided architectural design. **CAD/graphics** refers both to drafting-specific software and to generalized graphics software that is useful to architects and designers. The software is what allows the computer to be a helpful tool and it does not have to be "profession specific" to be useful for graphic communication. (In other words, graphic designers, furniture

Fig. 1–37 Software applications. There are numerous application packages useful to architects and designers that are available for different operating systems and platforms. (*Microsoft® Windows™, Canvas by Deneba Software; ArchiCAD by Graphisoft US, Inc.; and AutoCAD by Autodesk, Inc. Screen shot reprinted with permission from Microsoft Corporation*)

designers, animators, publishers, architects, and planners may all use some of the same software packages—although for different purposes.) Furthermore, within the generic graphic software types, different proprietary packages may have varying benefits for individuals (Fig. 1–37).

Raster Graphics—Painting

A **raster image** is one that is created solely as a series of dots or pixels (Fig. 1–38). There is no intelligence associated with the image other than the color of each dot in its specific location within the prescribed resolution. In its simplest format, a raster painting is only a flat two-dimensional representation that can simulate a three-dimensional model or movement in space by changing the color of individual dots. In some programs, however, one can create a painting that is rotated in space and applied onto (or wrapped around) a three-dimensional model.

Painting refers to the use of raster, or bit-mapped, software packages to create images. A software package is referred to as a paint program when one is only painting, or creating color (including shades of gray and black and white), on dots (Figs. 1–39, 1–40). The information contained in these drawings is completely dependent on the resolution of the image and in some instances can be tied to the specific graphics device driver (also known in some systems as a graphics card)—or at least file type—being used. (Note: It is possible to convert one file type to another and to convert color resolutions with image processing software.) The computer file associates information with each dot on the screen.

Fig. 1–38 Raster or painted image of Henry Hobson Richardson's Ames Library   (*Sara Gordon, NJIT*)

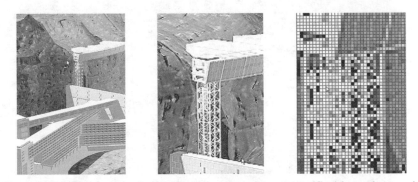

Fig. 1–39 Pixel-by-pixel editing. Images can be magnified in order to allow work on discrete pixels.   (*Amado Batour, NJIT*)

Fig. 1–40 Screen image of paint program. Tools are shown as icons (pictures) on the right of the screen. Color palette from which selections may be made is at the top center. (*Image by Sean McCarry, NJIT. Paint software is PhotoFinish by Softkey International, Inc. © 1995*)

Each dot has a color (or a shade of gray). The more dots available, the greater the file size of the image. The more colors possible, the greater the file size of the image.

The amount of information per pixel, or bits per pixel, determines the number of colors and the degrees of transparency available in the image (Box 1–M). For example, a 24-bit-per-pixel image will provide approximately 16.7 million colors—sometimes referred to as true color. The increased number of colors allows for smooth gradations between elements in shading and rendering. Limiting the number of colors can result in visible banding (a clear distinction between adjacent areas of color) when attempting to illustrate smooth transitions—like light falling on a curved surface. Nonetheless, it should be noted that the use of 32,000 to 65,000 colors selectable out of a palette of 256,000 colors is adequate to create well-composed, attractive images and requires less storage space for files. The number of colors needed depends on the particular requirements of the image and the way it will be created. *Images created by painting, in which the user maintains control by selecting every color, one at a time, can be created with fewer colors than one would need in a program where colors are selected by material or through some automated means.*

Paint programs can be used to add color, texture, or tone to a line drawing. Paint programs allow the artist or designer an opportunity to transform the precise definition of surfaces and edges to representations that

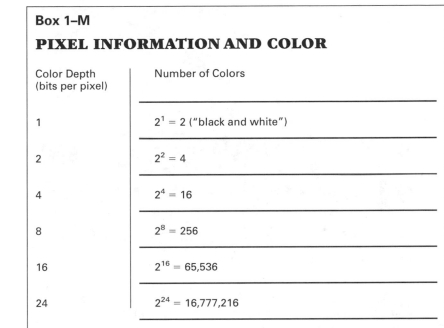

Box 1–M

PIXEL INFORMATION AND COLOR

Color Depth (bits per pixel)	Number of Colors
1	$2^1 = 2$ ("black and white")
2	$2^2 = 4$
4	$2^4 = 16$
8	$2^8 = 256$
16	$2^{16} = 65,536$
24	$2^{24} = 16,777,216$

Increase in color resolution results in increased file size. File size of bit-mapped images depends on *both* the amount of information per pixel (color depth) and the image resolution (number of pixels).

Conversion of files from a lower level of pixel information to a higher one within a graphics software package will not result in changes of existing colors. However, additional colors will become available.

Conversion of files from a higher level of pixel information to a lower one within a graphics software package results in a reduction of the number of colors within the image itself and may cause visible changes because some colors may have to be eliminated.

Because pixel information is binary (on-off or 0-1), the number of colors available generally will be a power of 2. (The above description represents a simplification of computer displays, which also deal with red, green, and blue guns, bitplanes, etc.)

include greater detail and provide opportunities to personalize the image by a method that most closely corresponds to traditional drawing or painting techniques. The pixel-by-pixel drawing involves selective editing by the creator and electronically returns a digital model to a sketch format, giving a freedom and directness similar to that of freehand rendering. As with a traditional drawing, one is applying line and color to a surface (albeit electronic and color emitting). Unlike a traditional painting, however, this image can be modified using electronic techniques—without destroying the original when it is saved in digital format. The pixel-by-pixel application of color allows the greatest flexibility in the presentation of the image and can give it unique style or character (Figs. 1–41, 1–42).

Fig. 1–41 Raster re-creation of "San Marco, Venice" (1881) by Pierre-Auguste Renoir (1841–1919). The facsimile of this painting, illustrating its style and character, was reproduced completely within a painting program. (*Peter Agnello, NJIT*)

Fig. 1–42 A single view of a three-dimensional model is painted in a personal style. (*Eric Trepkau, NJIT*)

Vector Graphics—Drawing and Modeling

In addition to storing information about colors of dots on a screen, the computer can store information about drawing elements by using their mathematical definitions. **Vector drawings** are those in which the lines, planes, and volumes are created and stored according to mathematical formulae that refer to coordinates in space (either two- or three-dimensional) and that are *independent* of the graphic resolution of the display devices used for viewing (Fig. 1–43). In other words, a line that is created in a vector drawing program maintains its length and digital precision in any computer capable of reading the file created. It has no relationship whatsoever to the resolution of the system being used to create or view the line. If one is viewing the line on a low-resolution system, jagged "stairstepping" might be visible in a diagonal line. However, because the line is straight in its mathematical representation, the line can be printed as straight and can be viewed as straighter on higher-resolution systems. (This is in contrast to a raster image described in the previous section, which is tied to the resolution of the file established at the outset of image creation.)

Vector drawings can often be transferred from one computer system to another, because the mathematical definitions of lines are clear. Vector drawings are the type most commonly used for model creation and drafting in CAD/graphics systems (Figs. 1–44, 1–45). (Drawings that can be saved in a common format may be able to be imported into a different program or application for further work.) The thickness and types of lines drawn, as well as a line's orientation, can be defined with mathematical precision. The principle of creating vector drawings is the same whether they are two-dimensional or three-dimensional. Two-dimensional representations have less information than three-dimensional ones and therefore have correspondingly reduced storage space requirements to save the information. Also, since there is less information to manipulate, the computer can calculate changes more rapidly.

When dealing with three-dimensional information, different computer programs choose to create and store information according to different model types. Drawings, or models, can be created with lines and points in three-dimensional space, with surfaces or planes, or with actual solid objects (Fig. 1–46). Although

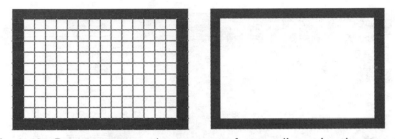

Fig. 1–43 Raster vs. vector data structure for two-dimensional rectangle. Image on the left is made of "just dots"—either black or white. Image on the right is four lines with mathematical formulae and vector coordinates associated. The two objects are created and modified differently. (Note that the square boxes would not normally be seen on an image unless magnified a few hundred times.) Raster = filling in dots. Vector = drawing lines and shapes.

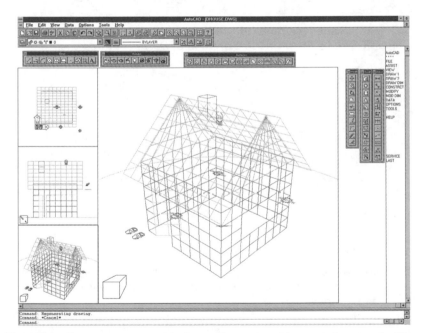

Fig. 1–44 Screen capture with three-dimensional image of vector drafting and modeling program (AutoCAD). (*This image has been reprinted with the permission from and under the copyright of Autodesk, Inc.*)

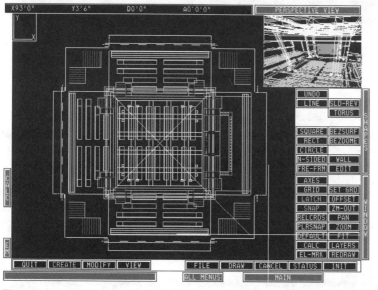

Fig. 1–45 Screen capture of vector drafting and modeling program (*MegaMODEL by MegaCADD, a division of Design Futures, Inc.*)

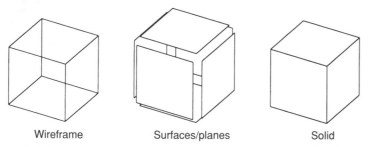

Wireframe   Surfaces/planes   Solid

Fig. 1–46 Three-dimensional models. All of the above may represent the same object, but because the data structure varies, the way the objects can be modified varies.

the digital information (and some graphic representations) defining the location in space may have some common qualities in the different model types, the mathematical definitions of the objects themselves vary. The type of model created determines the way in which the model may be manipulated later. (Note: Depending on the system, surfaces or planes or polygons may be able to be displayed as either transparent or filled.)

Whether dealing with site development, building design, or furniture design, it is likely that vector software will be used (Fig. 1–47).

File Formats

Each software application—whether raster or vector—usually has its own way of storing and organizing information. The data is organized into a file that conforms to the program's unique (and frequently idiosyncratic) way of doing things and that is referred to as its **native file format.** Even though a line or surface may be defined mathematically by the same equations, one program may not be able to directly read the file of another.

There are a variety of third-party utilities (programs created by entities that are distinct from those responsible for the CAD/graphics programs being used) that are available to convert one format into another—but the results do not always work acceptably. There are, however, a few common formats that programs can read and write. Two of the most common vector formats are International Graphic Exchange Specification (**IGES**) and Drawing Exchange Format (**DXF**)—a de facto standard created and trademarked by Autodesk, Inc. Many software applications can import and export to these formats. Be warned that because these formats can represent the "lowest common denominators" readable by multiple applications, the size of files can grow substantially during the conversion process—sometimes by a factor of 10, depending on the original drawing program! In order to keep file sizes manageable, and to keep the speed of the computer processing as rapid as possible, files should usually remain in the native file format for working and be converted only to transfer the file from one program to another. Additionally, because embedded elements created within any program may be defined in a number of ways, translations may lose some of the original information.

Common raster file formats have been developed by a variety of companies, and conversion from one to another is sometimes an easier task than trying to translate three-dimensional data from a vector modeling program.

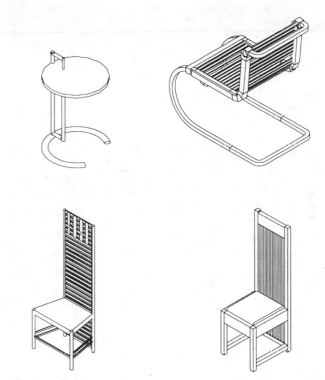

Fig. 1–47 Vector drawings based on (*clockwise from top left*) table designed by Eileen Gray and chairs designed by Mies van der Rohe, Frank Lloyd Wright, and Charles Rennie Mackintosh.

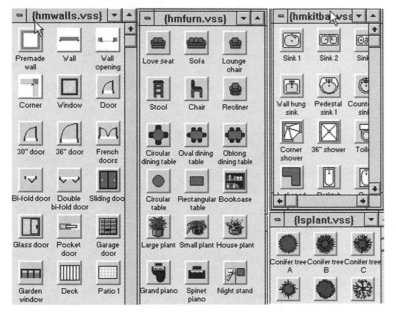

Fig. 1–48 Templates. Two-dimensional symbols used in creating drag-and-drop drawings. Walls, doors, residential furniture, bathroom fixtures, and trees are shown above. (*VISIO by Visio Corporation*)

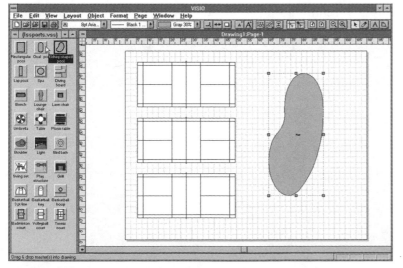

Fig. 1–49 Drag-and-drop drawing system with screen templates (*VISIO by Visio Corporation*)

1.2.3 Templates, Symbols, and Menus

Templates

Whereas templates are a convenience when drawing with traditional media, they are an integral component—and can form part of the conceptual base—of an electronic drawing system (Fig. 1–48). The principle of "drag-and-drop" (or, on some systems, "select-and-place") drawing relies on already-created shapes and forms that are chosen and deposited onto an image (Fig. 1–49). When using a traditional template, the specific size needed for the drawing must be selected and traced. However, when using an electronic template and drawing with computer, the selected element can be stretched to the appropriate size (either before or after final placement is made) and then repeated, rotated, and/or combined.

As in the case of traditional templates, electronic ones are frequently used by architects to save time when drawing and are available for many of the same purposes, including furniture layout (both commercial and residential), plumbing fixtures, electrical symbols, flowchart symbols, and a myriad of geometric shapes. However, electronic templates can also include a variety of wall types and thicknesses, as well as entire rooms that can be stretched to a desired size for either placement or experimentation during the design process. Templates contain groups of predesigned elements that have either use or geometric characteristics in common. Templates can save significant amounts of time when creating digital drawings.

(Templates can be obtained to work with different vector or raster programs, and it is also possible to create your own library of stencils or templates for frequently used repetitive elements.) Templates can be illustrated as part of a menu system for use when needed.

Symbols

Symbols are single predesigned shapes or elements for use in drawings. Templates or "libraries" can be made up of a collection of symbols that have some common properties. Symbols can be either two- or three-dimensional and, to be useful, must be available in a format that is compatible with the software being used. In addition to the traditional symbols found on templates, three-dimensional furniture, building and landscape elements, and people are particularly common and useful. Because symbols can be three-dimensional vector files, they can be placed in a building or space, resized, and turned or manipulated just as any other three-dimensional model in the program's file (Fig. 1–50).

Menus and Dialog Boxes

A **menu** is a list of operations visible on screen from which a user can select the desired command. The presence of a menu system relieves one of the requirement to remember every command without prompts or hints. Menus can be in the form of words (text) or pictures (icons)—or a combination of the two. Some menus

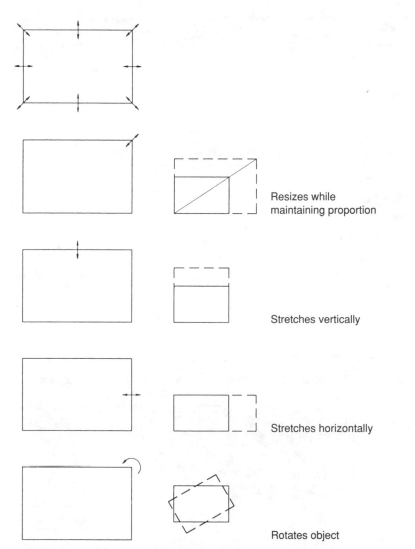

Resizes while maintaining proportion

Stretches vertically

Stretches horizontally

Rotates object

Fig. 1–50 To be useful, symbols selected from menus or templates must be able to be modified easily. The handle commands shown here are generic and will vary to some extent within any application. However, the use of handles, or control points, and their selection by mouse are fairly common. Note that the arrows represent commands and do not always represent control points—especially when rotating an object. (The diagram shows rotation about the center, a frequent default condition.)

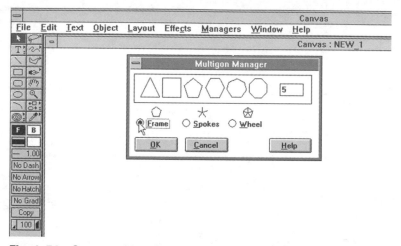

Fig. 1–51 Screen with menus of two-dimensional drawing program. The triangular arrows in the upper corners of the tool buttons indicate the presence of submenus. (*Canvas by Deneba Software*)

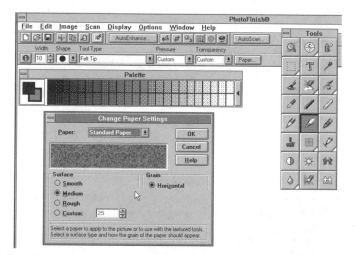

Fig. 1–52 Screen with icon-based menu for paint program. Small white triangles in lower right corner of tool buttons indicate the presence of submenus. (*PhotoFinish® by Softkey International, Inc. © 1995*)

have context-sensitive instructions that display text when the cursor is placed on the icon. The "help" instructions may appear at the bottom of the screen or in a text balloon at the icon. The tips help the inexperienced user of the software program and can, usually, be turned off when expertise is gained.

Menus can be located along the edges of the screen and/or arranged in "floating" palettes that the user can arrange in much the way papers and information are placed around a desktop when working with traditional media. Finally, some menus have **submenus** or **child menus,** which are second (or third, fourth, etc.) sets of menus or options relating to the original command that become visible upon a command's selection.

Dialog boxes are screen prompts in a graphically defined area giving and requesting information about an action selected by the user. Default, or preset values may be shown for an element that can simply be overwritten by the user (by placing the cursor over the element to be changed, highlighting or deleting the current value, and using the keyboard to enter new values). Under some circumstances, limited choices are given to the user from which selections must be made. Dialog boxes are program specific and may appear for everything from wall creation parameters to the selection of a printer for output (Figs. 1–51 through 1–53).

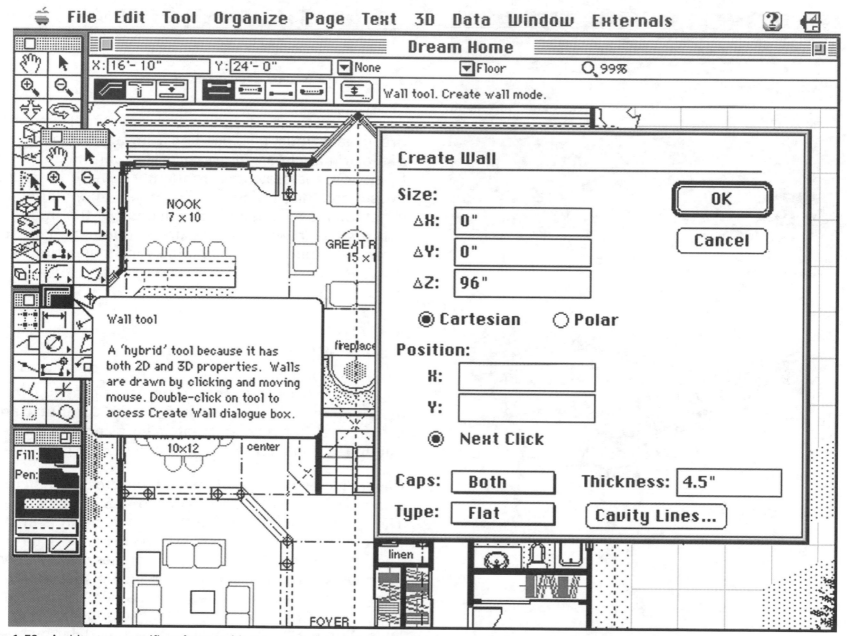

Fig. 1–53 Architecture-specific software with menu system on left. Pull-down menu categories are always along the top of the screen. The selected icon—a wall command in this example—is darkened, and the description of the command appears in a "help balloon." The dialog box appears, which allows the user to select the size of the wall. In this example, only the height (ΔZ) is listed, as 96". (*MiniCAD by Graphsoft, Inc.*)

Fig. 1–54 Desktop laser printer (*Hewlett-Packard*)

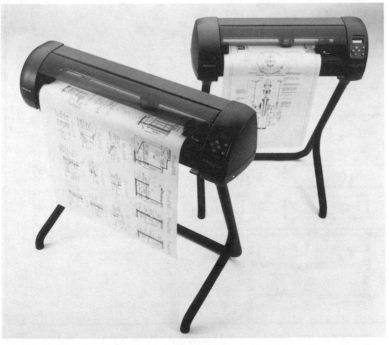

Fig. 1–55 Large-format ink jet plotters (*Photograph courtesy of CalComp*)

1.3 DRAWINGS AND OUTPUT

1.3.1 Paper and Drafting Film

As architects and designers use traditional media to draw, marks must be placed on a surface. Because one of the primary goals of graphics is to communicate information, the drawings frequently have to be reproduced and disseminated. The type of material on which marks are made is a reflection of the intended use of the drawing. There are a number of paper, film, and board types available for architectural use (Box 1–N).

1.3.2 Plotters and Printers

In order to be able to see and present drawings created with digital media away from the computer and screen, we often have to create a **hard copy**, or printed output (as opposed to a digital copy) (Box 1–O).

Depending on the type of image to be created, different printers (Fig. 1–54) and plotters (Fig. 1–55) can be used. The difference between plotting and printing is analogous to the difference between vector and raster images. Plotters create copies of vector files, or line drawings, which are resolution independent. Because the lines being plotted are based on mathematical formulae, there are no unintentional jagged edges on angled lines. Printers create copies of text and bit-mapped

Box 1–N

PAPER AND FILM TYPES AND CHARACTERISTICS

Tracing paper (trace, flimsy)

- *Thin, lightweight medium used for sketching or overlays.*
- Available in cream, white, and yellow.
- Relatively inexpensive, and most common material used for (freehand) design sketches. (The "back of napkin" type of sketches architects draw are frequently drawn on trace.)
- Available in a variety of sizes, typically 50-yd rolls varying from 12" to 36" wide.
- Best used with soft pencils, felt tip markers, and charcoal. Paper tears easily with hard leads.
- Can be used for presentation drawings with pencil and/or felt tip markers.

Vellum

- *White translucent paper suitable for use with pencil or pen.*
- Made from 100% rag vellum and available in pads and rolls with different sizes and weights (16, 20, and 24 lb).
- Available in rolls, pads, and cut sheets (with and without nonprint "layout" grid).
- Heavier and less transparent than trace.
- Lighter-weight paper is thinner and less expensive than heavier-weight and tears more easily from excessive pressure of pencils or from repeated erasing.
- Heavier-weight paper best for ink presentation drawings.
- Lighter-weight vellum commonly used for initial layouts of drafted material as underlays for tracing onto heavier vellum or other media.
- Vellum can "stretch" and expands with prolonged exposure to high humidity. (Under certain conditions, when vellum is taped down to a drafting table for tracing purposes and left overnight, the stretch can be noticeable.)

Drafting film (Mylar™)

- *Polyester drafting film is a dimensionally stable translucent material with at least one matte, nonglare side that is suitable for pen or pencil.*
- Various thicknesses available (0.003" and 0.004" most common).
- Available in rolls or cut sheets.
- Greater transparency than vellum or trace that makes it particularly suitable for overlays, as well as for a variety of reproduction processes.
- Drawing done on matte side. Available in single matte or double (two-sided) matte. (By allowing drawing on both sides, double matte allows for a variety of graphic effects for presentation drawings and/or for underlying organizational patterns that can later be erased without disturbing the finished drawing.)
- More expensive than trace or vellum. Double matte more expensive than single.
- Ink lines can be erased with vinyl erasers and a little water.
- Does not tear easily and is appropriate when a drawing is expected to be handled with frequency or by many people.

Illustration board

- *Thick boards (frequently ¹⁄₁₆" or ³⁄₃₂") with 100% rag facing suitable for pencil, pen, marker, watercolor, and airbrush, used for presentation purposes.*
- Boards are opaque, which requires that drawings be laid out directly on the board.
- Smoother boards tend to accept thin and crisp ruled lines better than nonsmooth.
- Erasing on boards must be done with great care to avoid marking or damaging the finish of the boards.
- Illustration boards can be used as a background and mounting surface on which other smaller drawings (photographs, prints, etc.) can be placed for presentation.

Box 1–0

PLOTTERS AND PRINTERS

Pen plotters

- *Pen points with ink are moved mechanically across paper or film to draw the lines defined by a vector drawing program.*
- Pen numbers, each potentially representing a different ink color or line weight (thickness), are assigned to lines within the drawing program.
- The number of pens (usually minimum of four) a plotter can hold varies with the particular plotter.
- Pens use a variety of point types and cartridges: disposable points similar to felt tip or rolling ball markers, as well as traditional stainless steel point with refillable liquid ink cartridges. (Pens and points are proprietary—each plotter manufacturer can set its own standards.)
- Numerous moving parts in the plotter result in high maintenance requirements.
- Liquid ink pen points need frequent cleaning.
- Plotting can be done with cut sheets or wide rolls with various media.

Thermal plotters

- *Direct imaging technology process occurs in special, temperature-sensitive paper in a manner comparable to that seen in large fax machines.*
- Relatively few moving parts, low maintenance requirements, and comparatively quiet operation.
- Capable of withstanding heavy use.
- Large-format rolls (36" wide) available.
- Operating environment is less significant than in the case of pen or electrostatic plotters. (Many thermal plotters can operate within a comparatively wide temperature range.)
- No toner, chemicals, or ribbons used.
- Thermosensitive paper can yellow over time when exposed to light.

Electrostatic plotters

- *Electrical charges are used on writing elements that are embedded in a stationary writing head to create tiny electrostatic dots on paper as it passes over the head. Liquid toner is attracted to the charged dots on the paper, which results in image creation.*
- Among the highest-quality vector output (both color and black and white). Excellent results with complex line drawings.
- Expensive.
- Relatively fast operation.
- Environmentally sensitive: requires temperature and humidity controls for continued operation.
- Print media available in rolls and sheets.

Laser printers

- *Microprocessor-controlled laser beam rapidly turns on and off and, together with an electrically charged rotating cylinder (drum), applies fine powder (toner) which is fused to the paper or film with applied heat.*
- Relatively inexpensive and high quality.
- Emulation available for standard plotters.
- Excellent for text printing.
- Common sizes range from $8\frac{1}{2}'' \times 11''$ (and $8\frac{1}{2}'' \times 14''$) to slightly larger than $11'' \times 17''$ to allow for "full bleed" images.
- Printing may be on paper, adhesive-backed applique, or transparencies.
- Life of the toner cartridge, which provides the powder for printing, depends on the amount of black area on the images being printed.
- Printing and plotting graphics usually require additional memory to be installed over what would be required for text only.
- Color and/or black and white printing.
- Color more suitable for business graphics than for photorealistic, true-color images.

Cont'd

Box 1–O

PLOTTERS AND PRINTERS, CONT'D

Ink jet plotters and printers

- *Prints and plots are created by spraying ink through small nozzles that travel across the page.*
- Capable of comparatively inexpensive prints in both color and black and white.
- Printing may be on a variety of coated and uncoated paper types. Coated paper, though more expensive, often produces better color prints.
- Small-format (8½"-wide) ink jet printers among the least expensive color printers available suitable for architectural graphics.
- Large-format ink jet printers accept rolls of paper up to 36" wide for full-color raster prints and filled polygon vector plots.
- Comparatively long printing time for color output. Short drying time may be required.

Dye sublimation printers and wax thermal transfer printers

- *A heated print head is used to transfer color from the "donor" medium (thin colored film) to special paper.*
- Three-color (CMY: cyan, magenta, and yellow) and four-color (CMYK: black ribbon is added) donor rolls are available. Four-color rolls are more expensive than three-color but can provide better black areas.
- Wax thermal transfer melts solid wax and deposits the liquid on top of the paper or film.
- Dye sublimation printers use dyes that are heated into a gas, which is then absorbed by the paper.
- Printers are available that provide only one type of print or both types.
- Full-color (16.7 million colors) printing possible.
- Dye sublimation can provide near-photographic-quality prints, but some prints may fade over time.
- Sizes of prints vary.
- Dye sublimation media are more expensive than wax thermal transfer media.
- Printing time can be slow. For any given printer, dye sublimation prints usually take longer to print than wax thermal transfer.

Dot matrix printers

- *Impact printers that rely on moveable pins striking an ink-coated ribbon to leave a mark on the paper.*
- Least expensive and noisiest printer type.
- Unsuitable for printing vector data.
- Lower-quality prints than ink jet or laser printing. Suitable for draft text and some forms. *Not suitable for printing architectural graphics.*

General parameters

- Resolution of printers generally expressed in dots per inch (dpi). More dots per inch translates into better, or finer, quality of prints.
- Black and white raster printers may express shades of gray with a series of black and white dots. The greater the number of dots in an area, the smoother the tone will look.
- Memory requirements vary with printer type and manufacturer. In general, graphics requires large amounts of memory to process the information. Either the memory must be in the printer or the host computer's memory will be used (thus delaying the time until the cursor is regained—making the computer unavailable for alternative use during the printing process).
- Within any printer type, memory requirements increase with both number of colors and resolution.
- Plotting memory requirements increase with the complexity of the image.
- When printers (like ink jet) accept vector data for plotting, the data must be converted to raster data (very fine dots) for output. When the conversion is accomplished by the printer, accuracy of output is generally enhanced as compared to files originally created as raster images that were dependent on the computer's graphic resolution. When the output device directly accepts vector data (even when printing dots), the industry generally refers to it as a plotter.

Fig. 1–56 Tabletop diazo print machine. Prints up to 48" wide can be made. (Ammonia developer and filter not shown.) (*Photograph courtesy of Diazit Co., Inc.*)

Fig. 1–57 Large-format document photocopier (engineering copier) (*Xerox Corporation*)

graphic images that are resolution dependent. (*Note: The distinction between plotters and printers is, admittedly, a simplification, and the line is somewhat blurry. There are hardware and software mechanisms available that allow plotters to print and printers to plot. For our purposes, plotting refers to the act of creating a hard copy of vector files.*)

1.3.3 Reproduction of Original Graphics

The reproduction of graphics for dissemination, presentation, and archiving is an ever-present requirement for architects and designers. The way in which an image can be reproduced varies with the type of original (Box 1–P).

Traditional and Analog Reproduction

Diazo prints can be created from work on flexible transparent or translucent media (Fig. 1–56). **Photocopies** are restricted to work that physically fits within the parameters of the photocopier—although large photocopiers are available and are generally referred to as engineering copiers or large-format copiers (Fig. 1–57). Various **photographic formats** are also capable of reproducing the different types of drawings architects create.

Photography is one of the most common methods of image and drawing reproduction used in the design

Box 1–P

REPRODUCTION OF ORIGINAL DRAWINGS

Diazo prints

- Drawings on a transparent or translucent medium can be printed on light-sensitive paper or film.
- The reverse of traditional blue prints, a diazo print is most commonly a blue, black, or brown line drawing on a white or cream background.
- Specialty papers with different backgrounds or finishes are available.
- Sepia prints, with brown lines on translucent media, can be used as "master copies" for additional printing while preserving the original.
- Chemical (often ammonia) development process used within print machine. Equipment needs ventilation.
- Architects frequently supplement prints of line drawings with pencil, color pencil, and/or felt tip markers.
- Prints available in a wide variety of sizes.
- Relatively inexpensive method of reproducing large-format drawings.

Photocopies

- Common and inexpensive process using heat, light, and (usually) powdered toner (which may be recycled when available in cartridge form).
- Documents can be copied onto a variety of opaque, transparent, and semitransparent media.
- Drawing details can be easily photocopied onto transparent adhesive-backed appliqué for placement onto other documents.
- Best at copying pure black and white; shades of gray can become muddy.

Photography: black and white line drawings

- Line drawings can be photographed as black and white images—with no shades of gray or tone—for crisp reproduction.
- Graylike surfaces can be created with "dot screens" applied with adhesive-backed applique that, because of their density, can approximate tones with only black and white.

- Background is "pure" white.
- Photographic touch-ups are relatively easy because the areas of the image are either black or white.
- Title blocks, unwanted borders, or entire areas can be masked on the photographic negative before printing and the background will not reveal the change(s).

Photography: continuous tone

- A range of grays results in more subtle and softer images.
- Needed to more faithfully represent images that contain shades of gray found in soft pencil and charcoal drawings.
- Touch-ups difficult because of the variations inherent in any background. (Continuous tone touch-ups are best accomplished digitally with raster paint software prior to printing.)
- Most color drawings that must be photographed in black and white are best shown in grayscale continuous tone photographs. (Alternatively, color drawings must have their shades converted to grayscale and then to a dot screen for pure black and white reproduction.)

Photography: full color

- Full-color photographs and slides are needed to faithfully represent an image created in color.
- Manipulation and touch-up most often accomplished digitally.
- Color images require careful compositional balancing that can be independent of the size of the form or line weight.
- Exact color matching of original to reproduction can be difficult.
- Film type has an impact on color balance.

STEPS TO CONSIDER FOR 35-MM PHOTOGRAPHY DIRECTLY FROM SCREEN

Lens size

- 135-mm telephoto or 50-mm macro are effective in "flattening" curvature of screen. Note: Unless the monitor is perfectly flat (and few are), getting too close to the screen will accentuate the curvature and distortion of the image. Stepping back with a telephoto lens or being close with a macro lens will minimize visible distortion.

Shutter speed

- One-half second or longer (to prevent capture of refresh lines).

Tripod

- Needed for stability with slow speeds.

Lighting

- Room should be dark, with lights off.
- Care should be taken to prevent glare or reflection in monitor.

Screen composition

- Image proportion resulting from most screen resolutions does not match 35-mm frame size of photography.
- In order to photograph the entire screen, background area and portions of the monitor are often included. Photographic enlargements may be cropped, and transparencies (slides) may be masked with reflective silver tape.
- Digital copies of the image can be cropped to 35-mm proportions with image processing software prior to photography, but very precise framing would be required of the photographer.
- Full-frame images can best be achieved by "zooming in" and cropping parts of the image directly when photographing.

professions and is an essential component of graphic presentation and communication. Presentations of photographed work can be made to prospective clients or employers in portfolios and/or slide presentations. Photographs are used for publication of work to show clients and peers.

One of the least expensive methods of creating a full-color paper copy of a digital color image is through **direct screen photography** (Box 1–Q). There are a number of issues that must be addressed and steps taken in order to create good photographs of screen images. When taking photographs from the screen, it is important to know that the image is continually being regenerated on the computer monitor. The rate at which this occurs (refresh rate) varies with each type of monitor and graphics card. If the refresh rate is slow, you see flicker on the screen. If the photograph is taken at too fast a speed, the resulting photo will capture the screen in "mid-redraw" and show a dark band across it. Photographs should be taken with a relatively long exposure (usually one-half second or longer) in order to avoid capturing the refresh lines of the screen. A tripod should be used when photographing at such slow speeds to inhibit camera movement during exposure.

Digital film recorders (Fig. 1–58) record directly from the computer to the camera without the need for a photographer to stand behind the tripod, focus, and shoot. Either the image can be photographed as part of an enclosed light box and be a photographic capture of the screen, or a file can be digitally transferred to the camera itself. Film recorders are most commonly available in 35-mm and 4″ × 5″ formats. Driven by software, the recorder must be capable of reading the particular file format needed. The speed of operation can vary significantly among different film recorders.

Digital Reproduction

One does not need to print or photocopy drawings in order to save them or transfer them to another party. Drawings created or modified in a computer can be stored on disk or tape (Fig. 1–59). Storing information, whether for temporary or for archival purposes, on disk or tape takes up less space than one would need if all of the information were stored in hard-copy format. (See Box 1–R.)

Images and models in the computer can be easily transferred to another person or group. If the other party has the same software program—or has a program capable of reading the file—the image or model can be read, printed, and/or modified. This information can be sent over telephone lines or through networks that allow rapid transfer and sharing of the graphic data. It is possible for designers working together on a project to be separated by distance but still work interactively on the same model or image. Furthermore, clients often need the graphic data that describes a building in digital format in order to use the drawings for their own purposes, which may include furniture layout or space planning, production of maps or brochures describing the physical plant, and facilities management. Some

Fig. 1–58 Desktop digital film recorder with camera back (*Lasergraphics, Inc.*)

Fig. 1–59 Digital storage media. Recordable magneto-optical disks provide large storage capacity, longer life than tape, and random access. (*Courtesy of Sony Electronics, Inc.*)

Box 1–R

REMOVABLE OR PORTABLE STORAGE FOR DIGITAL MEDIA

Floppy diskettes
- 3 ½": 720 KB, 1.44 MB, 2.88 MB
- 5 ¼": 360 KB, 1.2 MB

Floptical diskettes
- 3 ½": 20.8 MB

Magneto-optical diskettes
- 3 ½": 128 MB, 256 MB
- 5 ¼": 594 MB, 650 MB, 1.2 GB, 1.3 GB, 2.3 GB, 4.6 GB

Data cartridges
- 40/80 MB, 120/250 MB, 250/500 MB, 350/700 MB . . . (backup cartridges are available in many different capacities, some of which exceed 16 GB including compression)

Data tape cassettes
- 4 mm: 60 MB, 90 MB
- 8 mm: 15 MB, 54 MB, 112 MB

Proprietary cartridges and formats
- Bernouilli: 44 MB, 90 MB, 150 MB
- Iomega Zip disks: 100 MB
- SyQuest EZ135 Cartridge: 135 MB

CD-ROM
- 550 MB (63 min), 680 MB (74 min)

Note: New hardware, sizes, and media are being tested continually. In most cases, the largest-capacity storage devices are used for backups of hard disks and network systems and to transport or archive large graphic files (including animations). In general, within any given medium, the more data that needs to be stored or copied, the longer the time needed to accomplish the task. As new sizes are developed, some older ones start to fade away (eg., 5 ¼" 360-KB floppy diskettes). The above list is a sample and does not list all available storage media.

Without additional software, tape backup is linear and not random access.

For archives to be readable in the future, one must make calculated judgments as to the availability of devices and supplies capable of reading the storage medium selected.

clients will work with architects and designers during the design process by electronically sketching over the information provided to them on disk in much the same way they would by sketching over prints or photographs.

It is important to remember that drawings on disk can be changed and saved over the original. The concept of what is original and what is a copy can be easily lost. There is no pile of trace on the floor to go back to during the design process in order to evaluate earlier alternatives if all information is on disk. It is imperative that back-up copies of originals be saved and labeled to distinguish one version from another. Interim prints or plots are also useful throughout design as a record of the process. Storing and disseminating information to critics, consultants, and clients in a read-only format (e.g., CD-ROM) allows use of information while retaining the integrity of the original.

REVIEW QUESTIONS

1. What are the differences between the two types of *lead holders* used for drafting?

2. What are the different types of *compasses* used when drafting with traditional media? Which type is most likely to be used for a circle of very large radius?

3. What are the different attributes of *drafting machines* and *parallel rules*? Why are they each well suited for different types of work?

4. What are some of the precautions one should take to keep a drawing clean while drafting with traditional media?

5. Why is it important to understand the qualities of a *solvent* used in a particular *felt tip marker* before using it to enhance existing work?

6. What is the length represented by a 6″ line at a *scale* of ¼″ = 1′-10″; at ½″ = 1′-10″; at ¾″ = 1′-10″; and at 1½″ = 1′-10″? How long a line would have to be drawn at ¼″ = 1′-10″ to represent 50′?

7. Would a scale of 3″ = 1′-10″ be appropriate to draw a large office building? Why or why not?

8. What is a *pixel*?

9. Describe the difference between *raster* and *vector* graphics. What are the characteristics of each? Which type of image has a file size that depends on resolution and color and not on the number of lines drawn?

10. What is the importance of *dot pitch* on a monitor when working with CAD/graphics?

11. Why does the scanning of an old line drawing often need additional work to be made useable?

12. Describe some of the characteristics of the *diazo print process*.

13. What are the differences between *templates* used with traditional drafting media and *electronic templates*?

14. Rank, in ascending order, the following media in terms of potential storage space: 5¼″ magneto-optical disk, 4-mm data cassette, 3½″ floptical diskette, and 5¼″ floppy diskette.

2 ELEMENTS OF DRAWINGS AND TEXT

Fig. 2–1 Architectural composition of points, lines, and shapes (*"First Light" by Jeffrey Hildner, architect*)

In certain contexts, drawings can be thought of as graphic descriptions of points, lines, planes, and volumes in space. Clearly, drawings can express a great deal more, including order, rhythm, character, style, mood, and intent, as they are used for exploration and the communication of ideas (Fig. 2–1). In the context of architectural design, they can also specifically represent existing and proposed physical elements. When creating and evaluating drawings, simple shapes and forms (as well as areas and intensities of color) are also very significant and may visually absorb the components. The discrete elements used to create drawings are more—or less—significant and identifiable depending on the composition of the drawing and the media used.

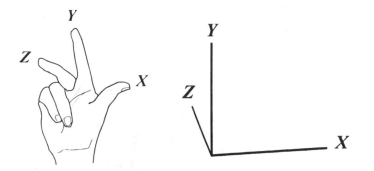

Fig. 2–2 Right-hand rule. Cartesian coordinate system with x, y, and z axes.

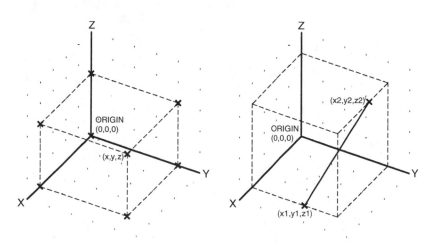

Fig. 2–3 *Left,* Cartesian position of a point in three-dimensional space. *Right,* Cartesian position of a line in three-dimensional space.

Fig. 2–4 *A,* Dot as a filled circle (pen, pencil, or filled vector shape). *B,* Dot as a single pixel (magnified). *C,* Dot as a group of pixels. *D,* Large dot made up of many pixels.

Strict mathematical coordinates can be overlaid onto almost any traditional drawing, but they are usually the base of a drawing only when relating part of a building to some other organizing principle like a structural column grid, premade standard office partitions, or other planning and design module. When drawing with the aid of the computer, however, the mathematical placement of elements can become more important and less transparent as part of the image creation process—regardless of the particular design issue being represented.

For the purpose of being able to create drawings and images in a variety of media, it is important to understand, and be able to manipulate, the graphic elements that represent many of the building blocks used for graphic communication in architecture.

2.1 POINTS AND LINES

2.1.1 Geometric Description

A **point** is a location in space that can be defined by three coordinates (x, y, and z) in a Cartesian coordinate system (Figs. 2–2, 2–3). Any point can be thought of as having a particular location. A point does not have any associated dimensional properties of size. A **line** is a one-dimensional element connecting two or more points. A geometric description of a line segment includes the length of the segment but no thickness. The

Cartesian coordinate system underlies virtually all common CAD/graphics programs used for architecture-specific drawing.

2.1.2 Points and Dots

Traditionally Created Points

A point on an architectural drawing is typically drawn as a "dot." With traditional media, the point can be created simply by touching the pencil or pen to the drawing surface with enough pressure to make a mark. Depending on the size and scale of the image, the dot may be perceived and drawn as a small solid circle. (Large pen points create larger dots than do small pen points.) Discrete dots are often used to mark places or locations. Many dots, in combination, are sometimes used to represent materials or texture.

Electronically Created Points

An electronically created dot on a two-dimensional raster drawing may vary (at the discretion of the artist) in the number of pixels it contains, with personal preferences usually able to be saved and reused on demand (Fig. 2–4). By selecting a "brush" or "pen" size within a paint program, one can create different-sized dots without actually forming filled circles or closed polygons. The point in a three-dimensional vector model is not

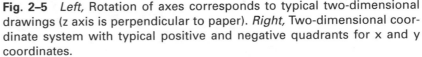

Fig. 2–5 *Left,* Rotation of axes corresponds to typical two-dimensional drawings (z axis is perpendicular to paper). *Right,* Two-dimensional coordinate system with typical positive and negative quadrants for x and y coordinates.

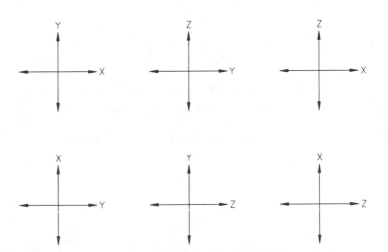

Fig. 2–6 Orientation of coordinate system. Coordinate system may be rotated such that any two axes are lying "flat" on paper or screen for two-dimensional representation and work. Depending on the particular software, different orientations may be the default. When transferring files, it is important to know the orientation of axes. Some software applications require a change of axes; some ask the users to change their own viewpoint. The net effect is the same.

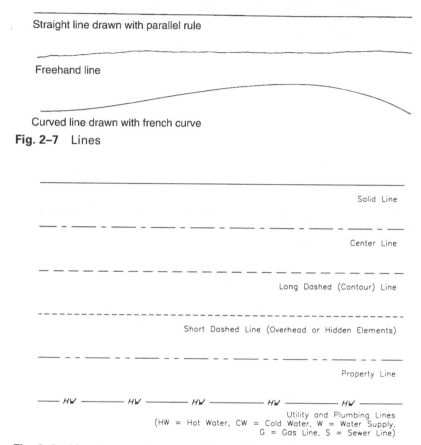

Straight line drawn with parallel rule

Freehand line

Curved line drawn with french curve

Fig. 2–7 Lines

Solid Line

Center Line

Long Dashed (Contour) Line

Short Dashed Line (Overhead or Hidden Elements)

Property Line

HW ——— HW ——— HW ——— HW ——— HW ———
Utility and Plumbing Lines
(HW = Hot Water, CW = Cold Water, W = Water Supply,
G = Gas Line, S = Sewer Line)

Fig. 2–8 Line types typically used in architectural drawings

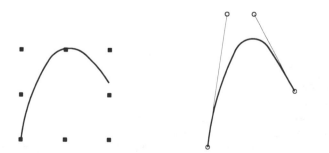

Fig. 2–9 Creation and modification of Bézier curve using control points and tangents (two-dimensional Bézier curve with four control points)

determined or defined by pixels; it is resolution independent and follows its geometric description. It represents a location in space.

A point on a two-dimensional drawing is distinct from a point in a three-dimensional model that is being represented by a drawing. The point on the drawing can be thought of as a visible dot or location on the two-dimensional surface of the screen or paper. The visible location of the point on a drawing will have two coordinates (typically x and y, x and z, or y and z), which are dependent on the coordinate and axis system of the drawing itself (Figs. 2–5, 2–6). A traditional way of hand copying original drawings (whether or not created with explicit grids) was to superimpose as small a grid as necessary to facilitate a box-by-box and point-by-point transfer by mapping the location of points on the grid of the original to the grid on the new drawing—either at the same or modified scale. *It is important to note that one need not draw over a grid to create two-dimensional images. The underlying coordinate system can be completely transparent to, and ignored by, the artist or designer.*

2.1.3 Line Creation

Lines can be drawn in a variety of ways: freehand, with parallel rule, with triangle against parallel rule, with french curve or compass, and with computer (Fig. 2–7).

In architectural and design graphics, the representations of points and lines must, of necessity, have dimension and are therefore not always viewed within their strict geometric definitions. They represent edges, materials, and objects, as well as representing conventions specific to the building design professions (Fig. 2–8). A line, as used in graphics, may be straight or curved, or it may be formed with a combination of straight and curved segments (a **Bézier curve**) (Fig. 2–9). The locations of various control points, the end points, and the angle of the tangent lines running between discrete segments determine the precise geometric shape of the Bézier curve.

There are some differences between media in the drawing of lines (and objects made up of lines). Whereas the use of traditional media *can* be based on explicit geometry, electronic media—especially vector-based graphics—*are almost always* based on geometric principles.

Traditional Line Creation

A variety of styles and media is available for traditional graphics. When drawing freehand, clear, steady strokes are usually best. When one draws too tentatively, the image suffers. Simple freehand sketches, when done well, can provide quick and elegant descriptions of architectural concepts.

In drafting, lines should meet crisply and with precision at all corners (Fig. 2–10). Lines that extend too far

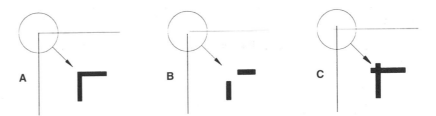

Fig. 2–10 Corner conditions. *A,* Exact meet, crisp corners. The preferred condition for clear definition of form—suitable for all drawings. *B,* Gap between corners (where the lines represent a condition of intersection). Leaves ambiguity in drawing as to whether the gap is intentional and represents an actual space between elements drawn, or the graphics just lack precision. *C,* Cross connection. Emphasizes endpoints of lines or forms and is a technique used, on occasion, for construction documents where dimensions and end conditions are the most significant elements. Excessive overlap distracts from the definition of the form (it focuses too much attention on the individual lines and is a technique inappropriate for presentation drawings).

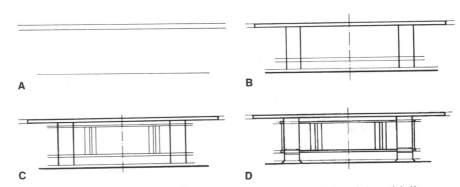

Fig. 2–11 Laying out a drawing with guidelines. *A,* Establish guidelines using lightweight or nonphoto blue pencil. *B,* Locate extent of drawing by finding centerline and/or margins of page. Locate and draw primary horizontal and vertical lines. *C,* Draw secondary horizontal and vertical lines. Add detail. *D,* Finish drawing by adding detail as needed. *Not shown,* If desired, trace as final presentation drawing with pen or pencil onto clean sheet. If drawing is to be traced, line weight is needed only to facilitate the tracing. If drawing is not to be traced, erase guidelines where still visible. *(Diagram based on a table design by Frank Lloyd Wright)*

METHODS OF ELECTRONIC LINE CREATION

Geometric specification

- Select line command from menu or activate procedure from command line or dialog box interface.
- Specify x_1 and y_1 coordinates (or x_1, y_1, and z_1 in three-dimensional, "real world" space).
- Specify x_2 and y_2 coordinates (or x_2, y_2, and z_2 in three-dimensional, "real world" space).
- Line segment defined by its two endpoints.

Point, distance, direction

- Select line command from menu or activate procedure from command line or dialog box interface.
- Specify x_1 and y_1 (and z_1) coordinates or select the start point with cursor.
- Enter distance of line segment in whatever units have been prespecified. (Change units as needed.)
- Specify direction of line segment either by selecting or pointing direction with cursor or by specifying rotational direction in degrees.

Click and drag

- Select line command from menu or activate procedure from command line or dialog box interface.
- Select start point with cursor. Click on point. (When available, coordinates of point may be displayed on screen during point selection.)
- Drag cursor to endpoint. Click (or, if required, double click) at end. Distance and coordinates may be displayed on screen during interactive line segment creation.

Drag and drop (template)

- Select template or menu system that contains desired line types.
- Select line segment from menu.
- Holding down mouse or cursor button, drag the selected element onto the drawing canvas.
- Stretch the line to its desired length.
- Drag the line to its required position in the drawing.

---

should be trimmed. Lightly drawn or nonphoto blue guidelines may be drawn to assist in the creation of precisely measured and drawn lines. Once accurately measured line segments are created, they may be darkened and/or inked (Fig. 2–11).

Although changes can be made (and frequently are) to traditionally drawn lines, one must still make an initial decision as to lead type and pen point size when drawing.

Electronic Line Creation and Snap Commands

When drawing by computer, a **line** or **draw command** is activated either by typing in a command or by selecting the item from a menu (text or icon). Lines can be created by a variety of techniques that are software dependent (Box 2–A). There are, generically, a limited number of ways in which lines can be created. In most cases, the line can be repeated and/or changed. Depending on the software used, line manipulation may, at times, be restricted to the same method used in line creation.

It is useful to be able to place the end of a line with some precision. In addition to the specification of actual coordinates, many drawing programs allow for an endpoint to be placed graphically at a precise spot. The **snap command** locks the cursor onto the nearest grid point, or other defined element, in order to place the exact location of the start or end of an object being drawn. Virtually all application programs have the capability to snap to a Cartesian grid underlay with the grid spacing defined by the user. Many programs allow the user to snap to other objects defined by user preferences (midpoints, ends, tangents, etc.). When snap is "on," no line may be started or ended at an intermediate point. Note that activating a snap command does *not* change the location of lines already placed at intermediate points when snap was inactive. Snap is a command that may be toggled on and off as desired. Snap commands are used to increase precision and speed. The snap command helps points to be exactly where they are supposed to be (Fig. 2–12). The precision with which electronic lines are created makes it very difficult to hide errors (unless they are printed so small that they cannot be seen). The snap command allows the designer to create lines graphically (without having to constantly enter numeric values and coordinates) and know that points that are supposed to align actually will.

2.1.4 Line Types

As mentioned earlier, the strict geometric description of a line does not include width, but lines do have weight, or thickness (and sometimes color and transparency), when used in architectural and design graphics. The thickness of a pencil line will vary with the sharpness of the point and the pressure of application. Various pen widths create lines of different thickness.

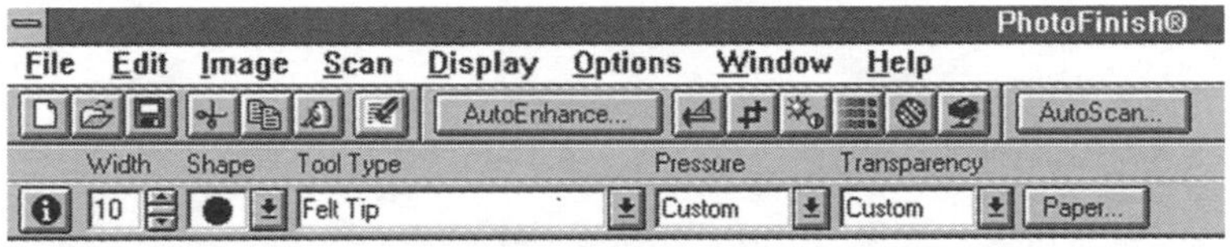

Lines and pieces of lines typically refer to various conventions when arranged in certain patterns. Combinations

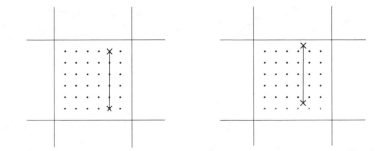

Fig. 2–12 *Left,* Line drawn with snap on. Ends of segments must start and stop at grid points. With appropriate grid setting, precisely dimensioned objects become easy to create. *Right,* Line drawn with snap off. Segments may begin or end at any location.

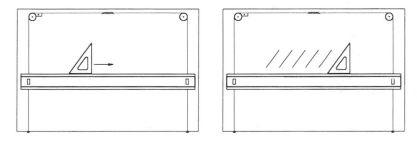

Fig. 2–13 Drawing angled parallel lines by sliding triangle along the parallel rule

Fig. 2–14 Tool bar menu provides options for selecting not only the tool itself, but also its width, shape, and transparency. (*PhotoFinish by Softkey International, Inc. © 1995*)

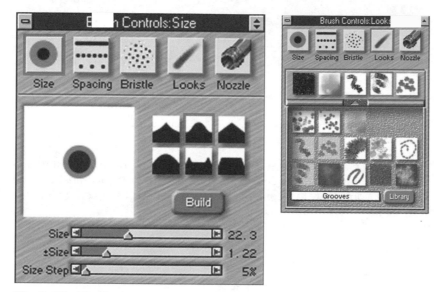

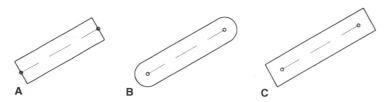

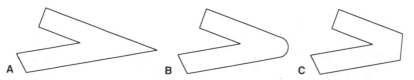

of lines and line types create other forms that have meaning to people reading the drawings. All lines on a drawing have (or should have) a purpose: either they directly represent something physical or they are used as graphic tools to enhance the description. When drawing traditionally, the line types, and combinations of lines, are created in a manner similar to that for the drawing of single lines. For example, angled parallel lines can be drawn simply by sliding the triangle along the parallel rule, with beginning and ending guidelines drawn first (Fig. 2–13). (Alternatively, the parallel lines can be drawn lightly, measured after creation, and then trimmed and enhanced.)

Lines drawn electronically have widths that are defined either by traditional pen widths, in absolute terms within the working units (inches, centimeters, etc.), visually by selecting from a menu, or by specifying the precise number of pixels defining the thickness (Fig. 2–14). (When modifying lines with desktop publishing or word processing compatible software, the line widths can often be described by "points," the same unit used to define text size [1 point = 1/72"].) Within paint or image processing software, transparency or opacity (expressed as a percentage of a completely solid line) may be specified. When software supported, pressure-sensitive tablets can also assist in visually determining line transparency based on the pressure of the pen and speed of application in a manner that is analogous to that used with more traditional tools. Various brush or pencil shapes can also be selected in most paint programs (Fig. 2–15), and very thick lines (used primarily for expressive pur-

Fig. 2–15 Brush size, pattern, and looks may all be defined interactively. (*Painter by Fractal Design*)

Fig. 2–16 Thick lines drawn with (*A*) butt caps, (*B*) round caps, and (*C*) projecting square caps. (*From Hearn, D., and M.P. Baker. 1994. Computer graphics [ed. 2]. Upper Saddle River, N.J.: Prentice Hall, p. 149. Used with permission.*)

Fig. 2–17 Thick line segments connected with (*A*) miter join, (*B*) round join, and (*C*) bevel join. (*From Hearn, D., and M.P. Baker. 1994. Computer graphics [ed. 2]. Upper Saddle River, N.J.: Prentice Hall, p. 149. Used with permission.*)

poses in rendered images) exaggerate the different end and joint conditions of line segments that exist with each brush shape (Figs. 2–16, 2–17). Under some circumstances in paint or image processing programs, brush or marker types can be selected in which gradients of color or opacity are created across the thickness of the line (Fig. 2–18).

When drawing with a stylus instead of a mouse, it may be convenient to rotate the digitizer pad and/or the page on the screen to more easily accommodate natural hand motions.

Line thickness in vector graphics programs may not always appear on screen. You *don't* always get what you see. Line thickness may be selected for plotting or hard-copy output. In some software applications, varying thickness may be defined by color, which, in turn, refers to pen number or actual line width. Lines are also related to the limitation of the output device (printer or plotter) being used. "Hairline" is the thinnest line the selected output device can produce (Fig. 2–19).

When drawing electronically, symbols of various line types may be available with the software, or can be created and saved for reuse, that are applied as if they were single lines during the process of image creation. Double lines; dashed lines; and "polylines," "multilines," "broken lines," "segmented lines" (different software-specific names for a variety of combinations or series of connected line segments that may be controlled or modified as an entity) are a few examples of commonly available line types on drawing menus or

Fig. 2–18 Gradients of color or shade can vary across the thickness of a line.

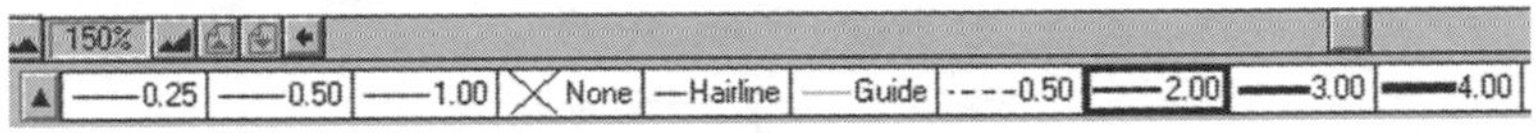

Fig. 2–19 Selection of line thickness by choosing point size in programs compatible with desktop publishing–or in word processing programs. Note: Hairline is thinnest line capable of display. Monitor displays as one pixel width. (*Intellidraw by Adobe Systems, Inc.*)

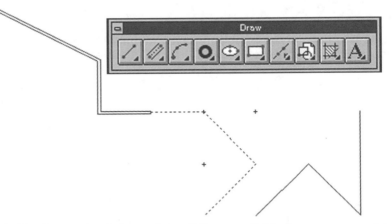

Fig. 2–20 A sample of the variety of lines available from menu system within CAD program: double or parallel, dashed, polylines, etc. (*AutoCAD by Autodesk. This material has been reprinted with permission from and under the copyright of Autodesk, Inc.*)

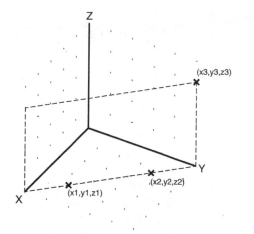

Fig. 2–21 Plane defined by three noncolinear points

Fig. 2–22 Regular closed polygons. *Left to right:* Triangle, square, pentagon, hexagon, heptagon, octagon.

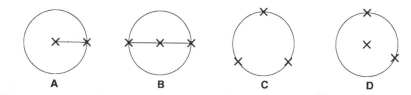

Fig. 2–23 Circle definitions. *A,* Center and radius. *B,* Center and diameter. *C,* Three points on circumference. *D,* Center and two points on circumference.

templates (Fig. 2–20). For ease of line modification, some software programs allow the insertion of control points, vertices, or segments within or at the end of existing segments.

2.2 TWO-DIMENSIONAL SHAPES

2.2.1 Regular Simple Shapes

Three points, not in the same line, can define a two-dimensional plane (Fig. 2–21). We are frequently interested in portions of a plane that can be defined by line segments (straight and/or curved). The geometric description of a planar figure includes length and width but not thickness.

The two common types of planar figures used in architectural drawing are polygons and simple closed curves (including circles and ellipses). A polygon, as used in graphics, is a two-dimensional closed figure with three or more sides. Shapes are simple if the line segments or curves do not cross themselves. **Regular shapes** include circles and regular polygons. **Regular polygonal shapes** are those in which the defining line segments are all the same length and the angles formed by the meeting segments (vertices) are all equal. Typical regular polygons include equilateral triangles, squares, pentagons, octagons, and so on

(Fig. 2–22). The definitions of, and distinctions between, various shapes have been important for traditional constructive geometry and take on increased significance in CAD/graphics.

Circles may be defined by center and radius, center and diameter, or three points—either three on the circumference or the center and two points on the circumference (Fig. 2–23).

Circles can be drawn with a compass by setting the center point and radius. In general, regular shapes can be constructed with compass and straightedge according to ancient principles of Euclidean geometry. They can be inscribed within, or circumscribed by, circles for ease of construction. Scales, triangles, and adjustable triangles are also useful for the creation of regular polygons (Fig. 2–24).

In many CAD/graphics programs, a variety of circles, ellipses, and polygons can be drawn with templates—either traditional or electronic. (When drawing with traditional media, circles, ellipses, squares, etc., may be drawn with templates that contain the precise size needed, but care should be taken to make sure the drawn shape [smaller than the stencil] is the size needed.)

Regular shapes are also called "primitives" and are frequently used as the building blocks of complex or composite shapes (Fig. 2–25). Many computer drawing programs rely on primitives as the basis for creating drawings of buildings. The shapes are selected, placed, and sized as part of the drawing process. By

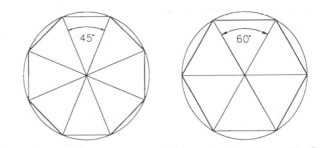

Fig. 2–24 Euclidean constructions. Many primitives found in CAD/graphics applications are based on the traditional constructions made with triangle, compass, and parallel rule.

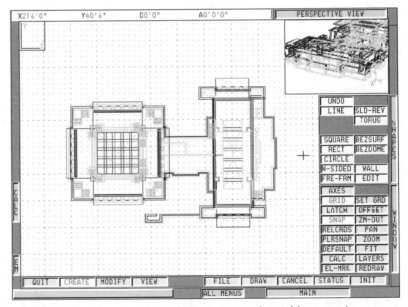

Fig. 2–25 "Shapes menu" on right uses text-based buttons (square, rectangle, circle, wall, Bézier dome, bezdome, etc.) to define primitives that are used to create floor plans. Users select the primitive and then draw it with the cursor. (*Plan based on Frank Lloyd Wright's Unity Temple, drawn by Michael Hoon, NJIT. MegaMODEL by MegaCADD, a Division of Design Futures, Inc.*)

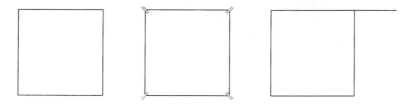

Fig. 2–26 Exploding or severing components in a shape allows for modification of individual pieces.

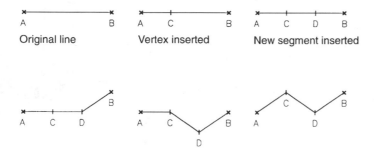

Original line   Vertex inserted   New segment inserted

Fig. 2–27 Modification of lines and new segments

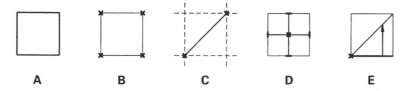

A   B   C   D   E

Fig. 2–28 Square definitions. *A,* Four sides. *B,* Four corners. *C,* Two opposite corners. *D,* distance of sides (or corners) from center. *E,* One corner and side with orientation. (Diagonals used to construct the rest of the square.)

drawing with primitives, the designer eliminates the need for drawing and locating each individual line segment. However, some software programs (especially vector-based drawing programs) may not allow modification of individual segments without breaking apart, or "exploding," the primitive (Fig. 2–26). Once individual lines of a shape are recognized, it may be possible to modify lines and insert segments or vertices in the same manner that discrete segments are modified (Fig. 2–27).

Perhaps the most common primitive used in the creation of electronic architectural drawings is the square. The square itself can be selected, or it can be created with four line segments. When created as four connected but discrete segments, it is usually not modifiable as a primitive without further effort in converting the lines into a group or object. The size and location of a square can be defined by its four corners, by the location of two opposite corners, by the location of the sides or corners relative to the square's center, or by one corner with the length of a side and its orientation (Fig. 2–28). (Note: The orientation of any polygon in three-dimensional space is defined by its "normal"—which is represented by a vector perpendicular to the face of the polygon.) *In practice, usually a corner is selected and either a length of a side is entered numerically or the shape is visually stretched to its appropriate size and orientation.* (Note: Some software programs will show a numeric value of the length of a segment and/or coordinates of the corners as the shape is being formed.) The construction of a square with traditional media is equally straightforward (Fig. 2–29).

The technique of selecting and sizing primitive shapes is found in both vector and raster drawing. When drawing a polygon with vector graphics, dimensions are usually full (real-world) size with defined units, or at times, a predetermined architectural or engineering scale when a paper size is defined. When drawing a polygon with raster graphics, the units can be defined either as pixels or as actual lengths (inches or centimeters) that will work with the size of the **page** (sometimes referred to as **canvas size**) established as the drawing size.

When creating any polygon, line thickness must be selected (Fig. 2–30). If drawing with traditional media, the thickness of the line segments that make up the polygon is determined by all the tools and techniques available and previously discussed. Electronic polygon creation also requires the selection of line widths for its border. Selection is made in a manner comparable to that of selection of widths when drawing single lines. Raster software, however, offers the opportunity to define polygons as either empty (showing the outline only) or filled. Furthermore, filled polygons may show the border and filled area as distinct or the same (in either color or pattern). When border and interior are distinct, they may be modified independently of one another. Once the border and pattern are merged in a raster image, they must be changed together unless a new border is drawn (Fig. 2–31). Vector polygons may be displayed as filled or unfilled without affecting the shape or orientation—even if the

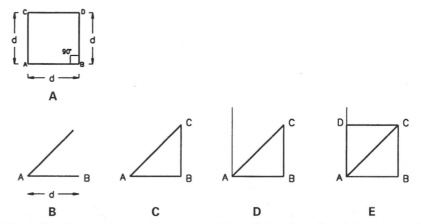

Fig. 2–29 Construction of a square with traditional media. *A,* Measure all four equal sides and construct right angle connections. (Alternatively, the rapid construction of a square can be accomplished with a 45° triangle and parallel rule by measuring only one side.) *B,* Find line AB and project diagonal of square from A. *C,* Draw line BC by projecting vertical to diagonal. *D,* Project vertical guideline up from A. *E,* Project horizontally from C to D.

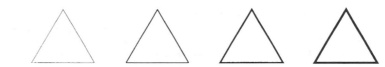

Fig. 2–30 Polygons may be drawn with different line thicknesses.

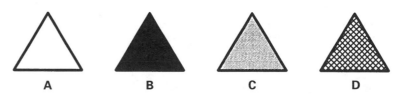

Fig. 2–31 *A,* Unfilled (empty) polygon. *B,* Filled polygon (border and interior the same). *C,* Filled polygon (border and interior different). *D,* Filled polygon (fill modified to hatch pattern).

Box 2–B

DRAWING A RECTANGLE WITH DIGITAL MEDIA

Rectangle: A simple, regular, closed
polygon with four right angles whose
opposite sides are parallel and of equal length.

Selection

- Select rectangle command from menu or activate procedure from command line or dialog box interface.
- When rectangle is not an available command, it may frequently be treated as a subset of polygon. The polygon command must be selected and the number of sides (in this case, four) must be entered.

Perimeter, interior

- Select the line type or line thickness for the border.
- Specify the interior (fill) of the polygon if an available option.

Position, size

- Position starting point—usually corner. (Note: It is frequently possible to define the rectangle by locating its center rather than corner.)
- Drag to fit or enter the specific length of the sides.
- If being created by dragging to fit, drag cursor to endpoint. Click (or, if required, double click) at end. Distances and coordinates may be displayed on screen during interactive polygon creation.

Modification

- Select object either by selecting appropriate icon or by activating a command from an "edit" menu.
- Modify line weight and/or interior as needed.
- Modify position as needed.

two-dimensional view of the object changes. Because so many portions of digital images may be implicitly or explicitly geometry based—made up of polygons—it is important to know the variables that can be manipulated.

It is possible to change the thickness of lines describing the border of the polygon. Selecting the polygon to change and modifying the defined border produces a thicker or thinner perimeter. The thickness of polygon borders created in paint or image processing programs may be "redrawn" electronically in a manner comparable to that of traditional redrawing.

2.2.2 Irregular Shapes

Simple, irregular closed shapes include noncircular closed curves and polygons. Irregular closed polygons are those in which all of the sides or angles at vertices are not equal. The group of irregular shapes includes ellipses, rectangles, parallelograms, and trapezoids, as well as those shapes in which no two sides are equal or parallel.

Nonsymmetrical, free-form, irregular, and nonsimple shapes are usually created in the same way one would create regular polygons. Irregular shapes may be drawn segment by segment using either traditional or digital media. Lines may be created with parallel rule and triangle or with mouse and/or stylus when free-form or irregular polygon commands are activated.

Rectangles and ellipses are specific and special cases of irregular shapes when drawing with computer (Box 2–B). Many painting and drawing programs provide commands for rectangles and ellipses as primitive shapes and treat squares as a subset of rectangles and circles as a subset of ellipses. Rectangles can then be selected directly by command or menu and defined by two sides, one corner, and its orientation. It is frequently possible to lock in proportions (either by pressing specific keys while dragging the cursor or by directly selecting shapes or proportions from the menu) that constrain the rectangle to a square. Circles and ellipses are treated in an analogous manner. (Alternatively, some programs allow the creation of rectangles or ellipses by the stretching of squares [Fig. 2–32] and circles once they are placed in an image.)

Irregular polygons (Fig. 2–33) are most often considered to be free-form and would be created by dragging the cursor to graphically define points or by numerically entering the coordinates of all corners of the polygon. Whether the shapes are free-form or rectangular, the possibilities of modification and definition when drawing electronically are the same as those available with regular polygons. It is therefore possible to create free-form nonsimple and/or irregular shapes as modifications of other shapes. By unlocking the fixed proportions and moving points in a square, a large variety of forms can be drawn—especially if a "skew" command (or equivalent) allows the crossing of lines.

Like lines, two-dimensional shapes may often be constrained by snap commands when it is convenient to do

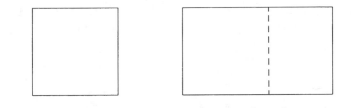

Fig. 2–32   Modifying a primitive. Stretching a square to create a rectangle.

Fig. 2–33   Irregular simple polygons

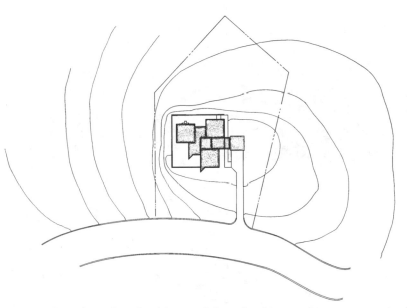

Fig. 2–34   Drawing of roof made up of closed polygons. At one conceptual level, the drawing may be thought of as a combination of primitives—both regular and irregular.   (*House in Chestnut Hill, Pennsylvania, designed by Mitchell/Giurgola Associates*)

so. With circles, the center and radius may be constrained. Depending on the specific software application, polygons may be constrained to have their vertices on snap points.

When drawing two-dimensional representations of buildings, building components can be drawn as composite shapes based on a combination of lines and primitives (Fig. 2–34). Rectangles can be drawn, stretched, and positioned (in any medium) to represent roofs, walls, and windows, as well as desktops, beds, and many other elements and materials. Speed and precision in drawing, modifying, and combining lines and basic geometric shapes is an essential skill in CAD/graphics when producing architectural and design drawings.

2.3 THREE-DIMENSIONAL MODELS

A clear difference between traditional and digital graphics becomes evident when discussing three-dimensional modeling. Two-dimensional *representations* of models are drawn with traditional media. Digital media are capable of creating virtual models that exist electronically as three-dimensional objects (Figs. 2–35, 2–36). As was the case with two-dimensional shapes, three-dimensional models can be based on clearly defined geometric properties. And, as in the previous case, three-dimensional snap commands are available in some software application

Fig. 2–35 The images shown represent just two views of the same model. The designer is capable of selecting any number of different views from any vantage point in a fully developed three-dimensional model. (*Amado Batour, NJIT*)

packages to help make the creation of the model easier and more precise.

When constructing a three-dimensional volume with vector software in a computer—regardless of the method of construction—we are "building" the model in a virtual three-dimensional space. The model can be rotated, moved, changed, and viewed from different vantage points.

In order to conveniently communicate the information in the model to others, we can "grab" or "capture" any particular view as a representation of the model (Fig. 2–37). That representation may look two-dimensional or three-dimensional but is, in fact, a flat representation once the view is frozen. The frozen view may be enhanced with raster software just as detail could be added to an outline of a painting. When information is added to the raster image, however, the information is *not* part of the three-dimensional model, and the file cannot be brought back to the vector format with the new information. It may be possible to save, or "export," a particular three-dimensional view as a two-dimensional flat vector drawing to modify the lines as part of a new two-dimensional image that is different from the three-dimensional model used as its original source. Similarly, when using traditional media to simulate three-dimensional models, we are creating two-dimensional representations, and any modifications we make to the drawing are for that drawing only. There is a significant difference between a drawing, image, or representation, and the model on which it is based.

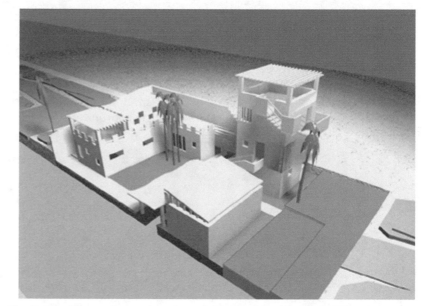

Fig. 2–36   Three-dimensional model   (*Andrew Guzik, NJIT*)

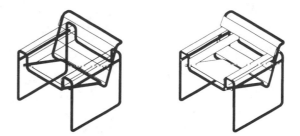

Fig. 2–37   Three-dimensional model showing vector data of Wassily Chair designed by Marcel Breuer in 1925 at the Bauhaus on left. Captured two-dimensional view with lines that would not be visible (hidden lines) removed on right. Once captured and modified, the view can no longer be moved or rotated. Enhancements made to the image are *not* part of the three-dimensional model.   (*Model by Dharmesh Patel, NJIT*)

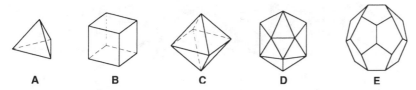

A   B   C   D   E

Fig. 2–38   Regular polyhedra. *A,* Triangular pyramid (four faces). *B,* Cube (six faces). *C,* Octahedron (eight faces). *D,* Dodecahedron (twelve faces). *E,* Icosahedron (twenty faces).

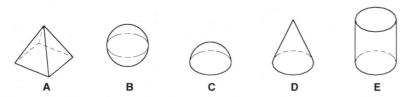

A   B   C   D   E

Fig. 2–39   Three-dimensional primitives frequently used in architectural drawing. *A,* Square pyramid. *B,* Sphere. *C,* Hemisphere (dome). *D,* Cone. *E,* Cylinder.

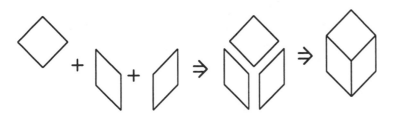

Square + Parallelogram + Parallelogram = Cube

Fig. 2–40   Three-dimensional representation made up of two-dimensional shapes

2.3.1 Regular Solids and Volumes

Three-Dimensional Primitives

Whereas we often use two-dimensional representations for architecture and spaces, three-dimensional modeling can remove a layer of abstraction when describing spaces or buildings. Models (whether built traditionally of cardboard and cork or electronically of bits of information) are three-dimensional. Paper and computer monitor—virtual reality notwithstanding—are (nominally) two-dimensional surfaces that can display flat representations. Two-dimensional images can effectively describe, and be useful in the study of, certain relationships in design. A building, however, is a physical object with mass and volume. When constructing or drawing a three-dimensional model of a building, solids and volumes defined by polygons are useful tools to employ.

Regular three-dimensional solids and volumes enclosed by surfaces can be thought of as the three-dimensional equivalent of two-dimensional regular shapes. The **sphere** is analogous to the circle. **Regular polyhedra** are those in which the faces are regular polygons (and are all the same size and shape—e.g., congruent) and all of the polyhedral angles are the same. These three-dimensional objects include the cube (six faces), octahedron (eight faces), dodecahedron (twelve faces), and icosahedron (twenty faces) (Fig. 2–38). Few CAD/graphics applications use *all* of these regular polyhedra as basic primitives because of the infrequency with which they are employed in architectural design.

Additional three-dimensional primitives that frequently do find their way into architectural compositions are the pyramid, cone, cylinder, torus ("donut"), and prism (Fig. 2–39). Hemispheres, or domes, are also found. For the purposes of architectural graphics, prisms are defined as those objects that have congruent polygons at the top and bottom, with the corresponding vertices connected by parallel lines. A rectangular solid, the shape of many tall buildings, is actually a rectangular prism.

When drawing with traditional media, volumes are drawn as a combination of shapes and lines. For example, a cube, depending on the view, may be drawn as a combination of parallelograms (Fig. 2–40). Because the image of a three-dimensional solid projected onto a two-dimensional surface is dependent on the view and contains so many variables, it has not proven economical to produce traditional templates.

Because the solids and volumes used in design are not view dependent and exist as coordinates in space, electronic templates of three-dimensional primitives exist in vector drawing computer programs. It is, in fact, possible to create three-dimensional electronic models of buildings as a combination of three-dimensional primitives put together with precision (Figs. 2–41, 2–42). For example, a solid wall can be described as a rectangular solid that could be rather thin compared

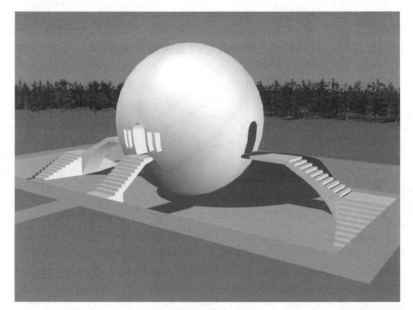

Fig. 2–41   Building proposed by Claude Nicholas Ledoux (c. 1780), Maison des Gardes Agricoles at Maupertuis, based on simple volumetric descriptions.   (*Model by Michael Hoon, NJIT*)

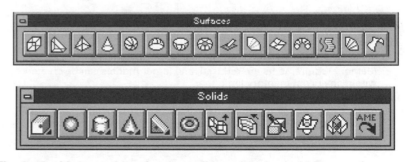

Fig. 2–42   Menu tool bar for three-dimensional primitives—surfaces and solids   (*AutoCAD by Autodesk. This material has been reprinted with permission from and under the copyright of Autodesk, Inc.*)

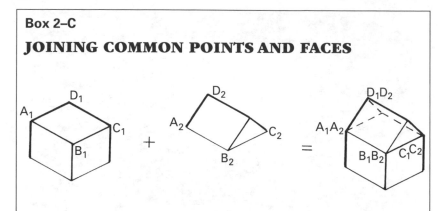
to its height or length. It should be noted that when one builds electronic models as a collection of primitives, there is the possibility of redundant descriptions of shared corners, edges, and/or faces. Many software programs allow you to "optimize" or "latch" the objects that make up larger models in order to maintain more manageable files by reducing the redundancy (Box 2–C).

Three-dimensional models can be defined by the coordinates of the vertices, but because of the number of points, they are often created with one or two corners and dimensions and sizes, or graphically by selecting, placing, and sizing. It is also possible in some three-dimensional modeling programs to start with regular polyhedra as primitives and then to modify or edit the shapes and change them into other geometries.

Solids vs. Volumes

Despite common representation, there are important differences between volumes and solids created with CAD/graphics. A volume has three-dimensional properties and can be thought of as having sides bounded by the planes making up the object. Remember that these planes are defined geometrically and usually have no thickness. To give the surfaces thickness, new surfaces must be created to make each original plane a volume. However, there *are* two sides to each original surface so that the volume has the potential of having both inside and outside faces.

From the exterior, a solid and a totally enclosed volume would be drawn the same way. Unlike the volume, though, the solid has no "inside" and is like a precisely defined block of clay or wood. As explained in Chapter 1, some modeling software creates solid models, some creates surface models, and some will create both types.

Finally, there are some computer models that create only the lines and vertices that make up the appearance of volumes and solids. When creating digital models, it is important to know the model type being created in order to be aware of the type of modifications and images possible. For example, a building created out of a solid model cannot be easily exploded to show interior views and a model defined only by edges and corners cannot easily have "holes" (that could represent windows or doorways in a building) punched in a surface.

2.3.2 Splines and Extruded Shapes

Three-dimensional volumes or solids may be extruded from two-dimensional shapes (Fig. 2–43). While this is true in general, it is important to note that extrusion is one of the ways that three-dimensional objects can be created in many CAD/graphics modeling programs. The objects may be constructed from the flat shapes by using the shape as a "base" and projecting the sides vertically. The simplest construction would have all sides of equal length and the top

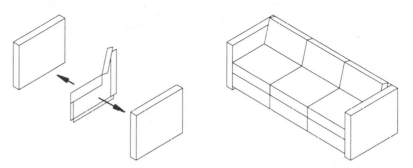

Fig. 2–43 Sofa modeled as an extrusion of simple shapes bounded by "arms" at each end   (*Sofa model based on a design by Charles Pfister and manufactured by Knoll International*)

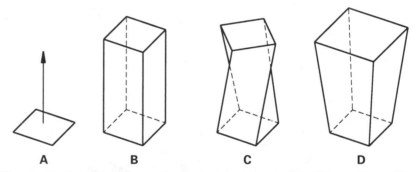

Fig. 2–44 Extruded three-dimensional elements. *A,* Base with vertical path of extrusion. *B,* Extrusion with top and bottom having same orientation. *C,* Complex extrusion with top rotated along path of extrusion. *D,* Extrusion generated by varying size of top.

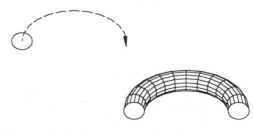

Fig. 2–45 Circle extruded along a curved path

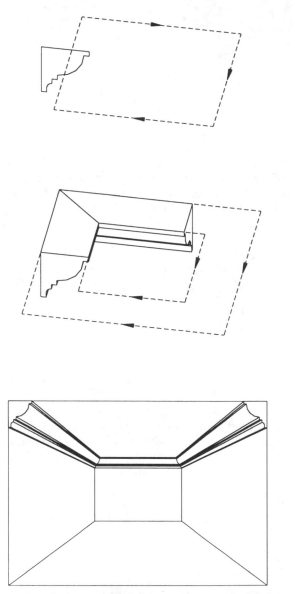

Fig. 2–46 Irregular shape extruded along a rectangular horizontal path to create crown molding for an interior room. The sides of the extrusion reflect the complexity of the original shape.

shape (or face of the volume) the same as the base shape. By varying one or more of the vertical lengths of the projected sides, the top face will be made to vary from the bottom in shape and/or size. Alternatively, the top and bottom faces can be constructed (either the same or different) and points on the perimeter be connected to form the sides of the three-dimensional object (Fig. 2–44). *In general, the process of creating a volume or solid by extrusion is to first define the shape being extruded and then to define the path of extrusion.*

The path of extrusion for a three-dimensional model need not be straight or vertical. It is possible to define a path, or spline, along which one can extrude, "loft," or "sweep" a two-dimensional shape that is horizontal, diagonal, and/or curved (Fig. 2–45). The process of extruding a three-dimensional element is conceptually the same regardless of the nature or geometry of the path. Furthermore, the shape can be rotated during the process of extrusion to form complex solids or volumes. The greater the complexity of the shape, the greater the complexity in the sides of the extruded object (Fig. 2–46). The greater the complexity along the path of extrusion, the greater the complexity along its length.

In addition to linear extrusions, volumes may be defined and created as surfaces of revolution through the operation of rotation. One can create a two-dimensional shape (rectilinear, curved, or faceted) and then rotate, or revolve, it around a central axis to create the three-dimensional volume (Fig. 2–47).

2.3.3 Meshes

Three-dimensional shapes and volumes can also be created directly as warped planes and meshes. **Meshes** are objects that are made up of common or interconnected edges and vertices with polygonal faces (restricted to triangular polygons in some modeling programs).

The method of creating meshes can vary significantly between software packages. There are, however, two ways that appear with relative frequency. Using the Cartesian coordinate system, a variety of points must be located either graphically or through numeric keyboard entry. Given sufficient data, a mesh command can interpolate between points to generate the appearance of a surface. Another option involves the use of surface meshes (Fig. 2–48) to generate certain open primitives (like hemispheric domes) for architecture. In those instances, there is no mesh command used and the user may or may not be aware that the dome is defined as a mesh. It is useful to be aware of how the primitive is created because modification of the element is affected by its makeup. A dome created as a mesh, for example, can easily be modified at each intersection, or vertex, of the mesh to create a distorted form.

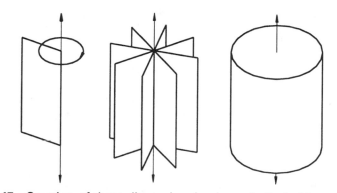

Fig. 2–47   Creation of three-dimensional volume (cylinder) by rotating a two-dimensional rectangular shape around an axis. Also defined as objects of revolution.

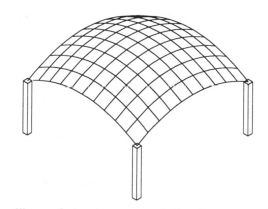

Fig. 2–48   Tentlike roof structure created directly as a mesh made up of small polygonal faces

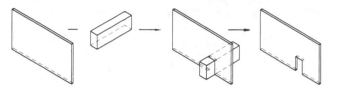

Fig. 2–49 Boolean operations. Subtracting one form from another to create an opening or hole using Boolean operation. The intersection of the two forms is removed.

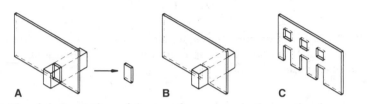

Fig. 2–50 *A,* Intersection of the two forms is only the portion in common. *B,* Union of the two forms is the combination of the two objects. *C,* Wall with window openings and doorways created by subtractive Boolean operations.

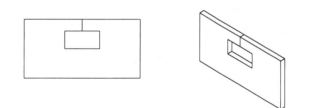

Fig. 2–51 Openings created by keyhole method when subtractive operations are not supported. (Wall perimeter is continuous and traced around openings.)

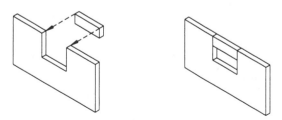

Fig. 2–52 Openings created by piecing objects together

2.3.4 Subtractive Shapes

Up to this point, all of the methods for creating three-dimensional digital models have been additive. In other words, all objects have been created either in whole or as a collection of elements. The elements may have been created within the same file and placed together, or they may have been created independently and merged together into a single model.

When permitted by the model type being created (which is software dependent), holes may be created through **Boolean operations** (Fig. 2–49). (The operations are based on a branch of mathematics developed by mathematician George Boole and are frequently defined as Boolean operations as a menu selection in architectural modeling software.) Subtractive design is taken literally in CAD/graphics modeling. Two elements are created, and one is subtracted from the other, leaving a void. By selecting the intersection of the two objects, and disregarding the remainder, one can create the element that is to be removed (Fig. 2–50). In both application of subtraction and intersection, the operations provide powerful tools in the creation of three-dimensional models. Window openings and doorways are often created subtractively.

When subtractive operations are not supported by the software being used, holes can be created by making "keyholes" (Fig. 2–51) or by building discrete pieces around the void (Fig. 2–52).

2.3.5 Architectural Object Building

A variety of architecturally specific software programs, as well as architectural additions (often called **overlays**) to generic modeling programs, have created primitive shapes corresponding to elements commonly used in buildings. Instead of creating walls out of rectangles that must be added together, a three-dimensional "wall" can be selected and sized. Windows, doors, and even typical roof types (hip, gable, flat, etc.) are included in many packages (Fig. 2–53). The use of these elements expedites the model-making process and relates directly to the creation of architectural drawings.

Whereas few designers will accept a rectangle or hemispheric primitive without modification, there may be, on occasion, a tendency to accept primitives that are associated with architectural objects. One must be careful, however, not to just accept default elements without design-specific modification. The use of only the standard windows and doors that come with the software, for example, may result in a generic-looking drawing or model that does not reflect, or take advantage of, the potential creativity of the designer. Furthermore, many of the primitives are only outlines, or partially created objects that need additional enhancement or work to accurately reflect the proposed design.

Architectural object building is particularly useful when creating models that will later be transformed into construction documents that require that building components be specified and dimensioned.

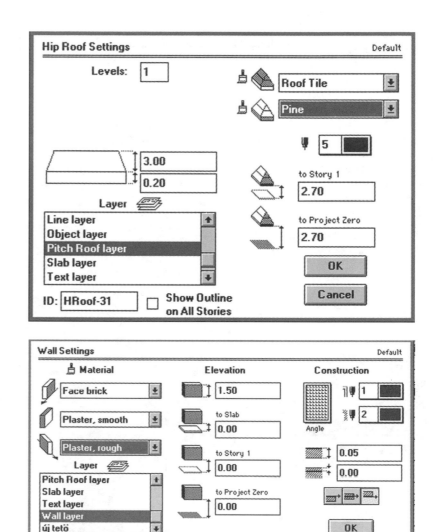

Fig. 2–53 Architectural object building. Rather than building with rectangles or geometric primitives, some applications allow for building directly with definable architectural elements. The programs usually accommodate associated data bases (sizes, materials, etc.) to be included as part of the model's information.   (*ArchiCAD by Graphisoft US, Inc.*)

Fig. 2–54 Reference planes. To create a box perpendicular to the sloped plane, one must select, or lock onto, the new reference plane. Next, one can constrain new drawings to perpendicular, define height, and create box. (*Lee Anderson, upFRONT by SketchTech*)

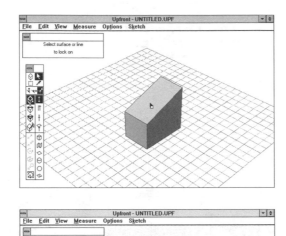

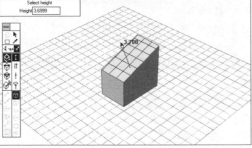

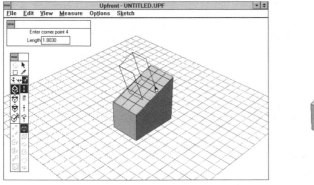

2.3.6 Reference Planes

Architectural objects often need to be created at angles that are skewed with respect to the x, y, and z axes. Usually, when creating an element, one starts the process in a plane orthogonal to the primary axes and defines coordinates relative to that default plane. It is not difficult to create an object using any of the previously discussed methods and end up with at least one surface facing an "odd" direction. It may also be important to add other elements that are attached to, and/or parallel or perpendicular to, that surface (e.g., a skylight or dormer attached to a sloped roof of a house). Rather than define each corner of the new sloped element with respect to the original x, y, and z axes, it is often easier to define its location based on the plane to which it is attached (Fig. 2–54). If the software allows, the new plane may be (temporarily) designated as the reference plane in order to speed up the modeling process. The ability or inability to define arbitrary reference planes does not allow for the creation of any particular model—it does not impact what one can create. It is, however, an enormous convenience that allows for more rapid model creation and lessens the chance of the software modeling process getting in the way of the creative design process.

2.4 EDITING AND MODIFYING ELEMENTS

At times, an image may need modification in order to better communicate a designer's intent. At other times, the design itself may need changing in order to best satisfy the requirements placed on the project. In any project, it is inevitable that modifications will be made. With digital media, it is important to maintain the distinction between modifying the image (what you see) and modifying the model itself. The ease with which elements can be removed or changed can be medium dependent.

2.4.1 Modifying Drawings Created with Traditional Media

When drawing with traditional media, line and shape removal is accomplished with erasing (with or without erasing shield), scraping, washing, or covering (Fig. 2–55). Under certain conditions (for example, ink on textured illustration board), significant errors cannot be removed effectively and drawings must be recreated. Under other conditions, erasure is easy. Modification of lines is usually accomplished by addition—new lines drawn over, across, and next to existing lines. Shapes are modified on a segment-by-segment basis. Finally, it is not uncommon for designers to simply draw over the original sketches—either using overlays or, at times, directly on the original when modifying the freehand sketches that are created early in the design process (Fig. 2–56).

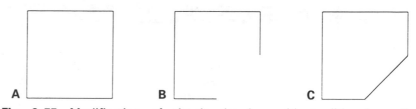

Fig. 2–55 Modification of simple drawing with traditional media. *A,* Original drawing with four segments. *B,* Erase portions of two segments. *C,* Redraw as chamfered corner.

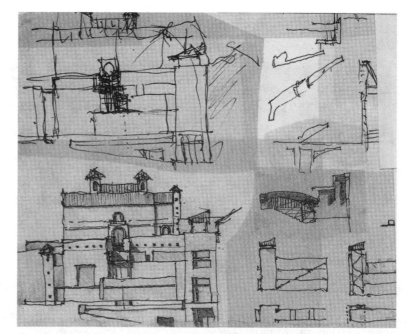

Fig. 2–56 Schematic design sketches. Modification of images with traditional media can be in the form of drawing and redrawing. Frequently, trace is used to facilitate the modification of one image by using an earlier version as a starting point. (*Jess Galloway, University of Texas at Arlington*)

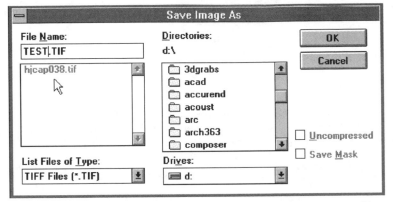

Fig. 2–57 "Save As" dialog box. It is important to save images or files under different names if modifications are to be undone easily. "Saving as" preserves the original while making a new copy. (*Painter by Fractal Design*)

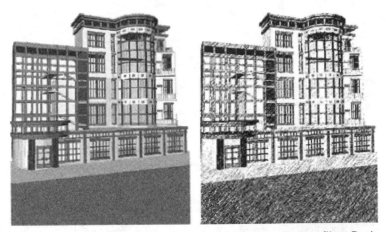

Fig. 2–58 Original and modified images saved as separate files. Both versions now exist in digital form, and each one can be treated as an "original" from which prints may be made or to which further modification may be made. (*Deborah Muñoz, NJIT*)

2.4.2 Modifying Drawings Created with Electronic Media

It is very important to remember to save a model or image before modifying it significantly. Once the model is saved, a copy of it can be changed. If a decision is made to incorporate the change, the new version may be saved directly on top of the old one (which destroys the original model). Saving on top of the old one is usually accomplished with a "save" command. The save command, more often than not, simply saves the working copy with the name of the model being used. Alternatively, a "save as" command (Fig. 2–57) may be employed, which saves the new model (with the modifications) with a new name and/or on a different disk drive. When saving the model or image with a new name, both the original and new models can remain intact (barring computer or disk failure) (Fig. 2–58).

Remember to save images and models in progress frequently. Never go a long time working without saving. Because of the inevitability of glitches or crashes (especially if working with unstable software—or software rushed to market prior to removal of all errors or "bugs"), one should save the files often to avoid loss of work.

Selection of Elements

The ability to easily change existing lines and models is an important attribute of CAD/graphics. Prior to changing any element, it must be selected for modification. Selection can be made simply by clicking the cursor onto the point, line, or object (Fig. 2–59) or through other means. Objects may be selected or chosen by color, object, name (Fig. 2–60), or material (if one was associated with the creation of the object). Objects may be selected by a window, mask, or boundary box (an artificial window described by a series of line segments—not necessarily rectangular—within the viewable area that describes a closed shape) (Fig. 2–61). When selecting elements within a boundary box, it is necessary both to draw the box and to define whether the items to be selected are those entirely within the box, those outside of the box, and/or those elements that exist both inside and outside the box (i.e., cross the boundary). Some types of raster software allow selection by color via a "magic wand" that, when clicked on a color, selects contiguous pixels of that color—or similar colors based on a user-defined tolerance. Once the elements are selected, operations may be specified that act upon them.

Erasure or Removal

Electronic erasure is relatively easy. The selected item may be simply deleted (Fig. 2–62). If the item is within a vector drawing program, the line or object is removed. In a raster program, the pixels are changed

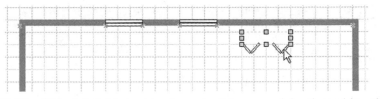

Fig. 2–59 Object (bifold double doors in this example) selected by placing cursor on object and double clicking.   (*VISIO by Visio Corporation*)

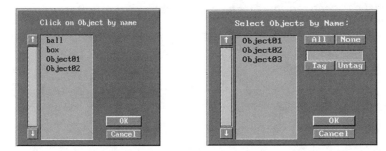

Fig. 2–60 Dialog boxes for selection of elements by object name in a three-dimensional model (*3D Studio by Autodesk. This material has been reprinted with permission from and under the copyright of Autodesk, Inc.*)

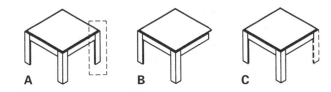

A   B   C

Fig. 2–61 *A,* Selection of element by creating a boundary box. *B,* Removal of element. *C,* Change of line type of element.

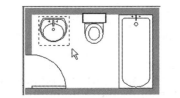
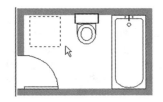

Fig. 2–62 Selection and deletion of element

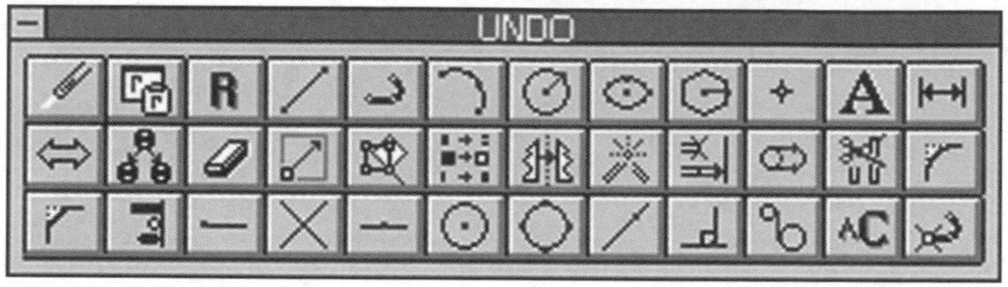

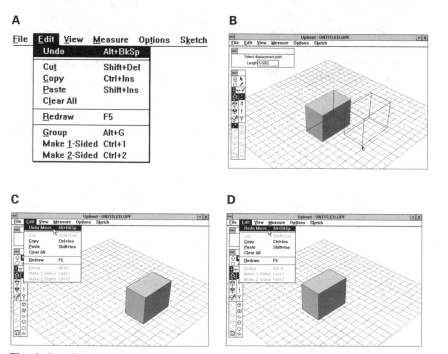

Fig. 2–63 Undo commands are frequently available as buttons or icons in a toolbox. A variety of programs make analogies to traditional media and use a pencil eraser as the image for undo. *(AutoCAD by Autodesk. This material has been reprinted with permission from and under the copyright of Autodesk, Inc.)*

Fig. 2–64 Undo may be selected from an edit menu (*A*). In this example, a box is made and a move is selected (*B*). After the move, Undo move is selected (*C*) to place the box back in its original position (*D*). Note that various programs allow you to "redo" the change, which permits toggling back and forth to evaluate the potential change. (*Lee Anderson, upFRONT by SketchTech*)

to a predefined background color (often white or black). Some raster programs retain the information and history of the creation of the image (or particular objects within the image) and may be able to restore the pixel descriptions (color) of whatever was previously drawn in the particular location where removal took place.

Undo

If it is software supported, and if there is enough memory in the computer system to retain a description of a model or image prior to making changes, an **undo command** will allow you to remove the last step (Fig. 2–63). The number of "levels of undo" describes the number of steps backwards you can take. Undo commands are often found in the edit group of menus (Fig. 2–64). Alternatively, some CAD/graphics programs allow you to "hold," "keep," or "maintain" a particular model or image in memory while making a series of changes. If the changes are acceptable, one can then save the new model. If the changes are not acceptable, one can go back and "fetch," "get," or "retrieve" the model that was held in memory.

Copying-Cloning and Pasting-Inserting

One should note that there is some ambiguity in the distinction between the creation of elements and the subsequent modification of those elements. Many drawing programs have either different modules or different submenus that distinguish between creating or drawing and modifying or editing. A **clone** is an exact copy of an existing element (Figs. 2–65, 2–66). The command to create a clone is sometimes found in an edit column or module and sometimes found in a create module. Regardless of where it is found, the ability to copy something created exists in virtually every graphic program used by architects and designers. (This command even exists in business and word processing applications.) A clone can be copied to a temporary file—or a "notebook" or "clipboard"—and can then be pasted or inserted into another location (Fig. 2–67).

Clones can be valuable as experimental "scratchpads." Similar to "fetch" and "hold," a clone can be worked on and saved as a separate file or discarded upon returning to the original.

Multiple Copies—Arrays

It is also possible to create multiple copies of an object once it is drawn. One can always select an element (line, shape, or model), copy it, and then paste it as many times as needed onto the drawing. However, it is frequently desirable to create a large group of multiple copies of an element. An **array command** allows the creation of multiple copies of a shape or object at prescribed intervals. The array command can specify the number of copies of the shape, as well as the linear (Fig. 2–68) or angular (Fig. 2–69) distance between them. Like the copy and clone commands, the array command is found in both

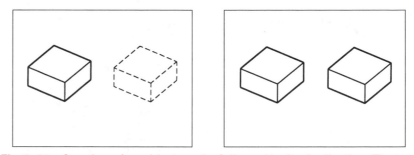

Fig. 2–65   Creation of an object can be followed by its duplication. The two boxes are now exactly alike except for position.

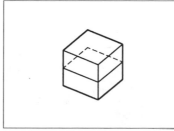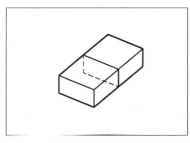

Fig. 2–66   Once copied, the box can be moved to create new composite shapes.

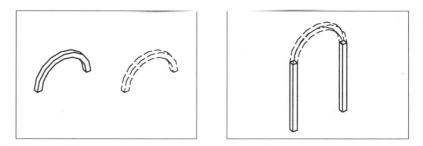

Fig. 2–67   Clones can be brought into a new file from a clipboard or from the original file. Clone of the arch is created, dragged, and pasted or inserted into another model, placed on top of two columns.

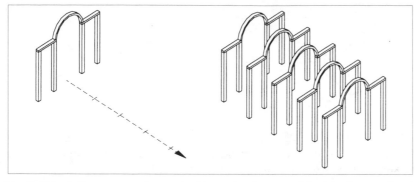

Fig. 2–68 A linear array is created by selecting an object and repeating it along a line at a prescribed interval. One can either select the length of the line and the number of elements to be spaced evenly, or the number of elements and the spacing between them.

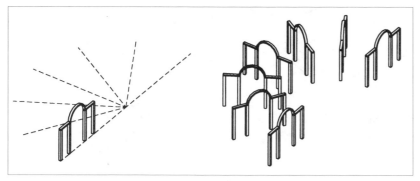

Fig. 2–69 An array can be created by specifying intervals along a curved path or by determining angular distances between elements.

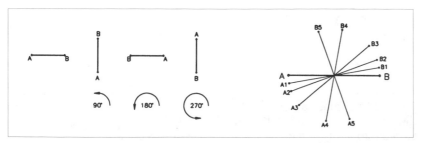

Fig. 2–70 Line rotation by specified degree (*left*) and by interactive free movement (*right*). Control point at center.

edit and creation modules in graphics software. Designers should be alert to the fact that building models or images with arrays reinforces the additive nature of creating.

Rotation

Rotation is the turning of an element in a model (or an entire model) around a specified axis or axes. Rotation can be by a specified degree, or it can be "free," which means it is determined interactively by moving the cursor (Figs. 2–70, 2–71). (A turning of a building in a model often reflects a desire to change the relationship between the building and its context. This may reflect a desire to test alternative impacts of the sun on a facade, pedestrian movement patterns at an entrance, or any other factor that may require study during the design process.) It is possible to select a particular element, or group of elements, for rotation while leaving the rest of the model in place (Fig. 2–72). It is possible to rotate one object about another object. Rotation of a portion of a model may involve rotating a building while leaving the site model in place, or rotating a piece of furniture in a room.

Scaling

Objects, polygons, and lines can be rescaled interactively by stretching or shrinking them by moving the cursor. Alternatively, it may be possible to specify a numeric value that represents the multiplier of the object's size. **Rescaling** is the change of size (either two-dimensional or three-dimensional) of an element or model (Fig. 2–73). (The rescaling of an element can be used for many purposes—from an exploration of the relationships between two forms in a composition to a study of monumentality in buildings within urban contexts.) An element may be scaled as needed along any combination of its principal three axes. Note: Be careful with proportion when rescaling. It is necessary to determine when existing proportion must be locked and maintained. When rescaling is not done in all axes simultaneously, re-proportioning can result.

Mirroring, Projecting, Skewing, and Moving

There is a variety of additional operational commands that are frequently found in modify and edit modules. Many of the commands refer literally to the changes made to the model or image. The **mirror** command, like the array command, creates new copies of a defined element (Fig. 2–74). However, a mirrored element, by definition, is a new composition with varying degrees of axial symmetry (Fig. 2–75). One can **project** a point, edge, or face of a three-dimensional object onto another surface, thereby causing the distortion of the original element. **Skewing** an element twists it without restriction to its principal axes.

To **move** means to relocate an element from one place to another. Once created, an object can be moved in any direction, or along any combination of axes. Movement can be created by specifying the axis or axes and the

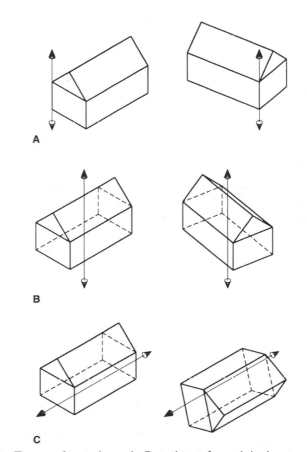

Fig. 2–71 Types of rotation. *A,* Rotation of model about vertical axis through corner. *B,* Rotation of model about vertical axis through center. *C,* Rotation of model about horizontal axis.

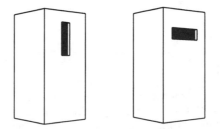

Fig. 2–72 Rotation of opening in a wall to evaluate visual impact

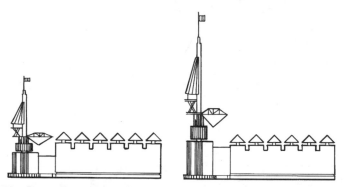

Fig. 2–73 Rescaling allows for stretching or shrinking of an entire object or a single element within a composition. (*Tom Andrasz, NJIT*)

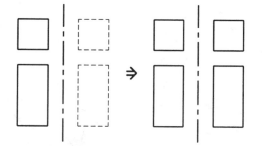

Fig. 2–74 Mirror commands allow for reflection of an element (or group of elements) about a defined axis.

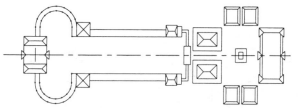

Fig. 2–75 Mirroring of elements reflected in diagram of symmetric organization of Eighteenth-Century Nancy (*Diagram based on a drawing in Peets, E., and W. Hegemann. 1922.* Civic arts. *New York: Architectural Book Publishing Co. [reprinted by Princeton Architectural Press], p. 74.*)

displacement (distance) or by selecting the element and visually relocating it (Fig. 2–76). Schematic design processes usually work best when you are moving objects visually and interactively (so you see what you are doing). Later in the design process, when exact distances become more critical, precise dimensions may be specified.

Moving the object (which is a modification of the three-dimensional model and/or the two-dimensional image) is different from moving the image around within the field of view. To **pan** across an image (which does not modify the data associated with the model) means to move the image within the frame of view, or screen. There are a few different ways in which applications allow for a pan that are software specific (Fig. 2–77).

Modification—within any operation or group of operations—is an attribute found in both raster and vector graphics programs, and it does not change the raster or vector characteristics of the image(s). It is important to remember that both two-dimensional and three-dimensional elements can be modified. The ease with which digital copies can be made provides a designer with a relatively inexpensive way to keep multiple originals and backup copies in case of "changes of mind" or computer failure. Maintaining copies of interim design or image files also provides a record of the design and drawing process that may provide useful insight for later modification.

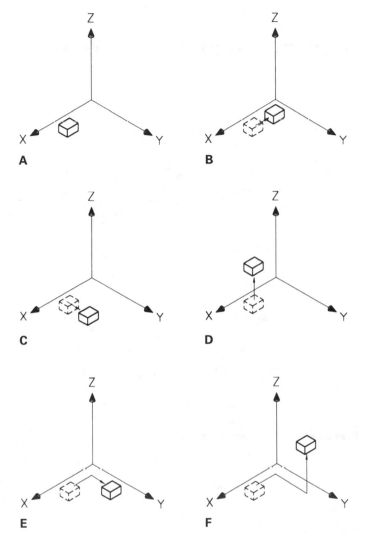

Fig. 2–76 Movement. *A*, Original position. *B*, Movement along x axis only. *C*, Movement along y axis only. *D*, Movement along z axis only. *E*, Movement in two directions (x and y). *F*, Movement along all three axes.

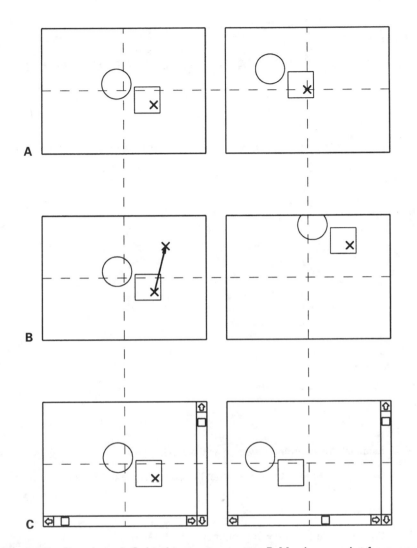

Fig. 2–77 Panning. *A*, Selecting a new center. *B*, Moving a point from one place to another. *C*, Moving horizontal and vertical scroll bars at the sides of the image. (Scroll bars are primarily used when the "desktop," "virtual screen," or "canvas" is larger than the actual screen. This can occur when the resolution of an image is larger than the displayable area on screen and reduction, or zooming out, is not desired.)

Example 2–1

CREATION OF A SIMPLE SHAPE: AN EXAMPLE OF THREE-DIMENSIONAL DIGITAL MODELING

Note: Most shapes can be created in more than one way—even within the same software program, using a variety of create and modify commands.

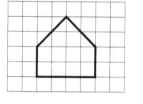

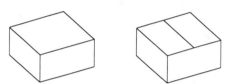

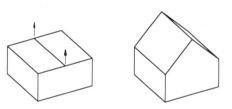

- Establish the coordinate system as the z axis.

- Set the grid to an interval such that the points of the object fall on exact grid intersections.

- Set snap on.

- Create profile with drawing commands.

- Define the x coordinates or select near and far points to create object

  OR

  Establish path and near and far points and generate extrusion.

- Create rectangular object sitting on x-y plane.

- Insert line and vertices.

- Move the new vertices in the z dimension (set vertical height).

Example 2–2

CREATION AND MODIFICATION PROCESSES USED TO CREATE A CORRUGATED PIPE: AN EXAMPLE OF THREE-DIMENSIONAL DIGITAL MODELING

Note: This exercise has been reduced to the basic general steps and commands. Many modeling software programs are likely to require additional program-specific steps for a satisfactory outcome. (The example is based on an exercise from *in·form·Z,* and printed with permission from auto·des·sys, Inc.)

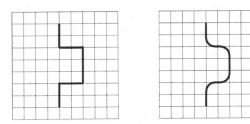

- *Left,* Software with smoothing options: simply draw the pattern with grid snap on. *Right,* Without smoothing option: use freehand or curve commands to create a pattern with rounded curves.

- Copy the element and create as many pieces as needed and joint one to the other. Alternatively, create a linear array.
- Smooth the rectilinear pattern. Although this represents an additional step in the process, it is still easier than creating the initial pattern as a curve.

- Add a top and bottom equal to the radius of the smaller dimension of the pipe.

- Rotate or revolve the profile 360° around the central axis. The greater the number of increments, the smoother the model but the larger the file.

- Create and attach as many copies as needed to develop the pipe to its proper length.

Example 2–3

BUILDING A DIGITAL SITE MODEL

General

- Site information may be obtained either from spot elevations on a site map or from contour lines (lines on a site plan that connect points of uniform spot elevation).

- The more detail on the site model (the smaller the increments between spot elevations or contours), the greater the digital size of the model and the more time it will take for the computer to manipulate the image and data. (Too large a file can greatly increase the time required by the computer to redraw views of an image or to render an image.)

- When the digital model size is very big—and the site is very large compared to the building(s)—it is sometimes desirable to *reduce* the amount of data placed into the digital model. For example, it may be possible to build a model using data from every other contour line. Care must be taken, however, to translate the correct vertical information to the site model. The reduction of data in the model reduces the file size and increases the speed with which the model can be manipulated.

- Landscape architects frequently require the visibility of contour lines on the site model to facilitate working back and forth in two- and three-dimensional images.

- Not all ways of building a site model will be possible with every three-dimensional modeling program. Generally, however, there are at least two different ways to build any model at any given time.

Stepped "cardboard" model

- Model is created by building up a stack of solids (or surfaces) the perimeter of which conforms either to the edge of the model or to the contour lines.

- The thickness of each slab is generally uniform. Depending on the overall size of the model and memory available, the thickness may conform to the vertical dimensions represented by the contour lines.

- It is possible to subdivide the vertical distances (usually in equal increments) and interpolate between contour lines to get smaller steps that more closely represent the slope of the site. Note that doubling the number of steps will usually double the size of the file. For those CAD/graphics packages with file sizes limited by RAM, too many steps may overwhelm the model. Note also that the larger the file, the more time it generally takes to manipulate it.

- *Advantages:*

  —Easy model type to create.

  —Virtually every three-dimensional modeling application has commands to create stepped models with freehand solid or surface models.

  —Easy to modify one slab at a time when working with site models.

  —Maintains visibility of contour lines.

- *Disadvantages:*

  —When sites are not actually stepped, the model represents an abstraction of a slope that may, on occasion, give a false impression to a viewer (or designer).

  —Complex contours can result in large file size of model.

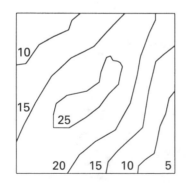

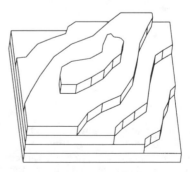

Example 2–3

BUILDING A DIGITAL SITE MODEL, CONT'D

Rectangular solid grid model

- Model is created by first building a grid of rectangular solids (or surfaces) and then moving the points at the top of each box to a vertical position that matches the height.

- The thickness of the original slab is generally small but, ultimately, has little effect on the final model.

- The number of subdivisions into small sections affects the memory required and the overall appearance and precision.

- Provides a good solution to get a sloped model (without steps) when there is no mesh, surface, or terrain command. (*It produces a model that is actually a "pseudoterrain" model.*)

- Creation can be very time-consuming when done as shown in this example.

- Some software programs allow for automatic creation of square mesh terrain models.

- Contour lines are *not* visible except in those instances in which they coincide with the square grid.

Terrain or mesh model

- Relies on *mesh, terrain,* or *surface* commands that are not available in all modeling applications designed for architects and designers. Is available in some design packages, however, and most GIS (geographic information systems) CAD/graphics applications.

- Generally provides the fastest way of producing a sloped site model.

- Depending on the software, the file can be smaller than the rectangular solid grid model.

- Contour lines are visible on model.

- Often created by first positioning the contours as lines at the appropriate vertical heights. (For example, the contours are created as line segments in the x-y plane, each with a constant z value corresponding to the height defined by the contour. One can either create the lines at the appropriate height initially, or create them all at the base and then move the lines to their proper position.) The next step involves the application of the terrain or mesh to conform to the contours. In the "best" situations, this application involves only one command.

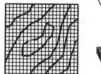

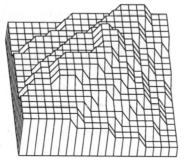
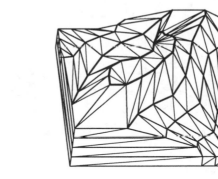

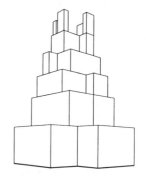

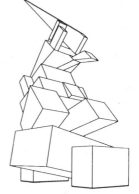

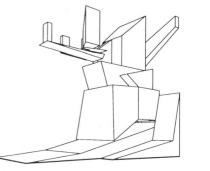

Fig. 2–78 Twiddling

2.5 TWIDDLING, TWEAKING, AND TWEENING

When designing with the computer, one can use automated processes in order to generate design and image alternatives. Twiddling, tweaking, and tweening all use combinations of previously described operations in order to generate and modify additional images and models. They refer not (necessarily) to a specific command, but rather to the process or the way the commands can be used.

2.5.1 Random Operations—Twiddling

Twiddling introduces a random component into the design and image modification process by allowing playful selection and manipulation of operations (Fig. 2–78). Just as a designer might sketch absentmindedly or playfully with charcoal at the beginning stages of a design, the computer permits this to occur whenever the designer wishes, throughout the design process. Random selection of different commands in any menu-driven drawing or design system can be used to generate new options for a design project. The design activity can radically distort the original intent. The designer is confronted with images that either have little or no design value, or may be unexpected solutions. The range of what is possible expands. Although the designer is performing random operations, it is the structure of the software that is developing alternative designs. The selection of what is appropriate—or better—becomes a more difficult and crucial task. The twiddling designer must remain open to the suggestions of the computer but critically and carefully analyze the possibilities that are presented. The primary design activity is the evaluation of multiple, and unpredictable, design ideas.

2.5.2 Incremental Decision Making—Tweaking

Tweaking is characterized by the linear and incremental sequencing of decision making, evaluation, response, and subsequent design activity (Fig. 2–79). Without pre-conceptualizing, a designer can explore sequential variations of any component in a design. Lines, shapes, surfaces, and objects can all be manipulated in size and proportion. The incremental exploration can be extended to include rotation, scaling, translation, and so on. Due to the speed of graphics processing, each tweak can occur almost instantaneously, can occur repetitively, and can be undone. Tweaking requires a level of design intent and a preselection of the operation(s) to be performed.

2.5.3 Intermediate Steps between Extremes— Tweening

Tweening (derived from the word *between*) is the process of creating intermediate images that fall between the extremes of a movement (Fig. 2–80). In computer graphics, these images are generated from key frames and are based on processes used by the animation industry. Tweening is, for our purposes,

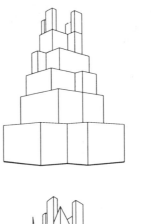

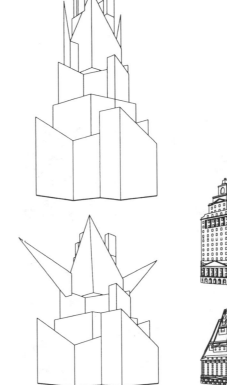

Fig. 2–79 Tweaking

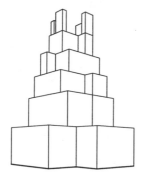

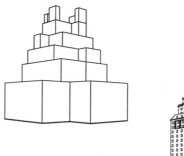

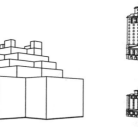

Fig. 2–80 Tweening

comparable to the "morphing" of one character or face into another that is commonly seen in film and advertising. But in architecture, the focus can be on the development of the stages between the extremes rather than on the fluid motion from one condition to another. Tweening allows a designer to study, consciously, the implications of parametric variations of scale and form. The relationship of a building to its context or a part of the building to the rest of the building can be studied. When the extremes are determined, a preset number of intermediate (or in-between) steps can be created and evaluated. If desired, fully developed images can be printed or displayed for each alternative to facilitate comparative studies. Tweening initially defines the extremes of a given context, develops the rules for intermediate variations, and results in a predictable and highly structured design exploration.

2.6 LETTERING AND FONT SELECTION

2.6.1 Uses of Lettering and Notation for Graphic Communication

Annotation on drawings is used to enhance communication. Although the use of graphics is a primary method of presenting information for architects and designers, words and labels are also useful. It makes no sense to spend hours drawing something that can be described as clearly in a sentence or two.

Sometimes, a combination of graphics and text is useful when a simple title improves the clarity of the image (Fig. 2–81).

When communicating information to contractors, labels and specifications are a critical component of the contract documents prepared by the building design team. Finally, text is used to identify the architect, interior designer, engineer, owner, contractor, project name and location, and so on, on a variety of drawing types (Fig. 2–82).

There are times when one is designing a package (or building sign) for which brand or company recognition is significant and the text is one of the most critical factors. There are times, also, when drawing titles or notations on diagrams are the only text. Regardless of the amount or type of text, poorly placed text, improperly sized text, or inappropriate text can detract from the image and distract the viewer from more important information. When used properly, text can be considered another graphic element on the drawing and becomes part of the overall image. It is important to remember that, in most cases, the use of text is to improve communication, and therefore it should be clear and legible.

2.6.2 Lettering Styles and Characteristics

Lettering is defined by its characteristics. *Font* refers to the style of the lettering and any particular characters or symbols associated with the style. Within any particular typeface, there may be a variety of styles—each considered a separate font—including italics,

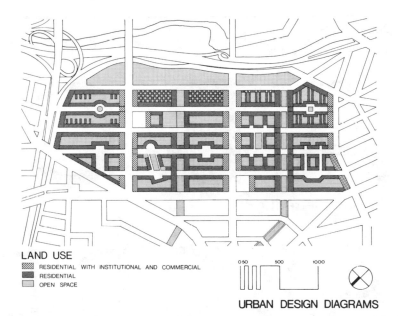

Fig. 2–81 Text on presentation drawings. Simple title blocks and labels help communicate information without detracting from image. (In general, avoid abbreviations in titles.)

Fig. 2–82 Facsimile of partial title block from architectural construction documents that usually includes the architect's name, address, and license or registration numbers. Typical title blocks would also include the client's name, name and location of the project, consultants' names and license numbers, drawing title and number, scale, and north arrow.

Box 2–D

SIZES OF TEXT

A B C

108-point lettering

A B C D E

72-point letting

A B C D E F G H I J

36-point lettering

A B C D E F G H I J K L M N

24-point lettering

A B C D E F G H I J K L M N O P Q R S T U V W X Y Z
12-point lettering

A B C D E F G H I J K L M N O P Q R S T U V W X Y Z 1 2 3 4 5 6 7 8 9
9-point lettering

Note: 72 points = 1" 6 picas = 1"

bold, and outline. **Point** refers to the size of the letter as measured at the maximum extension from the lowest to the highest letter within the alphabet. Note that this does not mean that every letter is the same size. When uppercase and lowercase are used, for example, 9-point type will have letters smaller than ⅛" even though 9 points = $\frac{9}{72}$" = ⅛". (See Boxes 2–D and 2–E.) **Leading** refers to the spacing between lines of text measured in points. **Kerning** refers to the spacing between letters that takes into account differing width of the letters themselves. Depending on the particular font, letters may be spaced evenly (fixed pitch) or proportionally (variable pitch) (Box 2–F).

The number of fonts available to a designer is enormous. Unless the text is the focus of the image, however, it is usually good practice to keep the text simple, clear, and legible. Text can be created with serifs (little "tails") or sans (without) serif (Box 2–G). Although not a rule, it is sometimes considered that serif text is traditional whereas sans serif (which, like modernist architecture, is ostensibly devoid of decoration) is modernist. Text may reflect the intended style of the building or, at times, may be selected as a contrast for added emphasis. Decorative fonts are also available to simulate signs or any other text that may appear on the building that needs to be represented in the image. It is possible, for example, to put signs on a door in a three-dimensional model that will be displayed and printed to scale in a representation of the space.

A designer should take note of digital fonts that mimic architectural-style hand lettering. Although it limits

Box 2–E

SELECTION OF LETTERING SIZES

- Understand the intended audience and final format for the drawing.
- If the final product is to be in 8 ½" × 11" book format, the text can be fairly small—as long as it is legible.
- Typical *minimum* sizes on architectural drawings are ⅛", or 10- to 12-point type size. (Note: It is common for architects and designers to create planning reports, proposals, program analyses, etc., that include large amounts of integrated text and graphics as part of the growing services the design profession provides.)
- Titles on large drawings or plots should be larger than drawing notes (at least ½") if they are to be seen from a distance in a public or group presentation.
- Text should be composed as part of the overall image.
- Multiple lines of small text can be grouped, viewed as, and moved about as a single graphic entity when composing a drawing or image that contains multiple elements.

Box 2–F

PROPORTIONAL VS. FIXED-PITCH FONTS

Aa Bb Cc Dd Ee Ff Gg Hh Ii Jj Kk Ll Mm Nn (Univers®)

Aa Bb Cc Dd Ee Ff Gg Hh Ii Jj Kk Ll Mm Nn (Times Roman®)

Aa Bb Cc Dd Ee Ff Gg Hh Ii Jj Kk (Courier)

- Proportional, or variable-pitch, fonts like Univers and Times Roman vary the spacing assigned to each character and space.
  - Variable-pitch fonts provide only enough space for letters so that visually equivalent spacing is provided between characters.
  - Variable-pitch fonts must be aligned visually in vertical columns or with preset "tabs" that align columns in tables.
- Fixed-pitch fonts like Courier have the same "amount of room" assigned to each character and space.
  - Fixed-pitch fonts assign the same width to each letter, regardless of the letter's width (an *i* gets as much room as a *z*).
  - Fixed-pitch fonts are easy to align in vertical columns because all letters—and spaces—are the same width: alignment is determined by counting characters and spaces.

Box 2–G

SERIF AND SANS SERIF LETTERING

Z, T, A

Sans Serif (Helvetica®, Univers®, Letter Gothic, etc.)

Z, T, A

Serif (Times Roman®, Courier, Souvienne, etc.)

Serifs are little tails on the ends of the letters that improve the readability of the letters—in part by implying horizontal continuity. (*Note the difference in the bottoms of the letters* A *and* T *in the illustration above.*) Serif letters are frequently used when large amounts of text are required (construction document specifications, written design proposals, etc., and consequently are sometimes found as the default type of font in word processing programs).

Sans serif (without serifs) letters are more blocklike than serif alphabets and are often used on drawings when they are viewed as graphic objects in themselves (rather than being considered *only* as text).

Helvetica, Times Roman, and Univers are registered trademarks of Linotype-Hell AG and/or its subsidiaries.

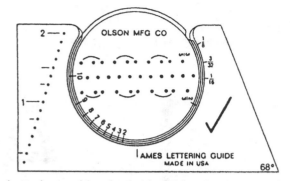

Fig. 2-83 Lettering guide. A multipurpose instrument that facilitates rapid creation of guidelines for hand lettering. By rotating the circular center portion, parallel guides (including intermediate guides) ranging from ⅟₁₆" to 1 ½" in height can be drawn. Sides can be used in lieu of a small triangle for assistance in drawing vertical and slanted lines when lettering. (*Olson Manufacturing and Distribution, Inc.*)

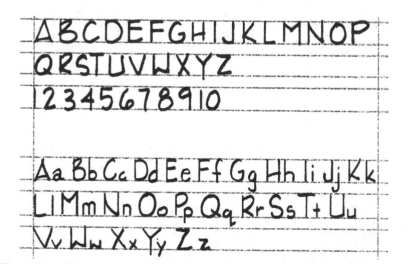

Fig. 2-84 Hand lettering. The creation of simple block lettering, drawn with guidelines, is an often-used graphic skill. If desired, small triangles or lettering guides can be used to draw the vertical lines to keep letters straight.

the style and expression of the lettering on an image, the use of a font that can be easily replicated by hand facilitates last-minute discrete changes on printed copy. *The purpose of the image and the likelihood of change are factors when considering font selection.*

2.6.3 Lettering Creation

Hand Lettering

Architectural hand lettering is most effectively produced with the aid of guidelines and straightedge (Fig. 2-83). Horizontal guidelines are drawn first, and a small triangle or lettering guide can be held against the parallel rule as a vertical guide while lettering. While many styles can be drawn, including calligraphic ones, simple block letters are most common (Figs. 2-84, 2-85). Outline fonts are used only for large letters, where the visual weight of solid letters would overwhelm an otherwise delicate drawing (one with fine lightweight lines and/or intricate detail). The lettering must be clear and of a size and weight appropriate for the drawing on which it is placed. Hand lettering can be done in ink, but architects most often use pencil. There are, however, tools that assist the drafter with ink lettering (Fig. 2-86). When pencil is used, it is important that the point not become too dull, or the letters will become distractingly inconsistent. Simple, clear, discrete strokes form the best letters. Spacing between letters must be done "by eye." Hand letters do not have a fixed pitch. In other words, the spaces between letters vary with the shape of the letter. Even spacing between hand-drawn block letters will look awkward and could result in miscommunication. One should strive (initially) for an *apparent* average spacing between adjacent letters.

Stencils and Transfer Type

Stencils (Fig. 2–87), available in a variety of styles and sizes, can be used for lettering in exactly the same way traditional templates are used for shapes and objects. Placement of letters on the page is facilitated by light guidelines. Sometimes, the guidelines can be offset so that the letters do not sit on the guides themselves. The offset can allow for careful erasing of the guides with erasing shields after the line is written. Stencils, like templates, can be used with both pencil and ink.

"Lettering machines" (Fig. 2–88) are available for titles and labels in a variety of fonts and sizes for use on drawings created for reproduction. The machine prints typed letters onto strips of adhesive film that can be pasted onto a drawing. The strips are relatively narrow (typically ½" to 1"), and the material varies with the intended method of reproduction (either diazo or photographic). Multiple lines of text are made up of multiple horizontal strips placed by hand onto the drawing. Because the tape is visible, text created with lettering machines can become somewhat inelegant on original drawings unless organized carefully to be part of the composition.

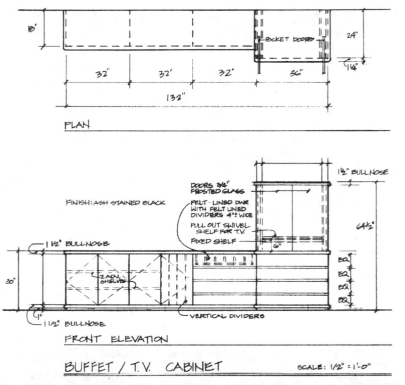

Fig. 2–85 Construction details with handwritten notes and dimensions.

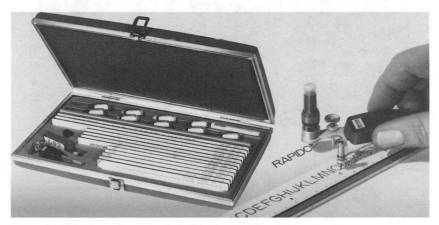

Fig. 2–86 Lettering set for ink lettering (*Koh-I-Nor, Inc.*)

Fig. 2–87 "Corbu" stencils. Metal stencils based on design of architect LeCorbusier. (*Charrette Corporation*)

Fig. 2–88 Lettering machine. Thermal printing process used to print lettering on strips of adhesive-backed tape. Characters can range in size from 6 to 60 points. (*Kroy, Inc., Scottsdale, AZ*)

Lettering can be transferred to drawings on paper or film with dry transfer type—sometimes called rub-on or press-on letters. Supplied by a variety of manufacturers, the transfer lettering is available in different fonts and type sizes. Using very light guidelines (often in nonphoto blue lead), one selects a letter, positions it, and rubs with a dull burnishing instrument until the letter is firmly in place on the drawing. Because each letter is placed on the drawing individually, application can be tedious. Transfer type, if left alone, does not always age well. Under certain conditions, an appropriate fixative may be sprayed lightly onto the letters (depending on the original drawing surface) to prevent damage during printing and handling. Nevertheless, the dry transfer type provides a crisp, printed letter on original drawings without any background or tape marks that are characteristic of other methods of lettering application.

Digital Fonts

Font selection is widest when lettering is created digitally. Designers have access to both bit-mapped and vector (polygon outline) type. Furthermore, with file capture and transfer programs, as well as automatic tracing and scanning software, one type can be converted to another. The resolution of type, when printed, depends on both the software being used and the particular printer or plotter. (For example, a dot matrix printer will not produce the variety and clarity of type that a 600-dpi laser printer will.) Although fonts can be created and stored by the designer, it is faster, and usually more than adequate, to use existing fonts and modify them on an as-needed basis. The number and type of fonts accessible will be based on whatever the CAD/graphics and word processing software support. Unless the text is the graphics, software selection and use is likely to be based on other criteria.

Designers have access to the myriad of lettering styles available in common business and home software packages (Figs. 2–89, 2–90). Additionally, CAD/graphics programs allow the importing and manipulation of fonts used in most common software programs (including Post Script and TrueType fonts). In other words, the designer's access to fonts and sizes is virtually unlimited and selection should be made carefully with consideration of the overall graphic impact. For example, large text—which may be needed for a presentation meant to be seen from a distance—on a delicate drawing may graphically overpower the image so a lighter-looking or outline text should be used. Also, too many varied font styles can be distracting to a viewer, unless a collage is carefully being created.

When drawings are created electronically, text is added just as any other component of the image is added. Once a text command is activated (either by menu and icon or command), text may be entered. The text icon in many programs is easily identified by a capital letter: either the letter *A* (which represents *alphabet* and is indicative of letters) or the letter *T* (for *text*). Although there are some applications in which text is entered directly in place on an image, text is commonly entered in a dialog box and then placed on the image. Any

Aero: AaBbCcDdEeFfGgHhIiJjKkLlMmNnOoPpQ

Big Top: AaBbCcDdEeFfGgHhIiJjKkLlMmNnOoPpQqRrSsTtUuVvW

Center City: AaBbCcDdEeFfGgHhIiJjKkLlMmNnOoPpQqRrSsTtUu

Chili Pepper: AaBbCcDdEeFfGgHhIiJjKkLlMmNnOoP

Courier: AaBbCcDdEeFfGgHhIiJjKkLlMmNnOoP

Gravure: AaBbCcDdEeFfGgHhIiJjKkLlMmNnOoPpQ

Harem: AaBbCcDdEeFfGgHhIiJjKkLlMmNnOoPp

Helvetica®: AaBbCcDdEeFfGgHhIiJjKkLlMmNnOoPp

Kidstuff: AaBbCcDdEeFfGgHhIiJjKkLlMmNnOoPpQqRrSsTtUuV

Letter Gothic: AaBbCcDdEeFfGgHhIiJjKkLlMmNnOoPpQ

Logan: AaBbCcDdEeFfGgHhIiJjKkLlMmNnOoPpQqRrSsTtUuVv

New York Deco: AaBbCcDdEeFfGgHhIiJjK

President: AaBbCcDdEeFfGgHhJiJjKkLlMmNnOoP

Souvienne: AaBbCcDdEeFfGgHhIiJjKkLlMmNnOoPpQ

Sterling: AaBbCcDdEeFfGgHhIiJjKkLlMmNnOoP

Surreal: AaBbCcDdEeFfGgHhIiJjKkLlMmNnOoPpQqRrSsTtUu

Fig. 2–89 A (small) sample of fonts (including decorative ones) available in digital and transfer-type formats. (*Adobe Systems, Inc., Expert Software, Inc., and The Monotype Corporation. Helvetica is a registered trademark of Linotype-Hell AG and/or its subsidiaries.*)

ARIAL regular, bold, *italics*

(clear, sans serif block lettering)

TIMES NEW ROMAN regular, bold, *italics*

(clear, serif lettering)

BRUSH SCRIPT regular, bold, italics

(script, decorative lettering)

TECHNICAL regular, **bold**, *italics*

(clear, "hand drawn" style of lettering)

CASPER OPEN FACE regular, **bold**, *italics*

(outline style of lettering)

Fig. 2–90 Variety of TrueType lettering fonts. (Not all lettering styles are available in each font.) *(Linotype-Hell Company, The Monotype Corporation, Adobe Systems, Inc., and Expert Software, Inc.)*

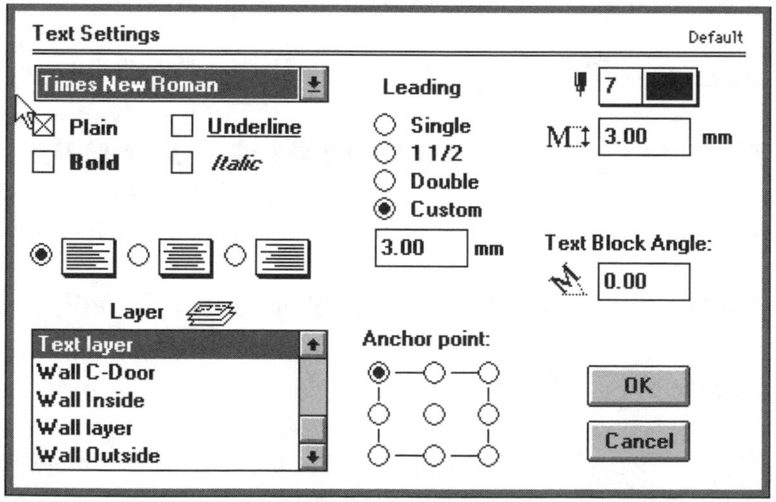

Fig. 2–91 Text dialog box with user settings and variables *(ArchiCAD by Graphisoft US, Inc.)*

individual text block usually remains as a group or block in the image and can be moved or edited as needed without affecting the rest of the image in vector-based images. Fonts and type sizes can be changed as part of the text-editing process (Fig. 2–91). Once text is added, and fixed in location, in a "painted" image, it becomes part of the pixel or image description and takes over whatever was underneath. Only in software that maintains various object layers can the text be moved and modified once set in place.

Text can also be created in raster software with tablet and pressure-sensitive stylus in a manner comparable to that of freehand decorative lettering. Once any lettering is in digital format, it can be manipulated with any of the electronic processes available.

Digitally created text is easy to add to traditionally created drawings and/or printed images. Title blocks, blocks of notes, specifications, and so on are easily created with any word processing program, printed onto an adhesive-backed appliqué suitable for laser printing, and placed onto a drawing. In fact, any printed text (limited only by size) can be photocopied onto adhesive-backed appliqué for use on drawings. Not limited to narrow linear strips, the appliqué can be cut to size to fit within predefined (frequently drawn) sections or boxes on an image to maintain a neat and well-organized composition. (Note that adhesive-backed appliqué is generally not completely transparent, and copies made of images can show a lightly shaded area, or "ghost," which corresponds to the limits of the appliqué. When the appliqué is in a predefined area, like a title block integrated with and surrounded by a drawing's border, the ghosting is frequently not objectionable or noticeable and—appears to be part of a text or title area.)

Finally, with various add-on programs, standard and decorative type can be further modified and individualized by varying individual characters through stretching, squishing, tapering, twisting, and so on (Fig. 2–92).

Fig. 2–92 Text can be modified and warped if it is to be treated as a piece of graphic design. The text may be added to a drawing either by directly importing it into the program being used or by printing it out onto adhesive-backed appliqué. (*Text created with Adobe Type Twister by Adobe Systems, Inc.*)

REVIEW QUESTIONS

1. Describe the *Cartesian coordinate system.* How many variables describe the location of a point?

2. Why is knowledge of geometry important in CAD/graphics?

3. What is a *primitive?* What are some of the different shapes or forms found as primitives in CAD/graphics programs? Look at the building in which you live, work, or study. List and describe the primitives you find.

4. Describe various ways a *line* can be drawn with electronic media.

5. What is a *snap* command?

6. Although *volumes* and *solids* may look the same from some viewpoints on the screen, they have different qualities—what are they?

7. What is the difference between a captured two-dimensional view of a model and the digital model itself?

8. What are the parameters for creating a three-dimensional object by *extrusion?*

9. What are *Boolean operations?*

10. Describe the difference between creating a digital model with *geometric objects* and creating it with *architectural objects.* Give an example.

11. How can the ability to create an *array* save time when building three-dimensional digital models?

12. In the context of digital modeling, what is a *mesh?* Describe some possible uses for meshes when creating three-dimensional models.

13. List and define at least three operations used to *modify* three-dimensional digital models in CAD/graphics programs.

14. List some possible uses for *adhesive-backed appliqué* on a drawing.

15. What is the difference between *serif* and *sans serif* lettering? What are some of the positive characteristics of each?

16. What is the difference between *fixed-pitch* and *proportional-* or *variable-pitched* lettering? To what does *kerning* refer?

17. Describe the advantages and disadvantages of dry transfer type lettering.

PRACTICE EXERCISES

1. Using 4H or 2H pencil, a triangle, and a parallel rule, T square, or drafting machine, draw a 20"-square, ½" × ½" grid centered exactly on a 24"-square sheet of vellum. Strive for accuracy in grid construction, and maintain consistency of line weight and a high level of craftsmanship in the way lines meet and end. On another sheet of vellum, repeat the exercise using a size 0 or 00 technical pen.

2. On 24"-wide white, yellow, or cream trace, use a very fine black felt tip marker and neatly trace freehand the grid created in exercise #1. Be careful not to tear the trace.

3. With soft pencil, carefully draw a detail found on a building. Draw the detail twice: once smaller than actual size and once larger.

4. On a 24"-square sheet of vellum, use a compass to draw ten evenly spaces circles with 1 ½" diameters, and ten with 3" diameters. Using a circle template and 2H lead, draw the same circles. Repeat the exercise with the circle template, and use a technical pen (size 0 or smaller). Again, strive for neatness, consistency, and a high level of craftsmanship. Centers of the circles should align horizontally.

5. Using traditional media (pencil), construct an octagon and hexagon that circumscribe circles. Construct a hexagon within a circle.

6. Using horizontal guidelines and a small triangle for verticals, practice lettering by writing the alphabet (uppercase) and numbers (0–9) ten times each at ⅛", ¼" and ⅜" heights in pencil on vellum.

7. From a color reproduction (print, postcard, calendar, etc.), copy—*without scanning*—a painting in public domain using a paint software package. Pay special attention to proportions. (Do NOT reproduce signatures or dates from the original.)

8. Create a two-dimensional drawing of the top view of a television remote control in pencil on vellum. Repeat the exercise with electronic media using a vector drawing program.

9. Create a three-dimensional digital model of a chair or table for which you have all dimensions.

10. Create a three-dimensional digital terrain model from the site data in the following contour map. (The base is elevation zero.)

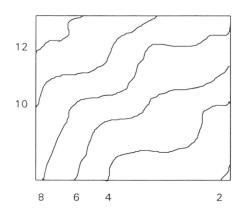

3 TWO-DIMENSIONAL DRAWINGS

Two-dimensional images are frequently used to *represent* three-dimensional objects or spaces (Fig. 3–1). *These representations are abstractions* in that the space or object being drawn is usually not seen by an observer in the kinds of views that are shown. They are also abstractions in that they are simplifications of the object and frequently do not contain all of the information actually found on or in the object. However, they *are* helpful in (usually) being easier to draw than complex three-dimensional images and in that they can show important design and construction information in clear and measurable fashion. Furthermore, they are excellent drawings to be used in the design and presentation processes when precisely locating objects or elements with respect to the two visible axes.

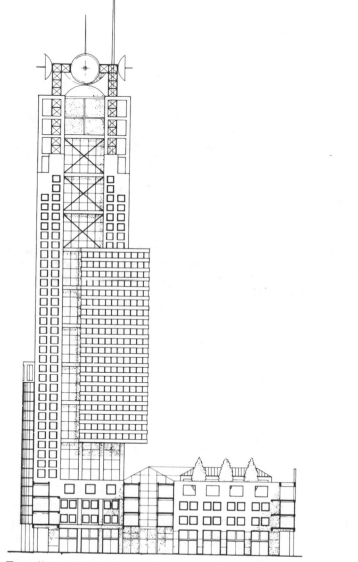

Fig. 3–1 Two-dimensional front view of a three-dimensional model (*Harold Raymond, NJIT*)

109

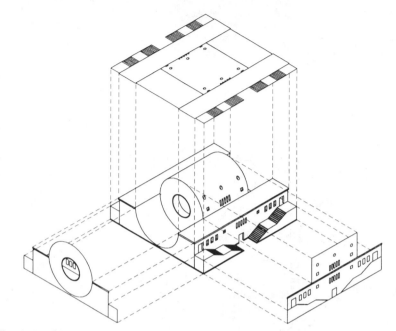

Fig. 3–2 Orthographic projection showing three-dimensional model with front and side elevation. At least two projections are needed to get a clear understanding of the nature of the object being described. (*Model by Michael Hoon, NJIT*)

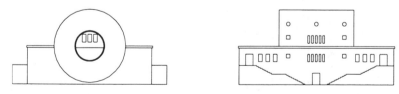

Front elevation   Side elevation

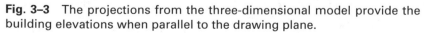

Fig. 3–3 The projections from the three-dimensional model provide the building elevations when parallel to the drawing plane.

3.1 ORTHOGRAPHIC PROJECTIONS

If we look at the front face of a building (facade) and imagine that we see it with a degree of measured precision, where right angles in the building are seen as right angles, and windows that line up vertically and horizontally are seen exactly that way—without appearing to diminish in size or recede at even slight angles—we are imagining an elevation of the building. An elevation is one type of orthographic projection of an object.

Orthographic projections are two-dimensional representations of three-dimensional objects in which the viewer's line of sight is perpendicular to the drawing plane, and representations of lines parallel to the drawing plane are shown without distortion—and are capable of being accurately measured (Figs. 3–2, 3–3). The parallel lines are represented either at a consistent fraction of true dimension—to scale—or, if part of a digital model that is displayed in a virtual work space on a screen, at actual full size. (Note: Full-sized digital models are usually "shrunk to fit" when printed copy is required, and a scale that conforms to architectural or engineering conventions can be produced on request. To view a full-sized model on screen, one must "zoom out" to give the appearance of a scaled-down drawing.)

Angled lines or elements that are not parallel to the picture plane are not represented with measured accuracy and would need to be shown in additional views to communicate precise information (Fig. 3–4).

Two-dimensional orthographic projections are useful to us in a variety of ways. The drawings can show us proportions that are part of the design that are independent from (and not distorted by) any particular view. Because they are measurable and to scale, we can easily draw orthographic projections with precision. Someone else can come and look at the plans and measure the length or width of an object with a degree of accuracy limited only by the precision of the original and the printing or reproduction processes. The clarity of orthographic projections makes them useful for design and presentation purposes, as well as to communicate information useful to builders and fabricators.

3.2 ELEVATIONS, SECTIONS, AND PLANS

The two-dimensional descriptive drawings used in design can also be thought of as slices through buildings and spaces. An **elevation**, or flat view of a facade of a building or object, is a vertical slice through the ground in front of, and looking at, the subject. The pieces of the building being drawn are projected onto the picture plane (or slice) in front of it for the purpose of representation (Figs. 3–5 through 3–7).

A drawing of a section of the building has the picture plane or drawing slice through the building itself. Depending on the scale and intent of the drawing, one can see the shape of the space inside a building or the nature of the materials used to construct it. A **section** is

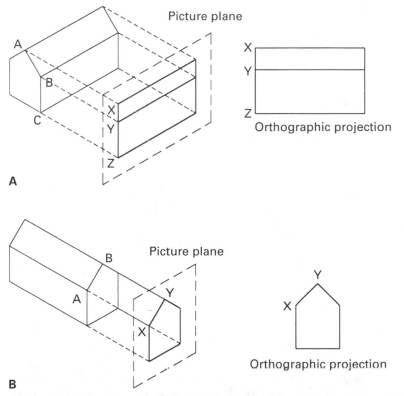

Fig. 3–4 Orthographic projections. *A*, Here, although lines AB and XY represent the same line of the object, the fact that AB is not paralled to the picture plane results in a line not to scale. XY is shorter than AB. Lines BC and YZ both represent the same line of the object, but because BC is parallel to the picture plane, BC=YZ. *B*, Here, AB is parallel to the picture plane, so AB = XY.

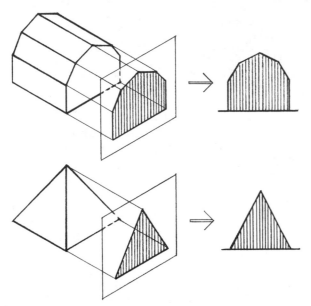

WEST ELEVATION

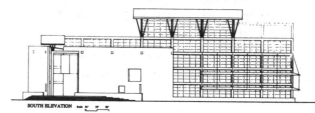

SOUTH ELEVATION

Fig. 3–5 Elevations of geometric forms

Fig. 3–6 Ink line drawing elevations of Evanston Public Library (*Francis X. Arvan, Architect*)

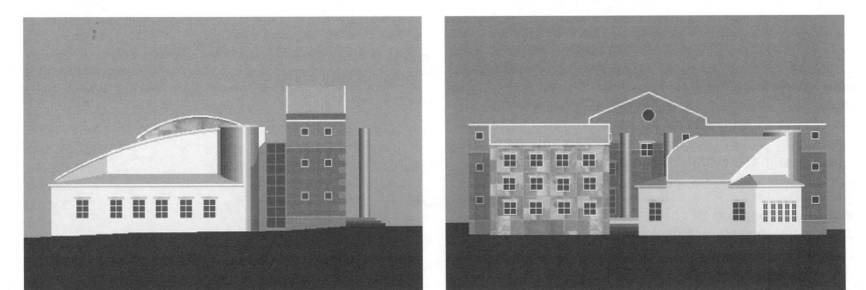

Fig. 3–7 Shaded elevations of three-dimensional model (*John DaCruz, NJIT*)

a representation of a vertical slice through an object, building and/or space (Fig. 3–8).

An object with varying angles can be represented by orthographic projections with the picture plane(s) oriented parallel to any surface of the object in order to obtain scaled views of the selected surfaces. The vertical slice can be taken at any angle parallel or perpendicular to any set of walls. By varying the orientation of the slice and point of view, one can create sections that show the interior facades or elevations of all walls in polygonal rooms. Every image conveys different information to the viewer and designer.

In addition to varying the angle of a slice, one can also vary the thickness and extend the concept of section into a series of pieces that are more like computerized axial tomography (CAT) scan images (Fig. 3–9). The designer can explore the relationship between interior and exterior, solid and void, parts and whole, and so on along the length of a building. Rather than each slice being created as a distinct two-dimensional drawing, these are created as "near" two-dimensional elements that simultaneously remain in a three-dimensional context and with relationship to the entire building. Conceptually, they represent a series of slices taken one after another throughout the building.

Sections may be taken and/or displayed at a variety of scales to show large buildings diagrammatically or small components in great detail (Figs. 3–10 through 3–12). Large site sections may be cut through the building and its context to show the relation between the building and topography (Fig. 3–13).

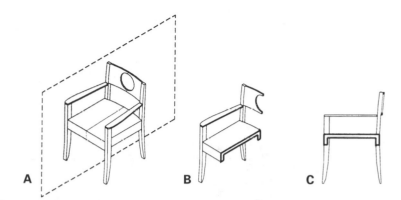

Fig. 3–8 Section and model based on "Oculus Arm Chair" designed by Michael Graves. A, Vertical cutting plane. B, Object removed from one side of cut. C, Section = orthographic projection of remaining piece.

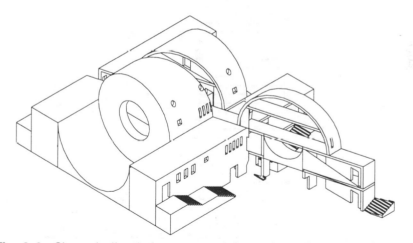

Fig. 3–9 Skewed slice being removed form three-dimensional model (*Model by Michael Hoon, NJIT*)

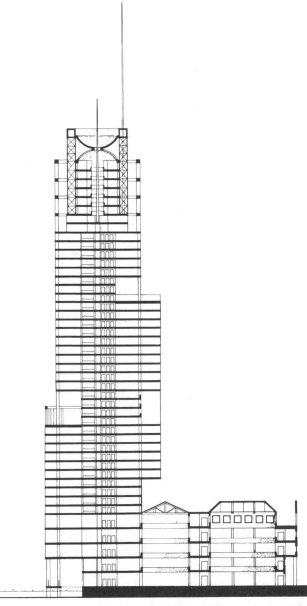

Fig. 3–10 Section through proposed building. The section refers to the same project illustrated in Fig. 3–1. (*Harold Raymond, NJIT*)

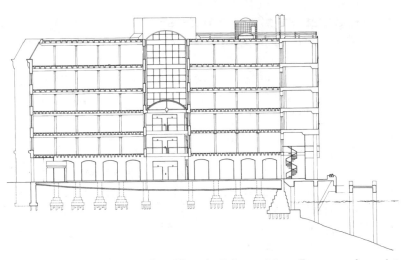

Fig. 3–11 Section through office building (*Jung/Brannen Associates, Architects; Neil Middleton, Principal Designer*)

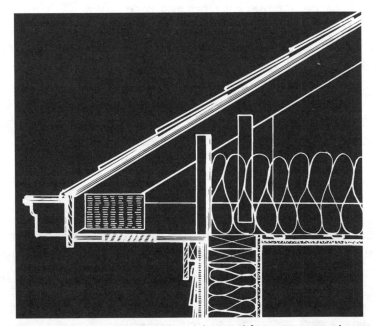

Fig. 3–12 Construction section through wood frame construction at roof overhang

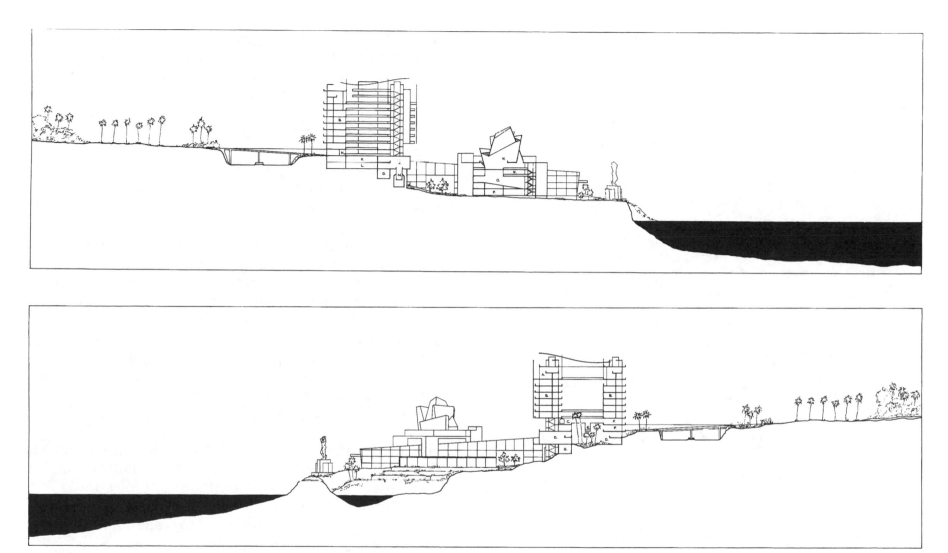

Fig. 3–13 Site sections through land and building, showing relation between architecture and context. Note that sections of a large scale are, of necessity, diagrammatic. (*Wainaku Mill Hotel; Hilo, Hawaii; Resolution: 4 Architecture; Joseph Tanney, Gary Shoemaker, and Robert Luntz; Partners*)

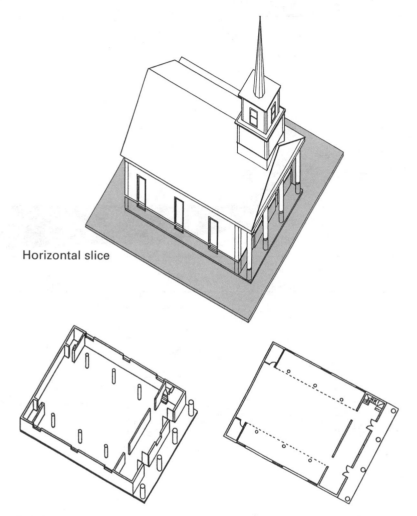

Horizontal slice

Section removed   Floor plan (detail and conventions added)

Fig. 3–14 The floor plan is created by slicing horizontally through the building. Additional conventions and detail to improve legibility are added to the two-dimensional floor plan. (Drawings based on the Meeting House at Old Sturbridge Village in Massachusetts.) (*Adapted from Muller E., and J. Fausett. 1993. Architectural drawing and light construction. Englewood Cliffs, N.J.: Prentice Hall, p. 47. Used with permission.*)

Under most circumstances, regardless of orientation, sections should be taken in such a way as to avoid cutting through columns or through the center of walls parallel to the picture plane in order to give the viewer a clearer picture of the shape of the space. In fact, it may be particularly useful to cut sections through wall openings and windows in order to graphically describe the flow of one space into another, or to better understand how light and air enter a room. (Possible exceptions would include an architect's or engineer's need to study the interior structure of a wall or column at certain locations through a building. Cutting through the wall may best show how one material is attached to another. Cutting through a concrete column may be the best way to see the size and placement of the steel reinforcing bars embedded in the concrete. These exceptions occur both in the design process of the details and also in the preparation of construction documents that communicate important information to the people who will construct the building.)

Similar to the vertical slices of a building, horizontal slices can be made. A **plan** is a representation of a horizontal slice through a building and/or space. The slice may be taken through a point in a building (typically 3' above the floor level) to represent a floor plan (Fig. 3–14).

Plans are used to convey a certain amount of information. Depending on the amount and type of information, the final drawing will be developed at different scales. A street map (plan) of the entire United States, to be useful and not too big, would only contain the major highways. However, if one looks at a city plan or street map, drawn at a relatively larger scale, all streets and monuments in the town can be seen. If one needs to search first at the state level and then at the town level, maps may be indexed or linked to one another. Similarly, in a building, one may need to look at—or explore—a project at different levels of detail: from the way a multibuilding office complex sits in the landscape to the furniture layout in one office. A print of a drawing showing all of the information could be too large to be useful and would lack the hierarchy needed to focus on relevant information.

The larger the scale, the more detail a drawing or display needs in order to look credible. It makes no sense to draw or display at one-half full size if the only information to be communicated is a schematic outline of a simple floor plan. On the other hand, a small-scale drawing would probably obscure important information if a designer were investigating the internal components of a construction detail. Because of the cross-disciplinary nature of the building delivery process, all members of a design team must be comfortable moving back and forth between different scales (Figs. 3–15, 3–16). (Note: Issues of scale selection are also applicable to sections and elevations.)

Digital models are not always drawn at a reduced scale: they may be viewed and printed to scale but can be created in full size with whatever unit of dimension is defined or selected by the user. Drawings developed electronically at full size often have too much information to

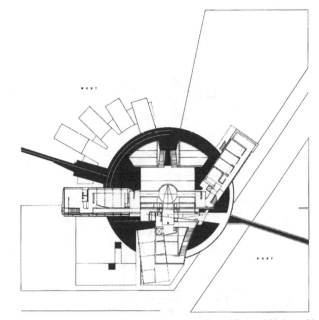

Fig. 3–15 Building plan at intermediate scale (*Brian Weber, University of Texas at Arlington*)

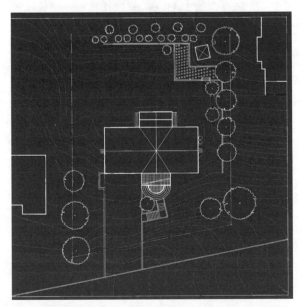

Fig. 3–16 Site plan and roof plan of single-family residence. (Original drawing scale @ ⅛" = 1'0".)

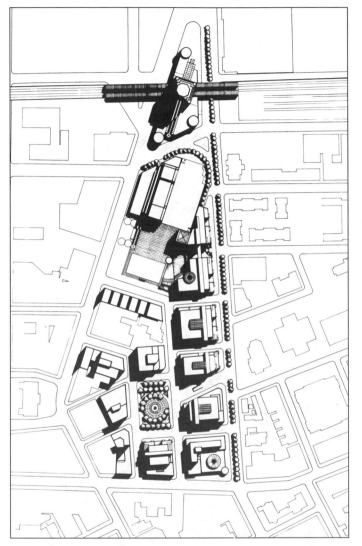

Fig. 3–17 Site plan of proposed urban development (*Emil Stojakovic, NJIT*)

convey clearly when reduced for printing or when viewed in their entirety (zoomed out) on a small screen. In these instances, one must make a decision as to which elements to "turn off" when printing or viewing in order to keep the output useful. While the image is on screen, one can enlarge it to look at specific details and continually recenter the image, or "pan" across the drawing. Large screens with high resolution facilitate working with images that have large amounts of information.

3.3 SPECIAL PLAN TYPES

3.3.1 Site Plan

The horizontal slice may be taken parallel to the primary floor levels but in a location *above* the roof of a building or group of buildings to see a roof plan and site plan. **Site** and **roof plans** are views of a building in its surrounding space—including neighboring buildings and landscaping in much the way the vertical slice in front of a building provides an elevation. These plans can show how the building fits into its surroundings, the proximity to neighboring buildings, the configuration of walks and roads, and so on (Figs. 3–17, 3–18).

When the scale of the site plan is small, one can see the pattern of built development or the extent of circulation (vehicular and/or pedestrian) systems. A street map, even for a small town, is a type of site plan usually drawn at a very small scale compared to the scale of building drawings. A site plan, for example, may be drawn or printed at $\frac{1}{32}'' = 1'\text{-}0''$ or $\frac{1}{16}'' = 1'\text{-}0''$. When the scale of the drawing is sufficiently large (e.g., $\frac{1}{4}'' = 1'\text{-}0''$), one may include such detail as landscape or street furnishings (benches, lighting, planters, etc.), representation of materials for walkways, and precise configuration of elements found on the roof itself (chimneys, skylights, mechanical equipment, etc.).

3.3.2 Reflected Ceiling Plan

One can also slice through the building and look up at the ceiling. More commonly, though, a **reflected ceiling plan** is created, by having an imaginary mirror on the floor and drawing the reflection of the ceiling. This convention allows us to orient the reflected ceiling plan over the same outline and in the same direction as the floor plan itself. Reflected ceiling plans are particularly useful in showing lighting design, as well as any ceiling grid, structure, or pattern that may be designed (Fig. 3–19).

3.3.3 Furnished Floor Plan

As abstractions, different two-dimensional plans can be used to quickly explore and communicate isolated design issues. Furniture layout can be quickly accomplished in plan. If the issue is the determination of how

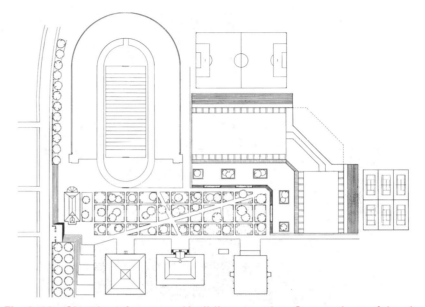

Fig. 3–18 Site plan of proposed building complex. Conventions of the site plan include elements such as paths, trees, tennis courts, and soccer field.

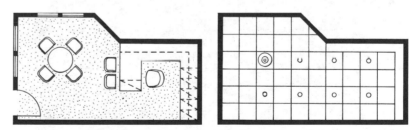

Fig. 3–19 Furnished floor plan *(left)* with reflected ceiling plan *(right)* showing ceiling grid, circular recessed lights, hanging light over conference table, and soffit above overhead cabinets. (Original drawing scale @ $\frac{1}{4}'' = 1'\text{-}0''$.)

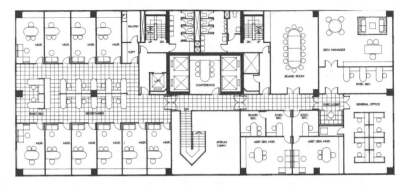

Fig. 3–20 Furnished floor plan of office building (*KMB Office Headquarters, Wong Chen Associates Ltd.; Nelson Chen, Architect*)

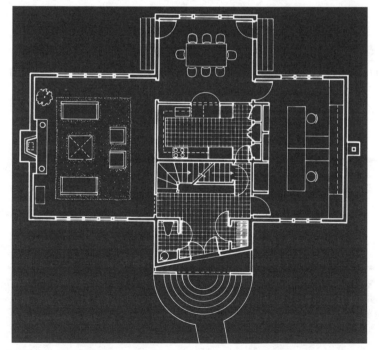

Fig. 3–21 Furnished floor plan of single-family residence

best to fit desks, chairs, tables, and so on into an office, one can draw furniture and the room at the same scale to see what fits and how much room is needed around the individual pieces. These furnished plans are abstractions, and one does not necessarily see the spatial implications of the layout. However, a designer can test to see if there is enough floor area for the necessary arrangement. In design, this is useful when doing space planning (working with a fixed area) or when creating new spaces that must accommodate specific functions (Figs. 3–20, 3–21). Inclusion of furniture also gives viewers a "sense of scale" that puts them in a position to better understand how a space works and how big it might be.

3.4 GRAPHIC CONVENTIONS FOR PLANS AND SECTIONS

Plans and sections contain information and conventions that are not part of a true slice through a building. Elements are added to a drawing to help make it more understandable. When drawing with traditional media or two-dimensional electronic media, these conventions become part of one's vocabulary and are added as the image is created. However, when starting with a three-dimensional digital model, the temptation may exist to merely slice the building and think that the drawing or image is done. In most cases, the image needs to be enhanced with either vector or raster software in order to conform to the language of architectural communication, as well as to improve its overall graphic quality.

3.4.1 Positioning the Slice

An exact slice of a building may not produce a plan or section that maximizes the utility of the drawing. Architectural conventions are employed to make the images better communicate the ideas and intent of the buildings and spaces. For example, when one is working on a furniture plan in a large open office space, a precise horizontal slice of the building might cut through partitions that are 5' high. If one were concerned about absolute accuracy in describing the horizontal slice, the cut partition would be shown as if it were a solid wall (although perhaps a little thinner than a building wall). However, the height of the ceiling may be 10' above the floor, and as one walks through the space (real or imaginary), the primary feeling may be of open space, since one can see over the partitions. In these instances, the best way to communicate the quality of the space will usually be to draw the tops of the partitions rather than expressing the cut partitions as solid wall-like elements. Similarly, in order to better convey and understand the implications of a design, a convention has been developed to show the tops of tables, chairs, and so on in furnished floor plans—regardless of the precise height of the horizontal slice. Windows that might not be apparent at the typical 3' slice height are also often shown. Although conventions can certainly be disregarded for certain purposes, they are usually followed. The common language used in architectural and design graphics also allows others

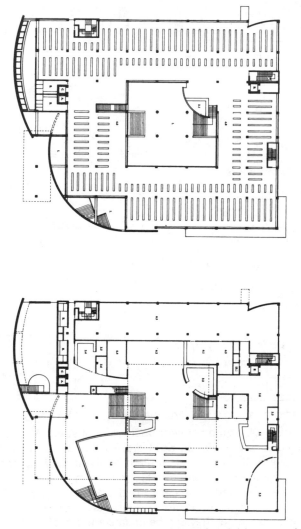

Fig. 3–22 Floor plans showing important furnishings and structure. Dotted lines on second floor plan (*bottom drawing*) represent opening overhead through to the third floor. (*Evanston Public Library, Francis X. Arvan, Architect*)

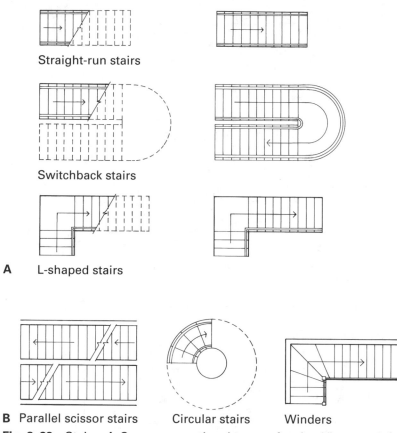

Straight-run stairs

Switchback stairs

A L-shaped stairs

B Parallel scissor stairs   Circular stairs   Winders

Fig. 3–23 Stairs. *A*, Some conventional types of stairs. Views on left are from lower floor, and views on right are from upper floor. *B*, "Specialty stairs." The use of these stairs is limited by most building codes. (Note: Winder stair treads have code-regulated minimum widths at their narrowest points and at specified distances from the narrowest point. They do not come to a point at the inside corner. Though easy to draw, simple split platforms should be avoided: they can be unsafe and are often not permitted.)

involved in the process to more readily understand the drawing.

3.4.2 Above and Below the Slice

There are a number of existing graphic conventions used in plans. Plans usually show the location of windows, even if located above the slice, in order to communicate information about entry points of light and air, as well as possible locations of emergency exits.

Changes in ceiling levels and other architectural activity above the horizontal slice are usually located with lines made up of short dashes on the plan to provide information about changes in the spatial quality of the room, as well as overhead clearances (Fig. 3–22). On rare occasions, engineers (and even more rarely, architects) will show hidden elements below the slice with dashed lines. Unless the purpose of the drawing is strictly graphic imagery, it is important that the intent of the lines be made clear with labels, diagrams, or additional drawings.

3.4.3 Stairs

Stairs almost always continue above and below the horizontal slice because they are used to connect different levels in a building (Fig. 3–23). Under most circumstances, stairs are cut with a diagonal broken line at about the 3′ mark with either an unlabeled arrow pointing in the "up" direction (towards the highest level being connected) or a labeled arrow starting at the level at which the floor plan is taken, pointing to the connecting level.

3.4.4 Doors and Windows

Doors are usually drawn as open at an angle of 90° (Fig. 3–24). Door swings are shown with portions of circles (usually quarter circles, but when needed, larger portions representing the maximum swing) in order to express the amount of floor space affected by the door as it extends beyond the door opening. Door swings describing doors that move in both directions are usually drawn as half circles.

Door swings are not actual elements in a building—they help us understand what is happening in a building or space. They are not part of the true three-dimensional model being sliced or described. Door swings, like many graphic conventions, frequently have to be added directly onto a two-dimensional drawing. They may be drawn line by line on an image, or symbols may be added in their entirety through the use of templates or electronic menus.

As is the case with many architectural elements, the manner in which windows are drawn varies with the size or scale of the drawing or proposed output. Elevation drawings at a very large scale can show the details of an entire window and surrounding trim, whereas those drawn at a small scale may be able to show only the opening with, perhaps, a double line indicating the window frame. Similarly, the details

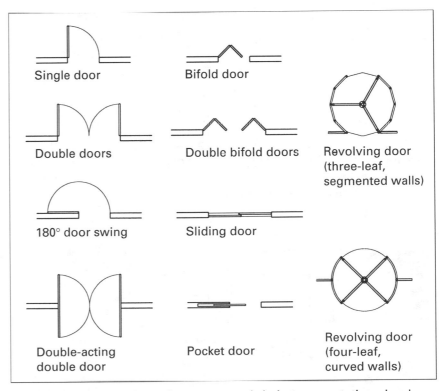

Fig. 3–24 Doors. Various door types and their representations in plan. Note that door swings, which do not physically exist, are drawn to give an indication of the space affected by the door's movement. (Dotted lines at revolving doors represent limit of overhead canopy.)

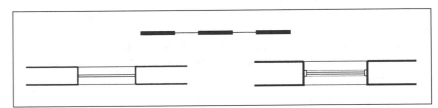

Fig. 3–25 Plan representations of windows. Increased detail with larger scale.

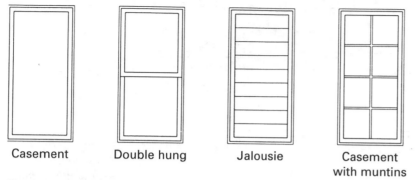

Casement   Double hung   Jalousie   Casement with muntins

Fig. 3–26 Elevations of window types

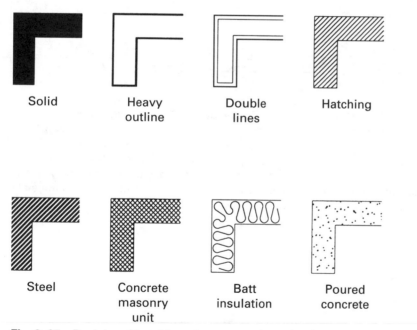

Solid   Heavy outline   Double lines   Hatching

Steel   Concrete masonry unit   Batt insulation   Poured concrete

Fig. 3–27 Poché and hatching plan conventions. Design and presentation lines are shown in the upper row. The lower row represents expression of construction materials.

drawn for windows in plan increase with the scale of the drawing (Fig. 3–25, 3–26). In both plan and section, it is important to show that the plane of the wall is punctured in a manner that allows light and/or air to enter the space. Windows can be an important compositional element in any design and should therefore be illustrated with precision in placement and proportion.

3.4.5 Hatching and Poché

The solid portion of wall cut by plan or section can be represented with various graphic conventions (Fig. 3–27). At a very small scale, the "cut lines" can be single, solid, black lines. When the scale gets larger, however, the relatively large area of cut walls (both in plan and section) can dominate an image if filled in as solid black in a black and white drawing. Rather than being allowed to focus on the expression of space in a section or the organization in plan, the viewer is distracted by heavy, ponderous black lines. As the scale gets larger, alternative ways of expressing solid components become more attractive. The outline of the cut areas can be drawn as heavier black lines, leaving the interior white. If the image is large enough, double lines (with the outer one darker) can be used to express cuts through solid elements. Hatching, or cross-hatching, is also a viable means of expressing cuts. In hatching, light diagonal lines are frequently used with heavier outlines. The solid or hatched fill between the lines in plan or section is also known as **poché**. To maintain graphic consistency in an image (thereby avoiding distractions from the message of the drawing), all hatching in an image should be drawn in a consistent direction.

Regardless of type of poché, there should be a clear distinction between walls and objects (including columns) that are cut and those elements that are not.

3.4.6 Line Weights (Widths and Thicknesses of Lines)

Line weights are used for expression in two-dimensional drawings. Images restricted to one line weight may be too light and flat, or too heavy and ponderous. Variety in line weight (and even media) can provide emphasis and hierarchy in a drawing (Fig. 3–28).

Cut lines, if not hatched, should be darker than lines seen only in elevation (even if it is only a "floor elevation"). When mixing pencil and pen on vellum, the section cut can be drawn with a very thin pen (2×0 or 3×0, depending on the scale), with all texture and elevational characteristics in pencil. When drawing in ink only, thickness and poché usually indicate cuts. Electronically, weight can be given directly to a line, or if the area or line is thick enough on a raster drawing, degrees of transparency can be used.

In addition to indicating cuts through objects, line weights provide depth clues and start to give the illusion of three-dimensional space. The outline around furniture should be darker than the texture of the floor

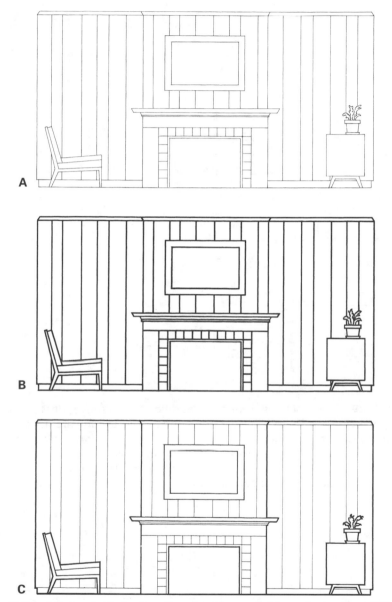

Fig. 3–28 Line weights in drawing elevations. *A,* "Anemic drawing." Thin lines throughout. Pale and weak. *B,* "Brutal drawing." Coarse lines throughout. Heavy-handed. *C,* "Expressive drawing." Subordination and emphasis of chosen lines. (*Adapted from Martin, C. L. 1968. Design graphics. Englewood Cliffs, N.J.: Prentice Hall, p. 21. Used with permission.*)

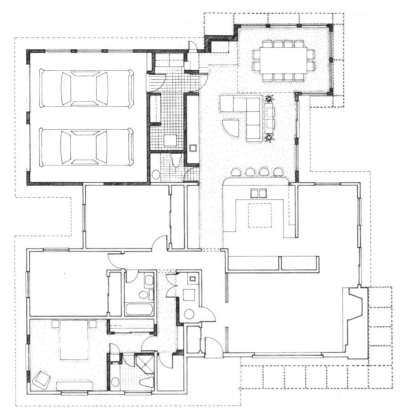

Fig. 3–29 Floor plan of proposed addition and renovation to single-family residence. Dotted lines, texture, and cross-hatching are used to improve design communication. Textured floor (stipple for carpet, grid for tile) represents new floor finishes. Dotted lines represent overhead construction (exterior overhang and trellis, interior skylight at kitchen, and change of ceiling plane separating dining area from family room).

or wall, because the furniture is in front of the background surface. Further refinement can be accomplished when one object is in front of another. Care should be taken not to make objects in a space stand out beyond the sectional cut lines.

Hierarchy of line weight is also possible in elevations, even when there is virtually no depth to represent. Texture of brick or siding should be lighter than the windows, or the mass of the brick lines may overpower the rest of the image. Expressed construction lines, or organizational lines, are usually even lighter.

Line weights are an important factor in creating an effective drawing that clearly conveys necessary information while providing graphic interest (Fig. 3–29).

3.4.7 Additional Information for Drawings

Leaders, Arrowheads, and Witness or Extension Lines

There are times when it is necessary to include information on a drawing that refers to an image, or part of an image, elsewhere on the same sheet. Based on the intent of the drawing, and its graphic composition, it may be desirable to visually connect related information. **Leaders** are lines that connect one element to another on a drawing: they lead the viewer to related information (Fig. 3–30). **Arrowheads** are the directional heads, or pointers, at the end of leaders or dimension lines (Fig. 3–31). Leaders and arrows are frequently used to connect a detail, or block of text, to a larger image. **Witness lines** (also known as **extension lines**) are light lines that are used to show the extent of a line or element being dimensioned (Fig. 3–32). Witness lines usually go near, but do not touch, the object being dimensioned. Dimensions may be between the lines, or outside them when the space is small.

Although dimensions on drawings are commonly associated with construction documents—providing necessary information for contractors—they are also important in many types of design and presentation drawings. For example, site plans that are presented to regulatory boards often need to show dimensions of buildings and setbacks, space plans for clients may need to include dimensions of offices, and so on.

North Arrows

Information about the orientation of drawings is important to further one's understanding of a project. Sunlight, energy flow, and predominant wind direction are but a few variables that can depend on the orientation of a project. To assist the observer looking at building plans, an arrow pointing north is often included (Fig. 3–33).

Scales

When a drawing is created or plotted, it is helpful for the viewer to know what the scale of the image is. Because it is not uncommon for drawings to change in size

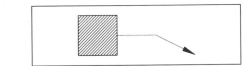

Fig. 3–30 Leader line (with arrowhead)

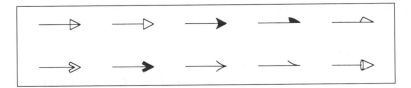

Fig. 3–31 Arrowheads. Selection of arrowheads should be consistent with overall graphic style without overpowering drawing.

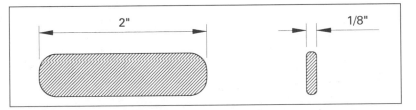

Fig. 3–32 Witness or extension lines offset about ¹⁄₁₆" from object. Dimension line between witness lines when area is sufficiently large, outside witness lines when area is small.

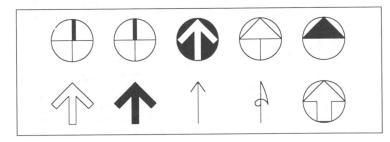

Fig. 3–33 North arrows

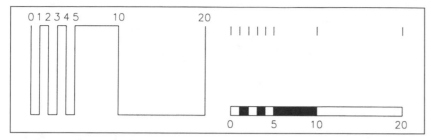

Fig. 3–34   Graphic scales

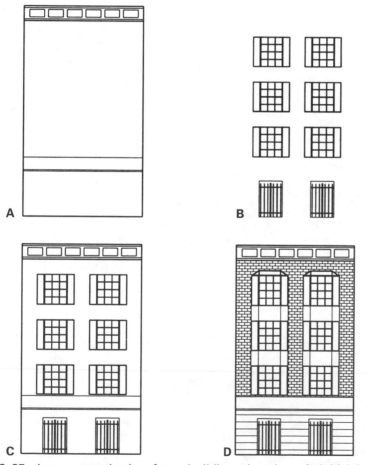

Fig. 3–35 Layer organization for a building elevation. *A,* Initial layer: building outline. *B,* Window layer. *C,* Building and window layers both visible. *D,* Building, window, and brick layers visible.

during reproduction (either due to the processes of reproduction or to purposeful enlargement or reduction), the use of a graphic scale (Fig. 3–34) that changes size with the image is often desirable.

3.5 LAYERS

Plan and elevation information can frequently be organized into subgroups, or **layers**. Typical subgroups might include site planting or landscaping, permanent walls, moveable partitions, windows, furniture, floor tile pattern, and structural grid. When drawing manually, each group may be drawn on a separate sheet and the sheets may be aligned by holes at the top held in place by pins (called overlay or pin-bar drafting) and then printed as a composite. Unfortunately, this procedure can be clumsy because the number of sheets can become unwieldy, and it is therefore used with decreasing frequency. To avoid dealing with multiple sheets of paper or film, one can restrict the layers to two, using both sides of a single sheet (walls or an organizational grid on the back, with other information on the front). With two-sided drawings, changes on one side need not impact changes on the other. During schematic design, however, it is not uncommon for architects to use tracing paper overlays to iteratively test ideas over a base sheet containing information that is constant or unlikely to change.

When drawing or designing electronically, layers become an important basis for file management. Most graphics programs are capable of handling at least fifty layers simultaneously (usually many more).

While drawing, layers can be assigned to major subgroups. Depending on the purpose of the image, layers might be assigned to different elements (Fig. 3–35). When producing a two-dimensional image only, layers facilitate expression of materials or sliced walls by assigning different colors or pen widths to different layers (Fig. 3–36). Raster graphics software may also support layers (Fig. 3–37).

When designing with a three-dimensional model, various materials are frequently assigned different layers to facilitate representation in both two-dimensional drawings (orthographic projections of the three-dimensional model) and three-dimensional perceptual images (renderings and perspectives). Because plans, sections, and elevations frequently are part of a three-dimensional model in a computer before slicing, graphic conventions needed for two-dimensional plans usually have to be added to the two-dimensional representation. These conventions can be placed on a separate layer so that they do not interfere with the building model when it is being used for other images or views.

Whoever looks at the drawing has the capability to turn layers on and off, deciding what gets looked at and eliminating, temporarily, unnecessary clutter and information. The layering system is also an effective means for controlling the selection of elements for editing when drawings are modified.

Although different software programs use different terminology, there a few basic modes for layers. The **active layer** is seen on screen and is the layer on which you

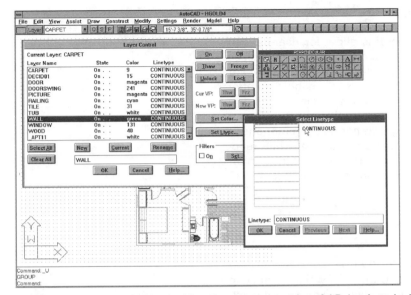

Fig. 3–36 Layer menus for drafting application (*AutoCAD by Autodesk. This image has been reprinted with permission from and under the copyright of Autodesk.*)

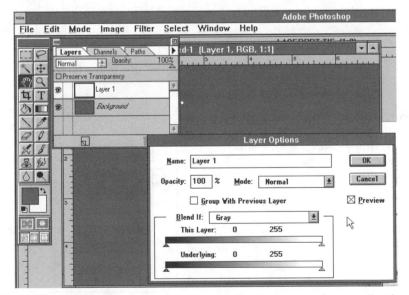

Fig. 3–37 Layer menu for painting or image processing applications (*Adobe Photoshop by Adobe Systems, Inc.*)

Fig. 3–38 Basic construction grid from CAD application. Various programs allow for user-defined major and minor grids to increase visual clarity on screen. Major grids are usually whole-number multiples of the minor ones. For very dense grids, some software programs permit the minor one to be toggled on and off while keeping the larger grid visible as an organization and drawing tool.

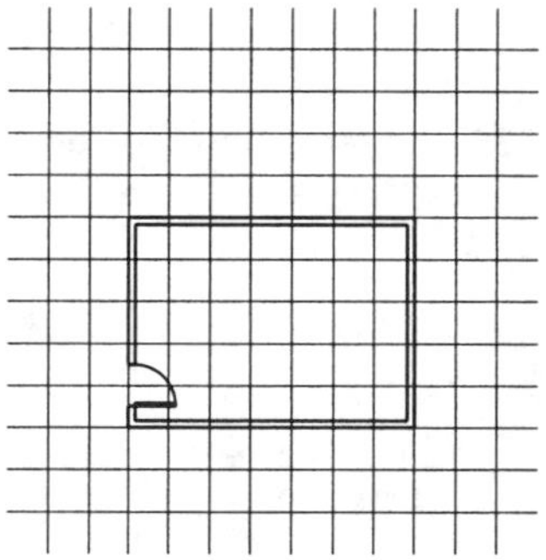

Fig. 3–39 Room plan drawn over grid. Corners of walls are at snap points. Wall thickness, in this example, is added to the inside of the walls.

Fig. 3–40 Construction or drawing grids can be rotated to any angle in many CAD/graphics applications.

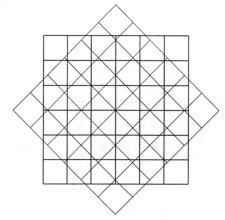

work at any given time. It is the layer on which current operations are performed and on which an element (or group of elements) can be selected for editing. Only one layer can be active at any one time. An **inactive layer** or **hidden layer** is turned off. You cannot work on it or see it. It is, however, still part of the data in the computer and is not lost. It is just temporarily "put away." A **locked**, **frozen**, or **reference layer** is visible on screen but cannot be added to or modified until it is made the active layer. The status of any layer is changeable upon command.

Careful use of layers in design drawings also helps a designer evaluate alternatives. By holding certain layers constant, a designer can alter specific elements for a careful comparison of unique variables. For example, the shape of a wall in an elevation may be determined before the exact configuration of windows. Either one can print the wall outline and draw different windows over the wall layer, or one can create alternatives on screen, assigning a new layer to each different window design. Various designs can be viewed in multiple windows on screen or printed for side-by-side evaluation.

3.6 GRIDS

Grids can be used to assist in the creation of two-dimensional images. The grid (Fig. 3–38) is treated like a reference or "base" layer—over which drawings are created. Graph paper can be used as underlayment to assist in the rapid creation of accurate drawings when drawing by hand. If the size of the grid conforms to architectural scales, one can draw plans or elevations by tracing the grid and "counting boxes" (Fig. 3–39). If the grid size conforms to a planning module that is relevant to the building's structure or fenestration, it serves as a guide to the layout of spaces and furnishings.

Grids are a useful tool in managing the level of precision afforded by electronic media. Electronic drawing uses grids both as underlayment for drawing layout and as fixed, or locked, points for locating the start and end of lines and objects during drawing creation (snap points). By limiting the software to a grid intersection for placement of points (the interval of which is adjustable by the user), one can establish a degree of accuracy for the base drawing based on the dimensions of the grid. Grids can be distinguished as (1) **construction grids** or **planning grids** (underlayment and base grids with the smallest useable interval for the drawing—frequently used to reflect a characteristic spacing [like that of columns] of the project), (2) **snap grids**, and (3) **visible**, **auxiliary**, or **screen grids** (grids shown on screen that may be at greater intervals than snap or planning grids to minimize drawing clutter). Any of the grids may be changed at any time during the drawing process (Fig. 3–40).

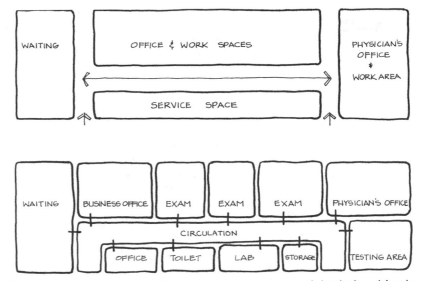

Fig. 3–41 Schematic plan diagrams exploring potential relationships between programmatic elements in a project. The upper diagram was created first and contains only the most basic, preliminary space planning ideas. The lower diagram is more developed and begins to subdivide the larger blocks into more defined activity areas.

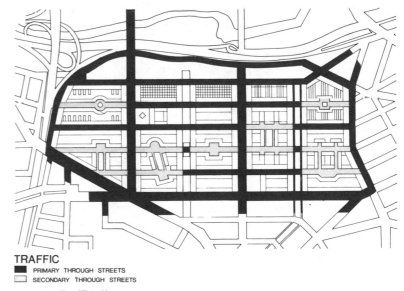

Fig. 3–42 Traffic diagram

Fig. 3–43 Circulation, geometric organization, and structural diagrams for single building (*Harold Raymond, NJIT*)

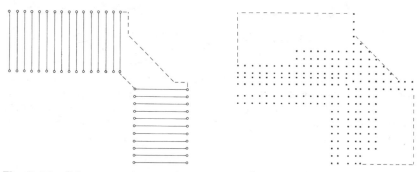

Fig. 3–44 Primary and secondary structural system diagrams

Fig. 3–45 Existing *(left)* and proposed figure-ground *(right)* diagrams for large urban proposal *(Emil Stojakovic, NJIT)*

3.7 TWO-DIMENSIONAL DIAGRAMS

We can use further abstractions to explore other ideas and various architectural organizations. Diagrams of plans and elevations, drawn with the purpose of evaluating specific design ideas (circulation, distribution of programmatic or activity-space elements, geometry, proportions, hierarchy, etc.), can help us make decisions by isolating the variables we are studying (Figs. 3–41 through 3–44). **Figure-ground drawings** are used to reduce parts of a design idea to an either-or, black-white, or yes-no condition. For example, in a site plan, all buildings can be drawn as black objects on a white background. The buildings become the "figure" and the site is the "ground." We can then quickly see the shapes of the spaces that are formed by the buildings to test for compatibility with our design ideas, or to analyze the conditions of existing places (Fig. 3–45). If useful, the black and white can be reversed to alternately emphasize the buildings or spaces. Similarly, figure-ground drawings in elevation are used to study proportions and placements of windows on a solid wall, or mullions on a glass wall, during the design process.

Diagrams can be a critical component of the design process, communicating significant information to the designer and other members of the design team. The use of two-dimensional diagrams makes it easier to perform a clear analysis of existing conditions as one evaluates both the built and natural contexts of a site and building. The ability to diagram the key components of one's own building design helps to bring order to the project and facilitates additional design development throughout the design process.

REVIEW QUESTIONS

1. What are *orthographic projections*? Why are they useful?

2. Under what conditions are angled lines drawn to scale in elevations?

3. What are the conceptual similarities between *plans* and *sections*?

4. Why do plans drawn or displayed at different scales need different levels of detail?

5. What is the purpose of a *site section*?

6. What is a *reflected ceiling plan*?

7. In what ways can varying *line weights* help make a drawing better?

8. What is a *witness line*?

9. Why is *layer management* important when drawing with electronic media?

10. What are some of the uses for *figure-ground drawings*?

PRACTICE EXERCISES

1. Draw an elevation of a teacup with a handle. Select a side to draw such that the handle is seen in full view (e.g., is parallel to the picture plane).

2. Draw the orthographic projections of a chair.

3. Draw a furnished floor plan of your bedroom. Pay attention to accuracy in measurement, as well as line weight.

4. Draw a furnished floor plan of a 6' × 8' residential bathroom containing one bathtub, a lavatory (with or without a vanity), a toilet, and an in-swinging 3'-0"-wide door. The surrounding walls are 6" thick. Draw the four interior elevations.

5. Obtain dimensional information about a house designed by a significant architect (Palladio, LeCorbusier, Neutra, Rietveld, Sert, Wright, H. H. Richardson, Moore, etc.). Draw the plans and elevations of the house. Drawings are to be created and/or printed at a scale of ¼" = 1'-0". Plans are to be furnished. The site plan is to be drawn or printed at a smaller scale (appropriate to the dimensions of the site).

4 THREE-DIMENSIONAL DRAWINGS AND MODELS

In order to reduce the level of abstraction during the design and presentation processes, it is often useful to represent the three-dimensional buildings and spaces we are designing in a manner that *looks* three-dimensional (Fig. 4–1). Although paper and screen are, for all practical purposes, flat two-dimensional surfaces, images that look three-dimensional more closely represent actual views of a proposed building—just as a still scene on television or in a movie looks like a space or building. Unless animated, however, architectural and design drawings represent discrete single views, frozen in time. The use of three-dimensional images helps the designer communicate architectural intent to individuals not regularly involved in the design professions (clients, regulatory boards, etc.) and provides a good way to work out complex spatial relationships.

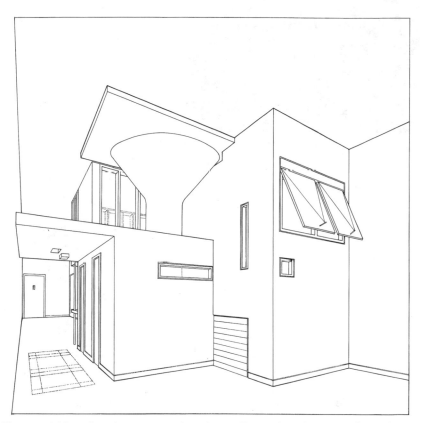

Fig. 4–1 Line drawing expressing three-dimensional space of architects' offices. (*Resolution: 4 Architecture. Joseph Tanney, Gary Shoemaker, and Robert Luntz; Partners*)

135

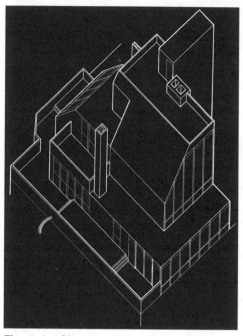

Fig. 4–2 Simple paraline drawing

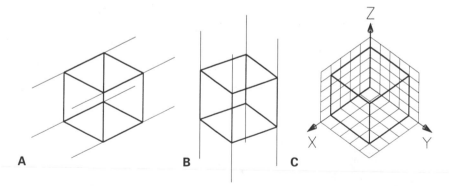

Fig. 4–3 Properties of paraline drawings. *A,* Paraline drawings have parallel lines drawn as parallel. *B,* Vertical lines are drawn as vertical. *C,* Lines parallel to the principal axes are represented to scale.

4.1 PARALINE DRAWINGS

4.1.1 Axonometric and Isometric Drawings

Paraline drawings are those in which parallel lines in a space or object are drawn as parallel in the image itself, *and* in which vertical lines are drawn as vertical (Figs. 4–2, 4–3). The images do *not* reflect actual viewpoints of an observer looking at the object. Furthermore, the distance between the observer and the object has no effect. Rather, paraline drawings are *measurable* representations of abstractions that are valuable in the exploration of the nature of the object being designed. *Lines that are parallel to the x, y, and/or z axes (in a Cartesian coordinate system) are created in accurate scale.* Because paraline drawings have elements that relate to actual dimensions and do not necessarily reflect perception of a building or space, they are often considered to be conceptual drawings that emphasize relationships between parts. The drawings are used because they are relatively easy to create and provide important information to the designer.

The most common paraline drawings used in architectural design and communication are **isometric** and **oblique** (plan and elevation) drawings (Fig. 4–4). **Elevation obliques** are sometimes called **cavalier obliques**. **Plan oblique** drawings are also called **axonometric** drawings and are probably the most widely used paraline drawings in architectural design.

Axonometric Drawings

In axonometric drawings, elements in horizontal planes (plan views in the x-y plane) are represented to scale and without distortion—they are merely rotated about the z axis. *The drawings are characterized by measured and angular accuracy in plan.* In plan, right angles remain right angles and circles are viewed as circles. For example, the representation of a flat roof or a floor plan in an axonometric can be created in much the same way as its two-dimensional counterpart. *It is important to note that lines or surfaces that are not parallel to the x, y, or z axis are not drawn as, and cannot be measured as, accurately scaled elements.* Vertical lines are projected directly from the plan and are at the same scale as the plan. "Horizontal" lines drawn in vertical planes follow the plan angle established at the base of the vertical plane. Elements that are not to scale must be plotted as points measured horizontally and/or vertically along the principle axes and then projected to their proper location (Figs. 4–5 through 4–7).

It is most common—but not required—for axonometric drawings to have a plan rotation of 30°, 45°, or 60° from the horizontal baseline (Fig. 4–8). Note that when the plan is rotated, the sum of the rotation and plan angles is 180°. Therefore, a cube, with an interior plan angle of 90°, drawn as a plan oblique, could be set at 45°-45° or 30°-60°. The conventions of the angles are based on traditional drawing techniques and the availability of 30°-60° and 45°-45° triangles. In fact, an adjustable triangle can be used as long as the

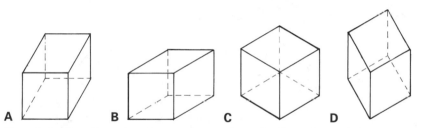

Fig. 4–4 Paraline drawings of a cube. *A,* Elevation oblique (60°). *B,* Elevation oblique (30°). *C,* Isometric. *D,* Plan oblique or axonometric (60°-30°).

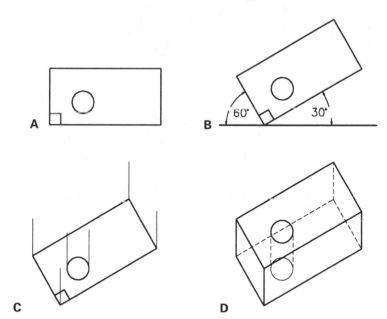

Fig. 4–5 Construction of axonometric. *A,* Plan view of rectangular element with cylindrical opening. *B,* Plan rotated about vertical axis. *C,* Vertical sides projected. *D,* Vertical lines measured to scale, and top drawn accurately to scale when horizontal (parallel to x-y plane).

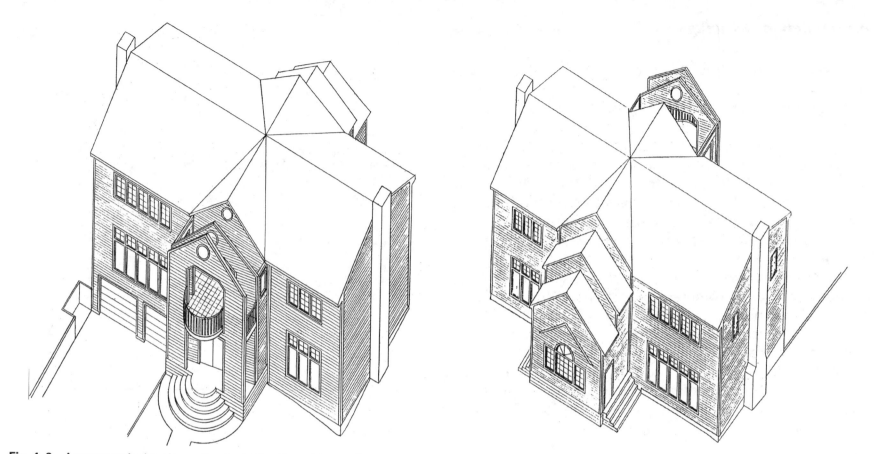

Fig. 4–6 Axonometric drawings of a single-family residence. Two axonometric drawings (in this case, 30°-60°) taken from diagonally opposite corners can show all four sides of a rectangular building.

sum of the plan angle and the other two angles remains 180°. *It is possible to draw a two-dimensional raster or vector paraline drawing with computer.* Most often, however, the paraline drawing will be a selected representation of a three-dimensional model of a building or space that has been created electronically. Digital axonometric drawings are not constrained in angle selection to triangle size. Although defaults, or preset values, can be established to produce the traditional degrees of rotation of the plan around the z axis, there is greater flexibility. Typically, one can specify the exact degree of rotation while looking at various "viewports" or windows of the three-dimensional model. It is also possible, if supported by the software, to interactively move the x and y axes about the z axis until one visually establishes the desired angle. (It is important to remember to fix or freeze the parameters that maintain the characteristics of paraline drawings prior to axes and model manipulation.)

Elements that are on the vertical plane (including circles), although drawn to scale, are skewed because of the angular rotation of the plan. Circles, which can be plotted with a series of diameters taken through the center point, appear to be ellipses when drawn (Fig. 4–9).

Elevation Oblique Drawings

Elevation obliques are paraline drawings in which a selected vertical (rather than horizontal) face is drawn to scale with both measured and angular accuracy. The

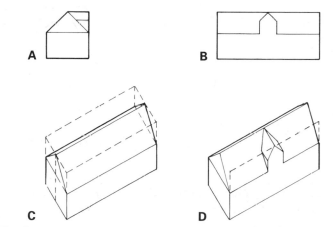

Fig. 4–7 Axonometric construction. *A, B,* Elevations. *C,* Construction of roof and diagonal element by plotting and locating points within accurately measured box. *D,* Addition of detail by locating necessary points on horizontal and vertical planes.

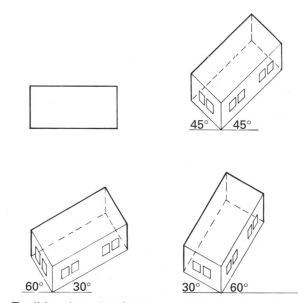

Fig. 4–8 Traditional angles for axonometic drawings. 45° axonometric drawing places equal emphasis on both exposed sides. When angles are not equal, the detail on the side with the smaller angle (in this case, 30°) is emphasized.

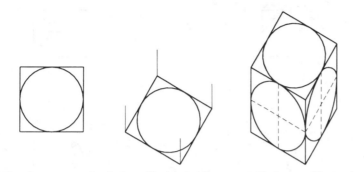

Fig. 4–9 Axonometric circles. Circles in plan are still circles. Circles in vertical planes drawn at angles are ellipses. Once centerlines are found, it is sometimes possible to use a template to draw the ellipses.

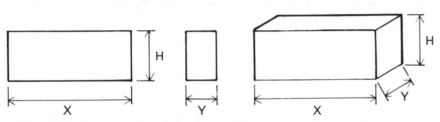

Fig. 4–10 Construction of elevation oblique. Front elevation is drawn accurately to scale with angular precision. Side is drawn to scale but is projected back at an angle (typically 30°, 45°, or 60°).

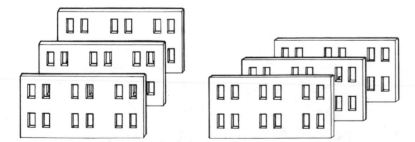

Fig. 4–11 The angle of the receding planes (known as the angle of projection) in an elevation oblique affects their emphasis and visibility.

The elevation of the object selected for the primary view is parallel to the drawing surface and, like its analogous orthographic projection, is drawn showing accurate proportions and relationships (Fig. 4–10). Any detail found within either parallel plane (x-z or y-z) is drawn to scale with angular accuracy. Depth of the facade, or information between planes, is expressed as a series of layered elevations in the oblique drawing with connected lines projected back on an angle (traditionally, 30°, 45°, or 60°) (Fig. 4–11). Side views are projected back, and any line parallel to one of the principal axes is accurate in scale. Only those planes parallel to the drawing plane have angular accuracy. To improve visual proportions, **cabinet oblique** drawings are sometimes created in which the receding lines are drawn at one-half scale, whereas lines parallel to the picture plane are still drawn at full scale.

Isometric Drawings

Isometric drawings are similar to axonometric (or plan oblique) drawings and maintain measured accuracy in plan when lines are parallel to the x or y axis, but they *do not maintain angular accuracy* (Box 4–A, Figs. 4–12, 4–13). A plan angle at the leading, front corner that would be 90° is actually drawn as 120°, leaving the side angles as 30° and 30° rather than 30° and 60°. The distortion of the angle results in an image that is shorter overall than a comparable plan oblique. Because the distortion is made to "improve the view" of the object (which would impact the way a viewer perceives the

ISOMETRIC DRAWINGS

Construction

*   Lines parallel to the reference axes (typically x and y) are drawn accurately with regard to linear dimensions and can be measured from a drawing or print that is accurate in scale.

*   Vertical elements parallel to the z axis are drawn vertically and to scale in the same manner as in plan oblique.

*   Plan angles are distorted such that 90° right angles in plan are typically either 120° or 60°, depending on their locations.

*   Elements on vertical surfaces (elevations) do not have angular accuracy under normal circumstances.

*   When created electronically from a three-dimensional model, isometric drawings require a redefinition of the angular relationship between the standard axes to account for the distortion in plan. (*Angular adjustment may have to be made to the default conditions directly, or it may be done automatically if isometric drawings can be created by the particular program being used.*)

Characteristics

*   The drawings do not have the same degree of overall accuracy as do plan obliques.

*   Isometric drawings are constructed with the same ease as plan obliques.

*   The angular distortion reduces the apparent height of an object in an isometric drawing and creates a "false view," and it imparts a perceptual characteristic to the image.

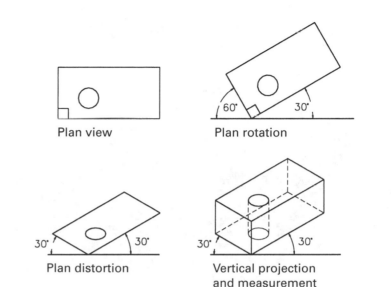

Fig. 4–12 Isometric drawings. Elements in vertical and horizontal planes are measured accurately to scale, but right angles are distorted to acute and obtuse angles to improve "realistic" nature of the drawing.

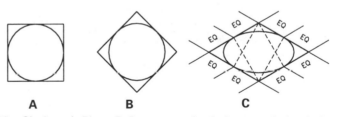

Fig. 4–13 Circles. *A,* Plan. *B,* Axonometric circles are circles in horizontal planes. *C,* Isometric circles are ellipses in horizontal planes because of the angular distortion of the right angles.

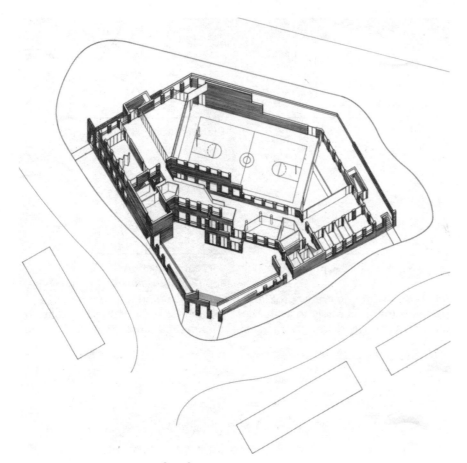

Fig. 4–14 Stepped 30°-60° cutaway axonometric

object), the drawing is considered to be part perceptual and part conceptual.

Isometric drawings are as easy to construct as axonometric drawings, and they provide a quick way to give a viewer a sense of what it might be like to view an object, because the effective viewpoint is lower than that found in a plan oblique.

4.1.2 Expressive Qualities of Paraline Drawings

Viewpoint Selection

The selection of a particular type of paraline drawing, and its angle of projection, affects the visual emphasis—the expression—of the image.

An elevation oblique puts the greatest emphasis on the elevation that is at the front of the image. Unlike a simple elevation, however, an elevation oblique can graphically portray a sense of depth. Elevation obliques are also particularly useful at displaying a series of parallel layers when they are a significant element in the design. The greater the projecting angle, the less will be the emphasis on, or visibility of, the sides, and the greater will be the emphasis on the parallel planes.

A series of axonometric drawings is particularly useful for viewing an object in its entirety. Two axonometric images of a rectangular object can be selected at opposite corners to show the primary sides. If all sides are of equal importance, or if square proportions are a significant design intent, 45° axonometrics that treat two sides with equivalence may be appropriate. (Note that diagonals in a 45° axonometric appear as vertical and horizontal elements in the drawing—a feature that emphasizes the nature of diagonals in a square.) A 45° axonometric also emphasizes the vertical element to a greater extent than do axonometrics of other angles. When 30°-60° axonometrics are selected, one (primary) face and planes parallel to that face are emphasized.

Axonometric drawings of buildings may have the "top" removed so that one can look at, and study, the relationships of objects and elements (including walls) within the space. Such drawings, called **cutaway axonometrics,** can be used to give level-by-level views of multistory buildings. Cutaway axonometrics can also be "stepped" to show multiple conditions in one image (Fig. 4–14). The cutting of the volume to produce this axonometric is nothing more than the type of slicing done to create the plan view of a building described earlier. Unlike the case with the plan, however, vertical elements that exist beneath the cut are shown in an axonometric. Cutaway axonometrics are most useful in the study of the relationship of interior organization of buildings and arrangement of furniture within spaces. Finally, cutaway axonometrics, together with plan views drawn as a base, can be helpful in describing the difference between existing conditions and proposed new

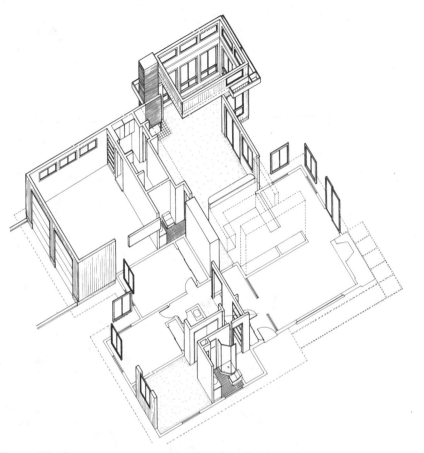

Fig. 4–15 Cutaway axonometric drawing. Projected elements represent new construction, whereas existing conditions are shown only in plan.

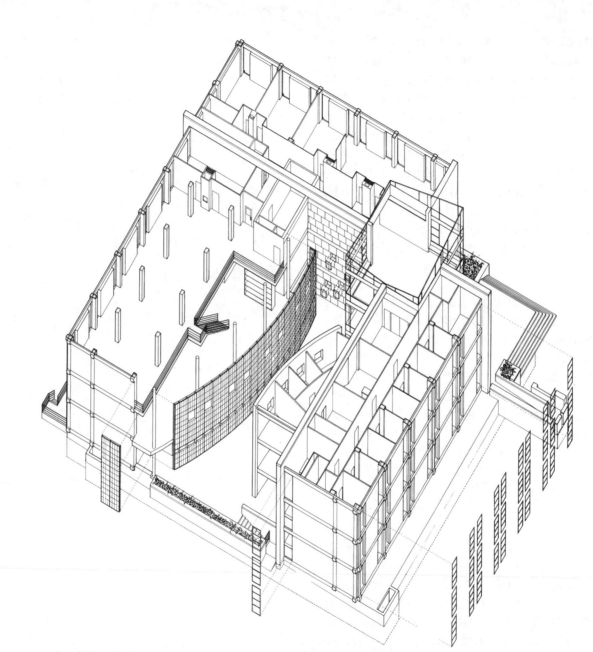

Fig. 4–16 Cutaway axonometric of Mandel School of Applied Social Sciences, Case Western Reserve University (*James Stewart Polshek and Partners, Architects. Drawn by Lisa Demankowski, University of Michigan.*)

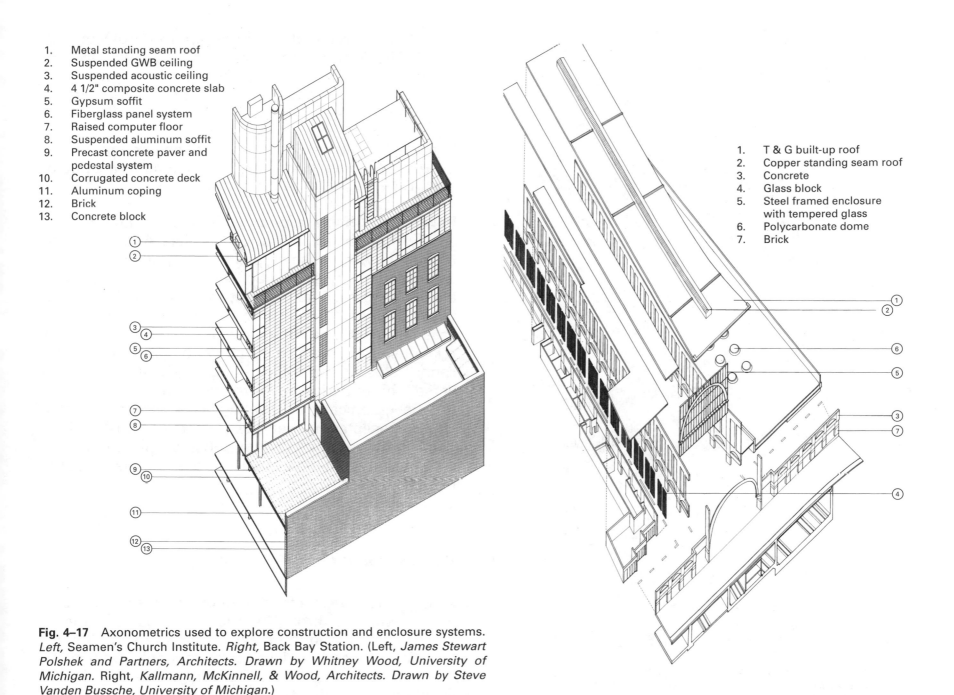

1. Metal standing seam roof
2. Suspended GWB ceiling
3. Suspended acoustic ceiling
4. 4 1/2" composite concrete slab
5. Gypsum soffit
6. Fiberglass panel system
7. Raised computer floor
8. Suspended aluminum soffit
9. Precast concrete paver and pedestal system
10. Corrugated concrete deck
11. Aluminum coping
12. Brick
13. Concrete block

1. T & G built-up roof
2. Copper standing seam roof
3. Concrete
4. Glass block
5. Steel framed enclosure with tempered glass
6. Polycarbonate dome
7. Brick

Fig. 4–17 Axonometrics used to explore construction and enclosure systems. *Left,* Seamen's Church Institute. *Right,* Back Bay Station. (Left, *James Stewart Polshek and Partners, Architects. Drawn by Whitney Wood, University of Michigan.* Right, *Kallmann, McKinnell, & Wood, Architects. Drawn by Steve Vanden Bussche, University of Michigan.*)

Fig. 4–18 Complex reverse axonometric showing relationship between interior space and building components (*Corvin Matei, University of Texas at Arlington*)

conditions in renovation and alteration projects (Fig. 4–15). The front, or near, walls of a cut-away axonometric may sometimes be omitted (or have their perimeter dotted or outlined) in order to more clearly show the inside elements.

Exploded axonometrics pull the building or object apart in order to explore, and inform how elements are put together (Figs. 4–16, 4–17).

Reverse, or **Choisy, axonometrics** look at the object or space from underneath the base plan. Although used infrequently, the image type made popular in the nineteenth century by August Choisy can show the nature of elements from a different viewpoint that can be instructive to designers. These drawings are useful, in part, because they are measured drawings that can explain the relationship between space and structure in a way that cannot be seen from above (Figs. 4–18, 4–19). The reverse axonometrics also provide an image type that can be graphically captivating as a component of a larger presentation. Because of the unrealistic viewpoint, however, they do not substitute for more conventional three-dimensional representations of buildings or spaces.

Expression of Depth—Line Weights

A straightforward method of depth expression in paraline drawings is through the judicious use of variable line weights. Without the expression of depth, the images look flat and are less understandable. Depending on the medium being used for image creation, the selection of expression type is likely to vary.

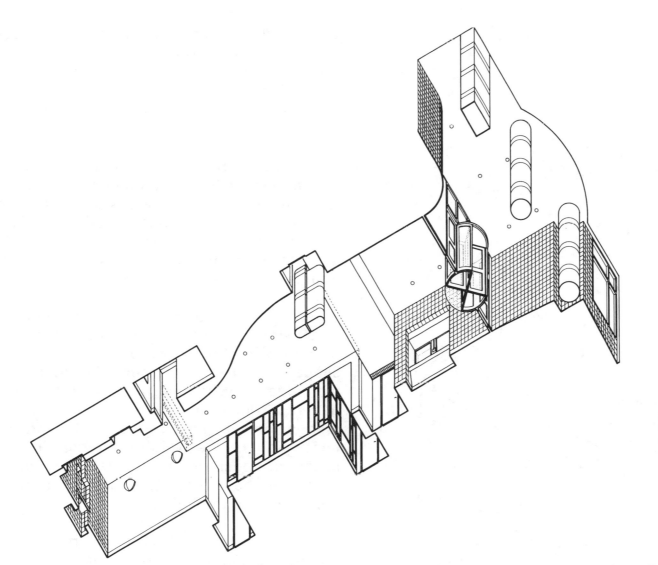

Fig. 4–19 Reverse axonometric showing interior lobby space and variable ceiling heights (*Powers and Associates, Architects. Drawn by William Bricken and Susan Morrow.*)

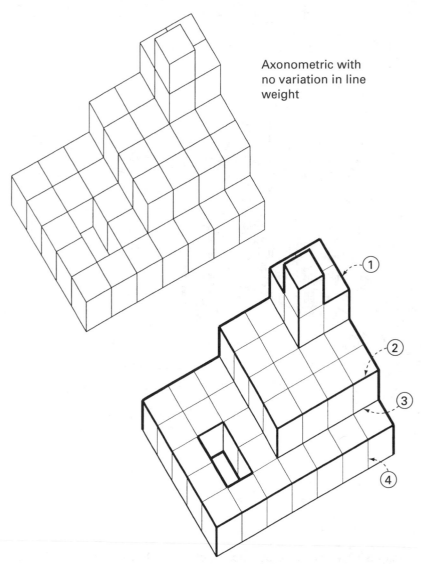

Axonometric with no variation in line weight

Fig. 4–20 Line weight applied (darker to lighter). *1,* Profile edge (only "air" behind it). *2,* Leading or outside edge. *3,* Receding or inside edge. *4,* Flush lines and grid lines (minimal or no change in plane).

Speed and ease of creation are considered assets when drawing paraline representations with traditional media. Line weight is an important element of the paraline image, which is often seen as a line drawing. Weights are assigned based on the relative position of lines in the view represented in the drawing (Fig. 4–20). Nevertheless, one should make adjustments for "local conditions" (especially when one object is meant to be seen as passing behind another) while drawing in order to improve legibility. Whereas the paraline drawing is primarily a conceptual one, the addition of line weights is generally for perceptual reasons and therefore may necessitate change to the image in order to make it clearer.

When paraline drawings are created with two-dimensional drawing or paint programs using electronic media, their creation is achieved one line or shape at a time. Adjustments are made to each line individually. When certain lines are grouped together for image creation, they may have to be exploded, or split apart, in order to add appropriate line weights. Line weights for paraline images are based on position in the selected view and not strictly on the two-dimensional geometric properties of the created image.

When the original design has been created as a three-dimensional model, a paraline view can be captured and converted to a two-dimensional drawing for line weight modification. (The ability to grab a view of a three-dimensional model and convert it to either a raster or two-dimensional vector image is software dependent and may require third-party utilities—programs separate from, but compatible with, the CAD/graphics programs used to develop the model.)

When the view is saved as a raster drawing, the image may be painted or rendered directly onto the lines, and the image resolution will be dependent on the particular display devices used. If the view is saved as a two-dimensional vector file snapshot of the model, one has created the initial paraline drawing of the model to which line weights can be added and which can provide a resolution-independent vector file for plotting with clear, straight lines. (See Box 4–B.)

4.2 PERSPECTIVE DRAWINGS

4.2.1 Perceptual Drawings

Perspective images are two-dimensional representations of a three-dimensional model that accurately reflect an observer's specific viewpoint and placement in relation to the space or object being described (Figs. 4–21, 4–22). The parameters include eye height and location, the target (the point at which the observer is looking), the angle of view, and the distance

---

Box 4–B

LINE WEIGHT IN PARALINE DRAWINGS

General characteristics

- Line weights proceed (darkest to lightest) from profile edges, to leading edges, to inside edges, to flush lines and grid lines that do not represent a significant break in surface.
- Individual judgment is required when lines pass behind other lines in order to portray an accurate sense of depth. (*Note: Adjustments are most easily made when building up the line weights incrementally.*)

Traditional media

- Trace over schematic layout with varying and appropriate weights of pen or pencil directly onto final drawing. *OR*
- Create lines without line weight differentiation by using lightest weight anticipated for the drawing. Build up drawing with successive applications of pen or pencil.

Electronic media

- Two-dimensional raster or vector paraline drawings may be created directly within painting or drafting software. Images created in this manner are electronic eqivalents of traditional drawings. *OR*
- Create images electronically from a three-dimensional model, adding line weight after the view is selected. The image may be exported to drafting or paint programs as a two-dimensional vector or faster image for line weight application if automatic application is not available.
  - The expression of line weights in a paraline drawing is *view dependent* (not intrinsic to the object) and therefore changes with each representation of the model.
  - When exporting or grabbing a two-dimensional view, it should be saved as a separate file—with a new file name distinct from that of the three-dimensional model used as its source. The three-dimensional model can be used as a source for a variety of views and images. Once a three-dimensional image is saved as a two-dimensional drawing, the image and file *no longer* have three-dimensional information associated with them and the view cannot be changed without going back to the original model.

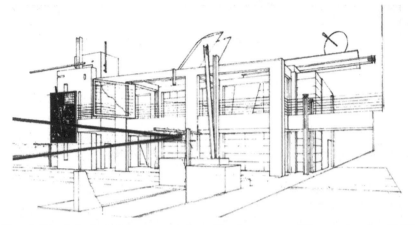

Fig. 4–21 Ink drawing perspective. Design competition entry for NJIT Student Center. (*Jeffrey Hildner, Architect*)

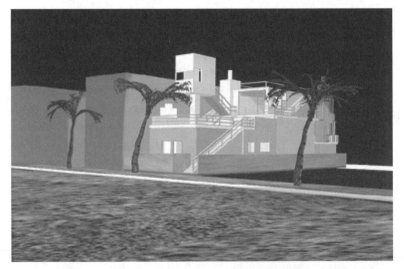

Fig. 4–22 Shaded exterior perspective. Model based on house designed by Frank Gehry. (*Elizabeth Regina Darmada, NJIT*)

between the observer and the object. Because the image depends on the observer in addition to the model itself, it is considered a perceptual image. For example, when a group of objects (furniture within a space, a collection of discrete buildings, etc.) is being shown in relation to an observer, objects near the viewer can obstruct those further back in the scene. The concept of "behind" or "further back" makes sense only in relation to someone looking at something.

Although perspective drawings are created with precision, requiring measurement and accuracy, they are not "scaleable" because elements vary with each of the observer's parameters. In other words, one cannot use an architect's or engineer's scale, measure a line drawn in perspective, and directly (without additional calculation) find out how large an object may be. Nevertheless, there is no image or drawing type used by architects, interior designers, planners, and other members of the building design team that can more accurately or more clearly show what a building or space will be like in relation to an observer.

Accurate perspectives are a valuable tool throughout the design process because they can give designers and clients a sense of "being there" and facilitate the previsualization of a design proposal. Perspectives can also be used to explain the nature of a design and how components fit together in a viewer-dependent manner (Fig. 4–23).

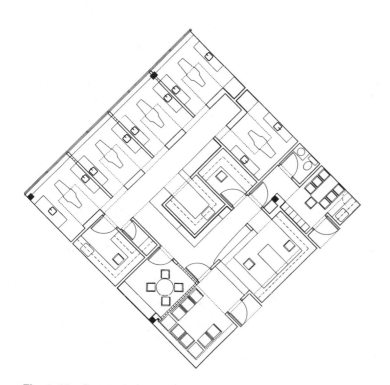

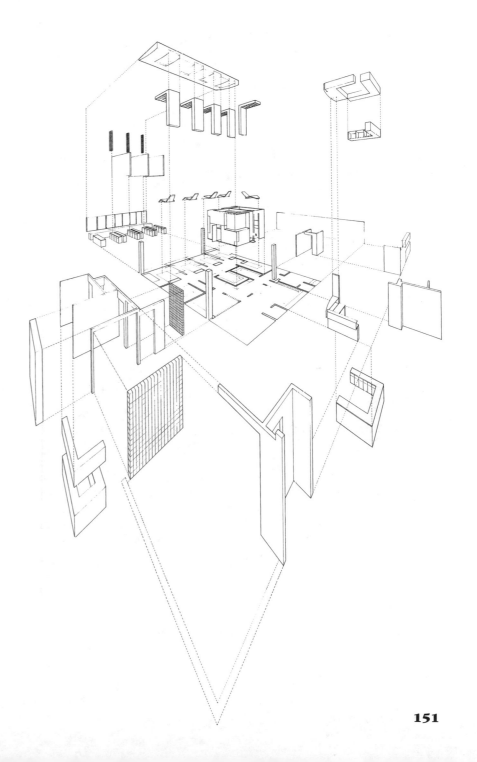

Fig. 4–23 Rotated plan and exploded perspective showing relationship of components in design (*Babushkin Dental Office, Resolution: 4 Architecture. Joseph Tanney, Gary Shoemaker, and Robert Luntz; Partners*)

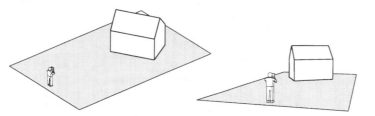

Fig. 4–24 Ground plane. The plane on which the observer (usually) stands and on which the primary objects rest.

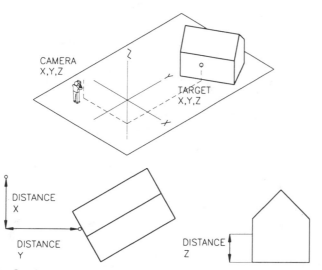

Fig. 4–25 Station point, camera position, or eyepoint. Observer's eye location in three-dimensional space. The location has both plan and elevation or section information. In general, it is defined by the distance from the target and the height above the ground plane. In CAD/graphics applications, both target and eyepoint are defined by x-y-z coordinates (although they need not always be specified by the user).

4.2.2 Basic Principles of Perspective Drawings

The rules for creating perspectives are clear, and whether created manually or electronically, the drawings conform to a common set of principles.

Because perspectives depend on the view of the observer, it is natural to consider the eye height and position of the observer relative to the object being described.

The **ground plane** (GP) is the plane or level on which the observer usually stands. It is also the plane on which the primary object(s) being described in the drawing are resting. When the observer is "flying overhead," the ground plane will be at a level considerably below the station point of the observer (Fig. 4–24).

The **station point** (SP) represents the height and location of the viewer's eye. It corresponds to "sight point," "eye location," "camera location," and so on in perspective creation (Fig. 4–25).

The **picture plane** (PP) is the frame of the image being drawn and corresponds to a transparent piece of paper or glass, located between the observer and the object, on which the projection of the object is drawn. It is perpendicular to the observer's line of site and it intersects the ground plane. In photography and electronic perspective creation, the picture plane may be identified by labels such as "camera view," "viewport," and so on (Fig. 4–26).

The **target** (T) or **center of vision** (COV) is the point at which the observer is looking. It is frequently in the center of the image being created, but adjustments within the field of view may be made once an image is composed. The importance of the target can be easily illustrated. If you are standing still and move only your head (or your "camera"), aiming at different places, entirely different views come into focus. With a stationary viewer and object, the relationship is constant, except for where the observer chooses to focus the attention (Fig. 4–27).

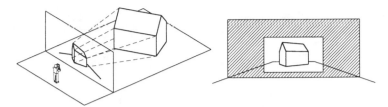

Fig. 4–26 Picture plane, camera view, or viewport. The opening, paper, screen, or window between the observer and the object, onto which the view is projected. The picture plane is comparable to the photograph printed on the flat photographic paper.

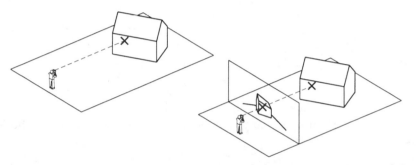

Fig. 4–27 Target or center of vision. The point at which the center of the camera is aimed is where the observer is looking.

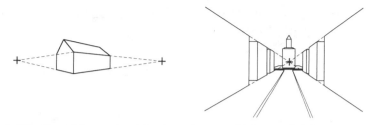

Fig. 4–28 Vanishing point. The location at which parallel lines converge. Two-point perspective on the left and one-point perspective on the right.

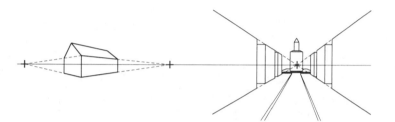

Fig. 4–29 Horizon line. The line on which the vanishing points of horizontal lines lie.

Vanishing points (VP) are the locations at which parallel lines give the appearance of convergence as they recede into the distance. All parallel lines that are not parallel to the picture plane appear to converge and therefore have a vanishing point. Parallel lines in different planes have different vanishing points (Fig. 4–28).

The **horizon line** (HL) is a line that lies on the horizontal plane determined by the eye position (station point) and target. It is the line on which the vanishing points of lines parallel to the ground plane lie. Lines above the horizon converge down toward the horizon, lines below the horizon converge upward, and lines on the horizon appear "level" (Fig. 4–29).

The **cone of vision** (also known as field of vision, field of view, angle of view, and viewing angle) defines the side-to-side limits of the observer's view in a manner analogous to the practical limits of undistorted peripheral vision (Fig. 4–30). The cone of vision is defined in degrees, and the angle is bisected by the line connecting the eye to the target. Typically, 30° to 60° has been considered the "normal" range for a cone of vision, although, depending on the observer's distance from the object, one can often go to a 90° cone of vision without significant distortion. When one is creating perspective views on computer, changing the field of view can be accomplished by entering the angular dimension directly and/or, depending on the focus of the program, by changing a "camera lens" with settings that correspond to the traditional photographic analogies of wide angle, standard, and telephoto (Fig. 4–31). Use of wide-angle lenses (35 mm and below) can result in larger fields of view but greater distortion. Telephoto lenses (85 mm and above) reduce the field of view and can be used for magnification of detail while limiting the breadth of the overall image.

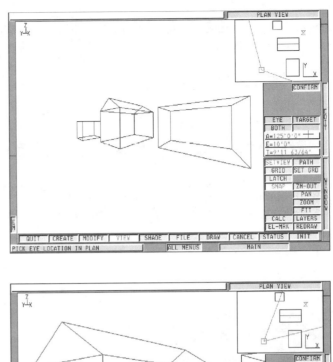

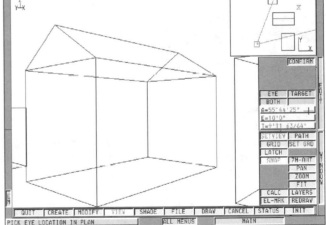

Fig. 4–30 Cone of vision or angle of view. Defines the limits of peripheral vision and the degree of distortion of an image. In the top view, the cone of vision ("A," for angle of view, on the menu) is 125°. In the bottom view, there is less distortion and the angle of view is slightly over 55°. Note that the cone of vision is graphically displayed in the upper right corner of each screen with two projecting lines emanating from the eyepoint. (*MegaMODEL by MegaCADD, a division of Design Futures, Inc.*)

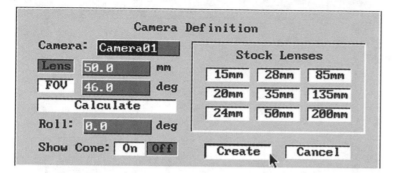

Fig. 4–31 Selection of cone of vision or field of view through camera lens selection (*3D Studio by Autodesk. This material has been reprinted with permission from and under the copyright of Autodesk, Inc.*)

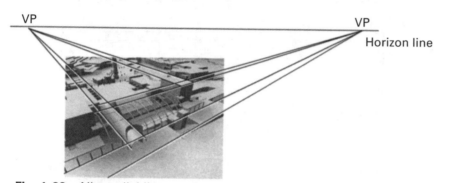

Fig. 4–32 All parallel lines vanish to the same point on the horizon line. When the horizon line is out of view above the drawing, the observers feel as if they are floating above the building(s). When desired, this view type can show the nature of a place in a manner that eye-level perspectives cannot. (*Original model by Elli Shani, NJIT*)

4.2.3 Viewpoint Selection

The selection of particular eye and target locations should depend on the purpose of the drawing. The question of what you want to see must be asked in order to decide where to look. Sometimes perspectives of objects or buildings are created primarily to explain a form, whereas other times they serve to make one feel that one is inside a room or space. The latter type of image requires that the observer be placed in a position that could be reproduced by a real observer after the space is built. The former type of image may require that the observer stand in a location that would not be considered "accessible" (in the air) but that may be valuable in explaining various qualities of a proposal.

Aerial perspectives can give the observer an overview of a space, object, or place—much in the way that paraline drawings can, but with modifications that take into account the viewer's position and relation to the object being drawn (Fig. 4–32). Eye-level perspectives have a unique opportunity to give an observer a sense of being *in* the space being drawn.

Even when the choice of perspective type is clear, one needs to decide where, *precisely,* the center of vision or target should be placed (Fig. 4–33). In practice, an architect or designer frequently sketches perspectives from different views, or electronically generates a variety of outline perspectives, in order to look at different aspects of a model and to decide which view (or views) should be developed in greater detail.

Although perspectives can be (and in the past, frequently have been) distorted to demonstrate or emphasize particular aspects of a proposal, personal interpretations are best placed in the rendering and expressionistic components of the image and not generally in the construction of the base view. The existence of mathematical principles that enable us to accurately reflect views from virtually any vantage point has created a climate in which people expect images to be accurate to the extent that the design process allows.

After deciding what you want to look at, you have to decide where you want to stand (Fig. 4–34). Because the eye level determines the horizon, where one stands affects the emphasis of the form. If very high above an object, the viewer gets to see the roof or upper-level details. If the viewer is standing on the ground or floor, eye height should usually be placed in the range of 5′ to 5′-6″ above the ground plane for a realistic station point. If the viewer is lying on the floor and looking up inside a room, there will be a greater emphasis on the ceiling than there will be on the floor. The distance from the object will also, of course, have an effect on the image.

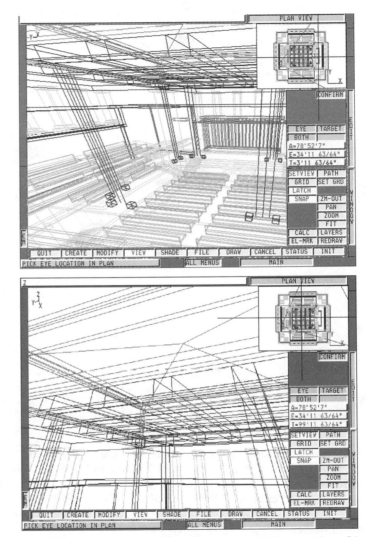

Fig. 4–33 Effect of varying target point in perspective creation. Observer, eyepoint, or station point is the same in both images. The height of the target ("T" on the menu) is raised from almost 4′ in the upper image to almost 100′ in the lower image. The ceiling is emphasized in the lower view of Frank Lloyd Wright's Unity Temple interior. (*Original model by Michael Hoon, NJIT. Screen capture of MegaMODEL by MegaCADD, a division of Design Futures, Inc.*)

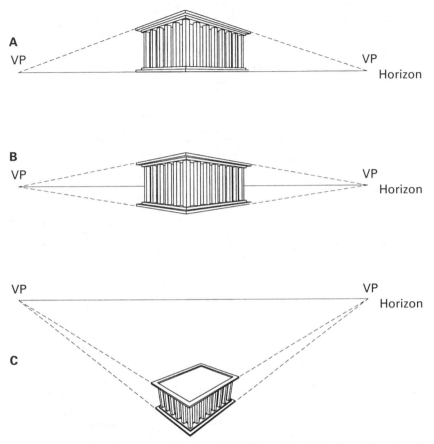

Fig. 4–34 Effect of horizon line location. (Note: Avoid horizon line that is even with top of building to prevent visual flattening of building.) *A,* Low horizon line. "Worm's eye." *B,* Horizon 5'-6" above ground plane. "Eye level." *C,* High horizon line. "Floating above." (*From Muller, E. and J. Fausett. 1993. Architectural drawing and light construction. Englewood Cliffs, N.J.: Prentice Hall, p. 381. Adapted with permission.*)

4.2.4 Two-Point Perspective Creation

Traditional Media—Office or Common Method

Two-point perspectives are, at times, referred to as angular perspectives because buildings or spaces are usually seen on an angle rather than full face or in elevation. Just as axonometric drawings are created by rotating a plan with respect to a horizontal base line, so too are angular perspectives. Furthermore, the angles of rotation (sometimes referred to as angles of view) are often 30° and 60° because the drawing is easier to create. Rotation of 30°-60° rather than 45°-45° allows the designer to place more emphasis on one side than another if desirable. A rotation of 45°-45° places equal emphasis on the two sides. The rotation of the plan holds true for both exterior and interior two-point perspectives.

Construction of Two-Point Perspective*

Step 1 Draw the roof or floor plan at an angle to the picture plane. (Alternatively, tape a copy of the plan to the board at the desired angle.)

The picture plane is often located at the nearest vertical corner of the building (Fig. 4–35).

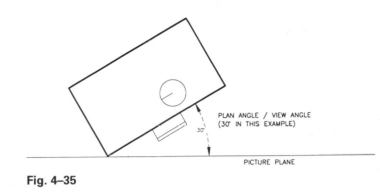

PLAN ANGLE / VIEW ANGLE
(30° IN THIS EXAMPLE)

30°

PICTURE PLANE

Fig. 4–35

Step 2 Determine at what point you want to directly look (target). Place the target at the center of interest (Fig. 4–36).

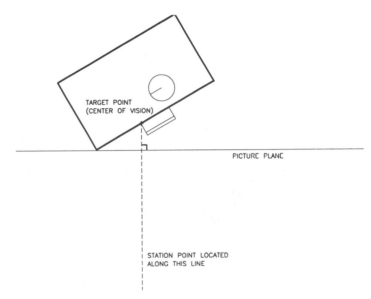

TARGET POINT
(CENTER OF VISION)

PICTURE PLANE

STATION POINT LOCATED
ALONG THIS LINE

Fig. 4–36

*Model used for Figs. 4–35 through Fig. 4–43 is based on Philip Johnson's Glass House and was prepared by Juhani Kelvin, NJIT. Diagrams were prepared by Michael Hoon.

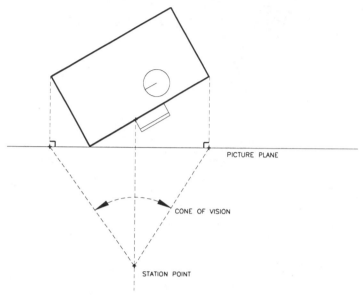

Fig. 4–37

Step 3   Determine the cone of vision such that the projection of the building to the picture plane fits. Typical values are between 30° and 60°, although for certain effects the range may be increased to between 15° and 90°.

Note that the closer the station point is to the picture plane, the wider the cone of vision and the greater the distortion if one is still to show the same "amount" of building or scene (Fig. 4–37).

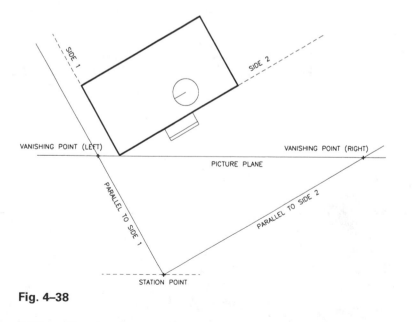

Fig. 4–38

Step 4   Project lines from the station point that are parallel to the principal sides of the plan. The vanishing points are at the intersection of these parallel lines with the picture plane (Fig. 4–38).

Step 5 Locate the horizon on the paper below the station point. Spread out the drawing far enough to avoid an excessive number of confusing overlapping lines. (The top of the perspective should be below the station point.)

Project critical points from the picture plane down to the horizon for perspective creation.

Any vertical element that intersects the picture plane exists (and can be drawn) at the same scale as the plan. This point of intersection, when projected down to the horizon line, becomes the "scale height" line or vertical measuring line (Fig. 4–39).

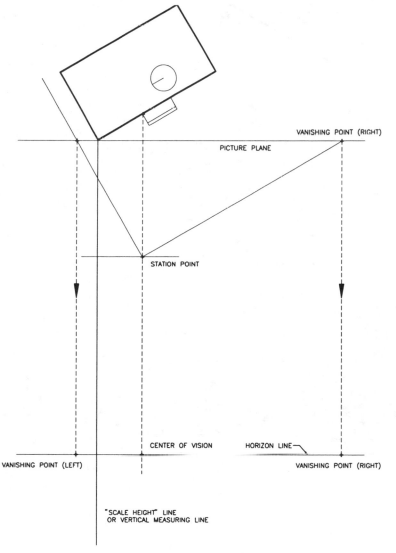

Fig. 4–39

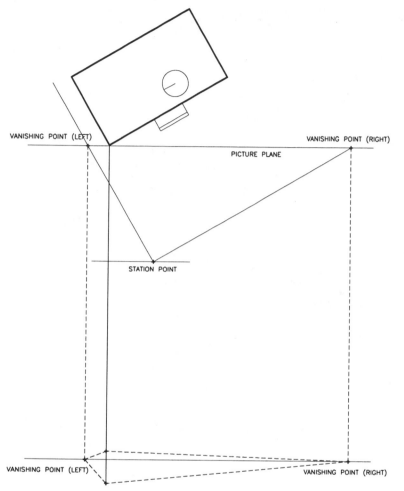

VANISHING POINT (LEFT)

VANISHING POINT (RIGHT)

PICTURE PLANE

STATION POINT

VANISHING POINT (LEFT)

VANISHING POINT (RIGHT)

Fig. 4–40

Step 6 Determine the eye height and the extent to which the center of vision is above or below the horizon—or whether it is *at* the horizon. (Quick freehand sketches, or measuring an elevation, can assist in this determination.)

Typical eye-level views are about 5'-6" above the horizontal datum (ground or floor), although other views may be equally valuable and should be investigated. (Note: The example in this text has horizon line higher than eye level.)

Measure, to scale, the vertical height of the building along the scale height line. Place the horizon at the desired eye level.

Project the building's top and bottom horizontals from the near corner vertically to the right and left vanishing points (Fig. 4–40).

Step 7 Find the limits of the building by projecting the intersection of the picture plane and the lines connecting the station point with the points to be located (in this case, the lines connecting the station point to the corners of the building).

Draw (or paste or tape) an elevation, to scale, alongside the perspective being created. Use the elevation to facilitate the location of horizontal elements on the facade. Locate the elevation far enough to the side so as *not* to cover up the vanishing point. (*The vanishing point and elevation were superimposed for the purposes of this diagram.*) (See Fig. 4–41.)

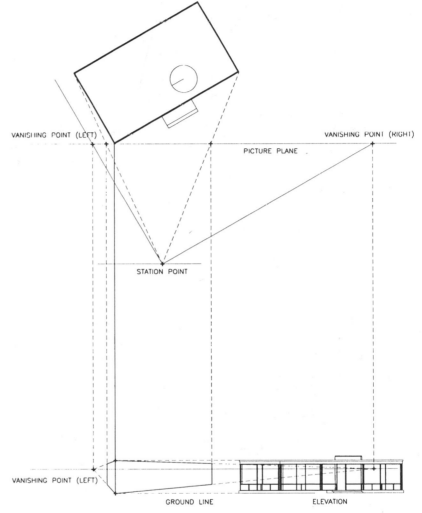

Fig. 4–41

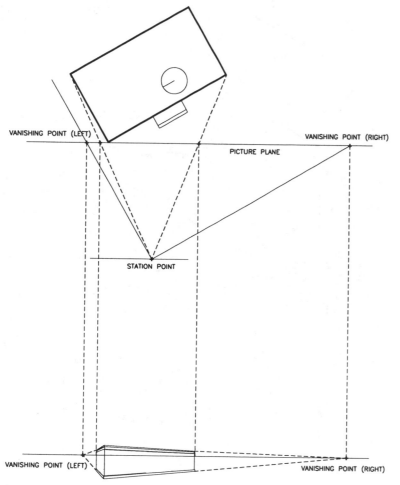

Fig. 4-42

Step 8 Find and project intermediate elements.

The scale height line can be used to project horizontal elements back to the vanishing points (Fig. 4-42).

Step 9 Project remaining lines in order to complete the drawing. All secondary lines and angled lines on building elevations can be found within a grid established by verticals and horizontals.

If desired, a final presentation drawing can be traced over the constructed perspective.

Vertical lines can be found in the same manner as the building limits were found (Fig. 4–43).

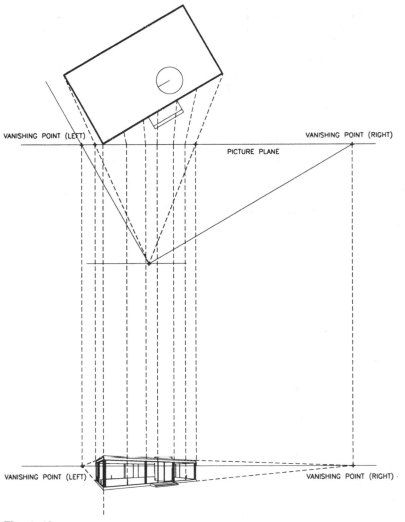

Fig. 4–43

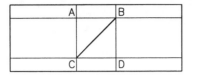

Orthographic projection

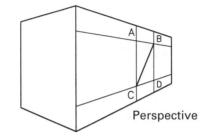

Perspective

Fig. 4–44

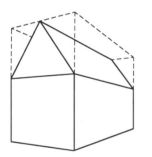

Fig. 4–45

Special Conditions in Two-Point Perspective

Diagonal Lines on a Surface

Diagonal lines can be found by locating the endpoints using typical vertical and horizontal constructions and connecting the points (Fig. 4–44).

Diagonal Objects (Sloped Roofs)

Construct the box that contains the sloped construction. Locate the various points determining the line segments and connect them. Make sure to trace back horizontal lines to the appropriate vanishing points (Fig. 4–45).

Finding Accurate Locations without Projection

Note: These processes work well both with traditional perspective creation and with raster modification of perspective models created electronically in which vanishing points, station points, etc. are not readily available.

Equal Horizontal Subdivision

Subdivide, to scale, the vertical measuring line.

Divide the back line into the same number of equal segments.

Connect (using a straightedge if needed) the corresponding points to get equally spaced horizontal subdivisions in perspective (Fig. 4–46).

Equal Vertical Subdivision

Diagonals connecting opposite corners of a rectangle intersect at the center.

Using the diagonals drawn in perspective, one can find the center of a face in perspective without projecting the lines from the plan.

Additional vertical subdivisions can be found by continually dividing components in half (Fig. 4-47).

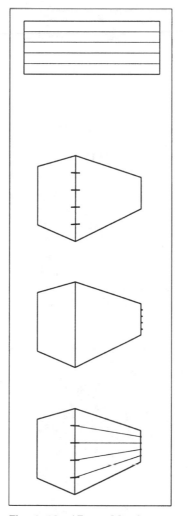

Fig. 4–46 (*From Martin, C. L. 1968*. Design graphics. *Englewood Cliffs, N.J.: Prentice Hall, p. 161. Adapted with permission.*)

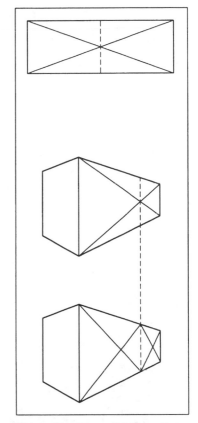

Fig. 4–47 (*From Martin, C. L. 1968*. Design graphics. *Englewood Cliffs, N.J.: Prentice Hall, p. 161. Adapted with permission.*)

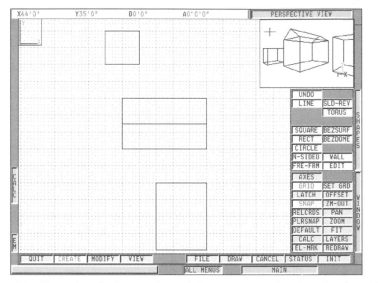

Fig. 4–48 Plan view in "create" module on screen simultaneously with a live perspective view in upper right corner (*MegaMODEL by MegaCADD, a division of Design Futures, Inc.*)

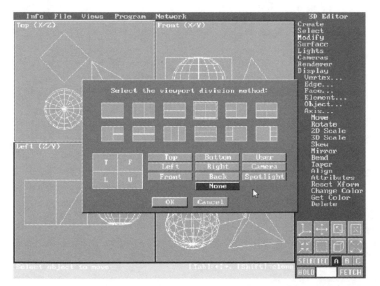

Fig. 4–49 Multiple windows showing live orthographic projections and perspectives. User can customize the screen and select both the layout of the windows and the views to be shown. (*3D Studio by Autodesk. This material has been reprinted with the permission from and under the copyright of Autodesk, Inc.*)

Electronic Media

Virtually every three-dimensional modeling program allows the user to view and print or plot the model in perspective. Some software packages always maintain "live" or active three-dimensional views, whereas others require calling up, or shifting to, different modules or components of the program (Figs. 4–48, 4–49). (Typical names for the perspective modules include view, user view, viewpoint, perspective, 3D, and camera. The different modules are activated by menu selection and/or by hitting "hot keys" or keyboard shortcuts like "F1" or "CTRL" that automatically trigger the change.) One still needs an understanding of the principles of perspective in order to be able to control the variables that affect the view. Although each program has its own idiosyncratic labels for items and commands, they all need someone to define the target and eye position. It is wholly within the power of the designer to control the view or emphasis of the image. Even default views can be quickly changed. Additionally, individual variables, like the cone of vision or angle of view, can usually be modified directly within the menu or command structure. At times, the field of view or camera location can be moved in a view while one is watching a window, or portion of the screen, change interactively. Perspectives can be established either graphically by selecting locations and criteria, or by entering relative values through commands. Many software programs provide options for entering selections.

It should be noted that a number of powerful and useful software packages capable of creating architectural and interior design perspectives were not initially developed for use by architects or designers. Many programs were developed for the film and video industries and have interfaces and menu systems that draw strong analogies to those professions. Therefore, it is likely that you will find yourself changing camera *lenses* and/or moving a *camera* on a *dolly. It is important to remember that the interface is only providing different names for the traditional perspective variables and that these variables can be modified for expressive purposes.*

The image that one sees can be modified by using specific commands that are applicable to views other than perspective. Zooming or panning does not affect the model—only what you see. When panning across an image, you are asked to select the new center of the image. After a perspective is created, however, panning will not create a new target or center of vision, so the center of the image will probably not be the center of vision. Panning creates a new image that can be captured in order to add additional information.

The concept of clipping is important in perspective creation. A **clipping plane** is one that cuts off, or slices, information from a model and excludes it from an image (Fig. 4–50). A near clipping plane cuts off all information between the eye (station point) and the plane. A far clipping plane cuts off all information behind it. Just as a section can be seen as a slice of a building, one can clip

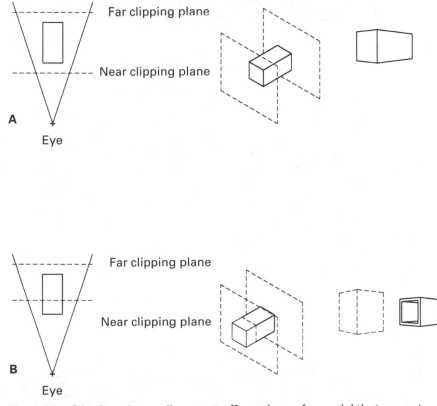

Fig. 4–50 Clipping planes clip, or cut off, portions of a model that are outside the planes. *A,* Entire object is between clipping planes and will therefore be visible. *B,* The object is intersected by the near clipping plane and is sliced at that point. Everything between the eye and near clipping plane is removed. When objects contain an interior, a section is created. (*Diagram adapted from illustrations in MegaMODEL manual by Mega-CADD, a division of Design Futures, Inc.*)

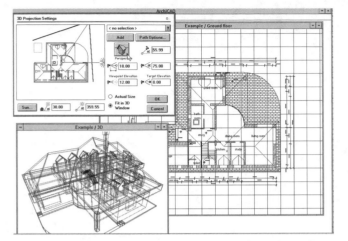

Fig. 4–51 In addition to allowing the user to select views interactively, some programs have a series of default, or predetermined, selections that can be used or modified. (*ArchiCAD by Graphisoft US, Inc.*)

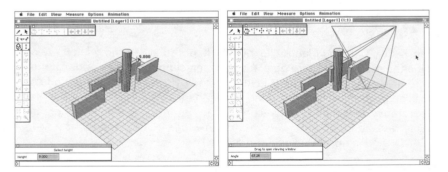

Fig. 4–52 Three-dimensional viewing frame can be established that defines both the perspective view and the limits of the image. (*Lee Anderson, upFRONT by SketchTech*)

a slice of a model and display only that slice in perspective. Although not available in all programs, clipping planes can be useful, when setting up interior perspectives, in removing portions of the three-dimensional model that would otherwise obscure the space being viewed. Clipping is also useful for separating objects into discretely viewable pieces. (Note: Some software packages offer the option to "cap" the edge of the model that was severed by the clipped plane and create a new surface. Capping the near clipping plane defeats the purpose of clipping to expose the interior in perspective creation.)

Creating an electronic perspective is usually so much faster than creating one entirely by hand with traditional methods, that many renderers will create a block-like electronic model that is used to set up views, vanishing points, horizons, and so on. The model can be used to test a variety of viewpoints and drawing compositions prior to selecting one (or more) for further development (Figs. 4–51, 4–52). The rough electronic perspective is then printed and used as an underlay, or guide, over which a drawing with traditional media (freehand or hard line) is created. Grids, or horizontal and vertical guidelines at important intervals (structural bays, window sills and heads, etc.), can be located on the model and then be part of the perspective underlay to facilitate drawing.

The ease with which perspectives can be changed by computer has allowed the image type to become an integral part of the digital design process. Although perspectives have always been used as an important part of the design process, more versions of more views taken more frequently—and in sequence—have allowed issues of serial vision to be included in schematic design discussions of architectural projects. Furthermore, the same three-dimensional model can be used as the basis for both design and presentation.

Fig. 4–53   Line drawing, one-point interior perspective

4.2.5 One-Point Perspective Creation

One-point perspectives are created when there is only one vanishing point for lines perpendicular to the picture plane (Figs. 4–53, 4–54). Unlike the case with an angular perspective, the front face of the building or object is parallel to the picture plane (and perpendicular to the observer). All lines parallel to the picture plane remain parallel in the one-point perspective.

Sections of buildings can be converted to **section perspectives** (Figs. 4–55, 4–56). As with sections, one slices through a building or object, but in this case, any space beyond the slice is seen in perspective rather than elevation. The scale of the section slice itself determines the amount of detail within the section and perspective. When drawn at sufficient size, or at a large enough scale, section perspectives provide a unique opportunity to study the relationship between how something is built and how the materials and construction systems impact on architectural form

Fig. 4–54   Shaded and enhanced exterior perspective of street scene (*Sean McCarry, NJIT*)

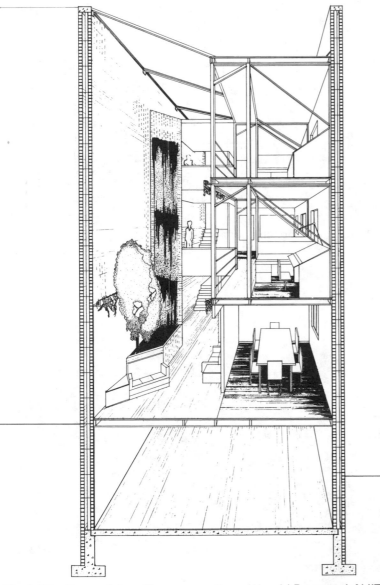

Fig. 4–55 One-point section perspective   (*Harold Raymond, NJIT*)

and detail. The section perspective is an excellent tool to study the perceptual and experiential qualities of a space and still maintain the conceptual information found in a section. When the slice of the building is parallel to the picture plane (i.e., not skewed with respect to primary axes), a one-point section perspective can be created. Although section perspectives can be, in theory, two-point perspectives, they are usually created as one-point.

One-point perspectives are most commonly used when trying to graphically describe bounded, or defined, spaces such as interiors of buildings and exterior urban sites (parks or town squares surrounded by buildings, streetscapes, etc.).

Traditional Media—45° Method

One-point perspectives can be created in a manner comparable to the two-point office method with the plan square to (parallel and perpendicular to) the picture plane. However, the nature of a one-point perspective provides opportunities for a simpler (but still accurate) method. Rather than projecting from a plan, one can create the perspective directly from the section, or vertical plane (Fig. 4–57).

Although lines perpendicular to the picture plane have one vanishing point, it is somewhat of a misnomer to call these drawings one-point perspectives. In fact, there are many vanishing points. A diagonal

Text continued on page 177.

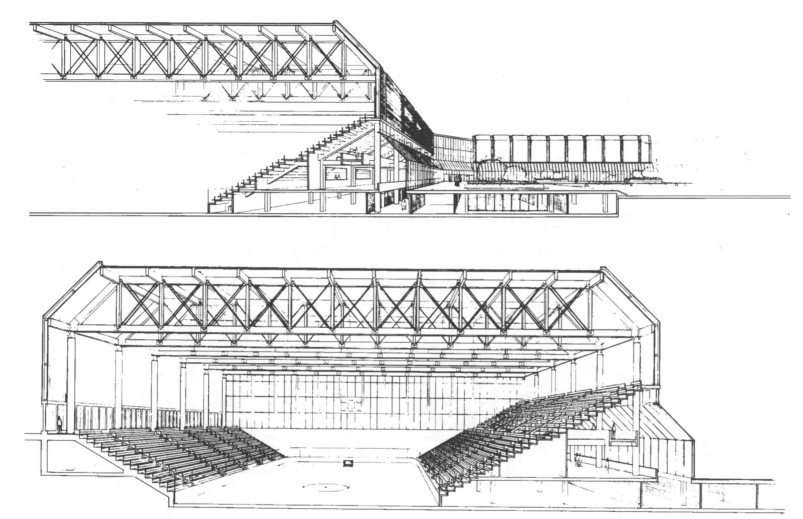

Fig. 4–56 Schematic design (pencil on vellum) one-point section perspectives used to explore the relationship between construction and space

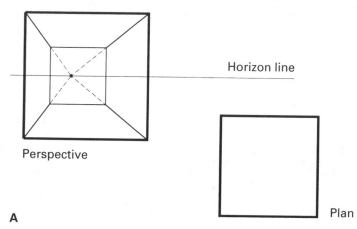

Horizon line

Perspective

Plan

A

A, Imagine a "hollow" cube with the front face off. The resulting image is a section perspective.

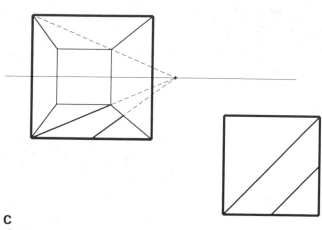

C

C, Any 45° diagonal parallel to the diagonal of the square will vanish to the same vanishing point. In a one-point perspective, any two parallel lines will vanish to the same point.

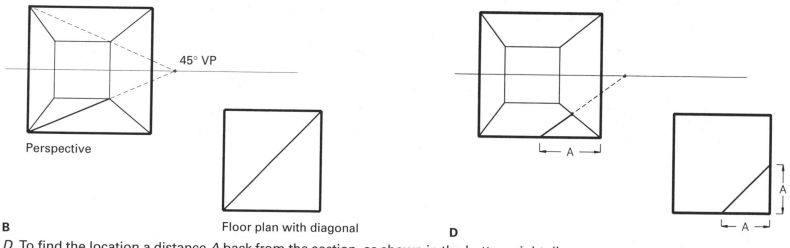

45° VP

Perspective

Floor plan with diagonal

B

D

D, To find the location a distance *A* back from the section, as shown in the bottom right diagrams, measure along the horizontal of the section from the same side as that of the 45° VP. Draw the 45° diagonal connecting the measured point to the 45° vanishing point.

The intersection of the receding line with the diagonal represents a point at distance *A* from the front section. Note: The diagonal constructed must be parallel to the one that is vanishing. (A 45° diagonal with a right triangle creates two equal legs and the hypotenuse.)

Fig. 4–57 Creating a section perspective —45° method

Cont'd

Example

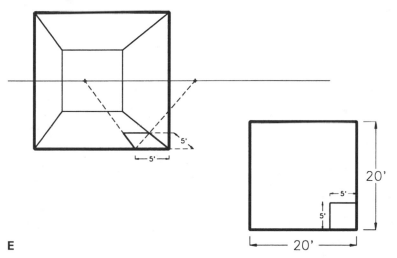

E

E, Any object can be located by using a combination of the standard central vanishing point and the 45° vanishing point.

Once the depth is located, the location can be "chased" over horizontally until the line connecting the vanishing point is intersected.

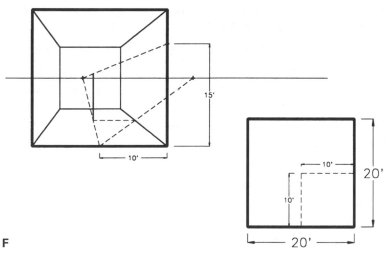

F

Fig. 4–57, cont'd

F, Similarly, the height can be found by chasing points back from the vertical.

In order to accurately chase points, the front section must be drawn accurately and to scale.

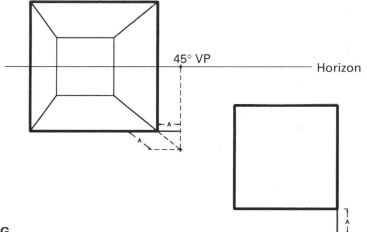

G

G, Locating objects in front of the picture plane

To find the depth location of an object at a distance A forward from the section, measure along the baseline *outside of,* and *away from,* the section.

Project *forward* the line that is perpendicular to the picture plane at the corner of the section.

Draw a line segment connecting the 45° vanishing point and the projected line, *going through the point measured on the horizontal baseline.* The intersection of that line with the forward-projected line represents a point at distance A in perspective, forward from the section cut.

Note that this technique can be used for a one-point perspective that is not a section perspective but that instead, is one projected from an elevation at the rear of the scene.

Cont'd

Determination of 45° vanishing point

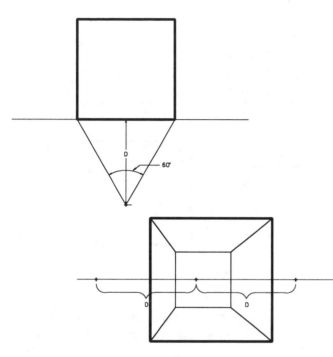

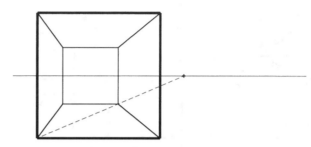

Option #1: the 45° point is located (to scale) at a distance *D* equal to the distance between the station point and the picture plane. (Note: This is a coincidence that works well to set up the drawing.)

Fig. 4–57,   cont'd

Option #2:

1. Visually determine how deep you want the section perspective to look. At times, you may be willing to accept some distortion in order to better describe the space.

2. Using squares in plan, find the location of the 45° vanishing point.

In most cases, it is a good idea to keep the 45° vanishing point *out-side* of the limits of the section, or at least at its edge. If the 45° vanishing point is inside the section, there may be excessive distortion.

line on the ground plane will vanish to a different point on the horizon than will a line perpendicular to the picture plane. In a one-point perspective, any two parallel lines will vanish to the same vanishing point. A diagonal of a square represents lines drawn at a 45° angle to the picture plane. The vanishing points for the 45° diagonals, together with our knowledge of the geometry of squares, can be used to correctly determine the locations of objects and the limits of the space within a one-point perspective (Figs. 4–58 through 4–60).

Electronic Media

The way to create a one-point perspective when imaging with computer is to select a target and eye-point in such a way as to have only one vanishing point (Fig. 4–61). Because, in most systems, the computer does not care what kind of perspective you want while it is rapidly calculating all the relevant vector information based on perspective variables, you have to limit the variables. It is necessary to be "looking at" the object in full-face view (Fig. 4–62). In other words, if this is a perspective of an exterior building, the full elevation of the building is parallel to the picture plane. If one assumes the x-y plane is the ground and the z-axis refers to the vertical dimension, the eye and target location would have the same x (or y) and z coordinates, whereas the y (or x) coordinate would differ.

In a one-point overhead exterior or interior plan perspective, the eye and target location would have the

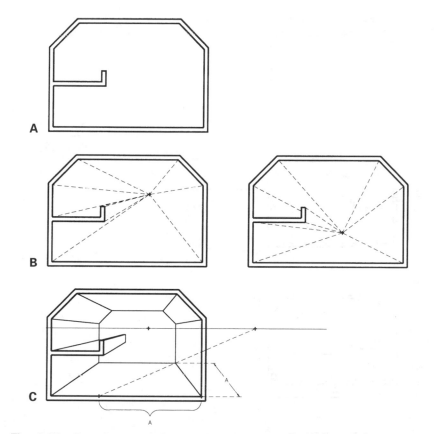

Fig. 4–58 Drawing a section perspective. *A,* Draw the section to scale. *B,* Choose vanishing point and project critical lines to it. Investigate options. *C,* Find station point in plan with 60° (±) cone of vision and determine 45° vanishing points. To mark off distances, measure in on base, vanish to 45° vanishing point, cross line, and project up.

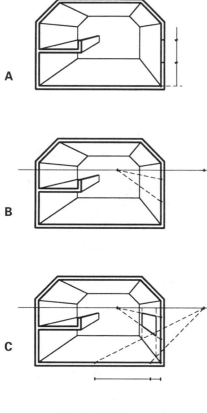

A

B

C

D

Fig. 4–59 Locating an opening or window in side wall in one-point section perspective. *A,* Locate top and bottom of opening to scale along section. *B,* Project horizontals back to the vanishing point. *C,* Find location of vertical with 45° vanishing points and project up until verticals intersect projected horizontals from previous step. *D,* Project horizontals and verticals attributed to thickness of walls in section.

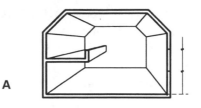

A

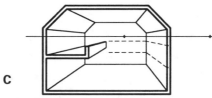

B

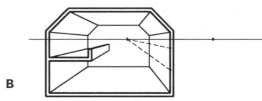

C

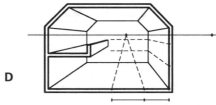

D

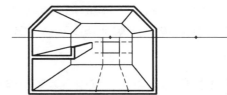

E

Fig. 4–60 Locating an element or opening in the rear wall of a one-point section perspective. *A,* Locate top and bottom of opening to scale along side wall of section. *B,* Project horizontals back to the vanishing point. *C,* Construct horizontal guidelines at the points of intersection of the back wall, the side wall, and the projected lines from the side wall. *D,* Locate horizontal size of opening along front section and project back to vanishing point. *E,* Project up from bottom wall to determine extent of opening. *Not shown,* Project thickness of opening as necessary.

same x and y coordinates with only the z coordinate changing. (The ground plane would be parallel to the picture plane.) In an interior or section perspective, some of the major walls will often be parallel and perpendicular to the picture plane. The vanishing point coincides with the center of vision. Near clipping planes can be used effectively to create accurate section perspectives. When selecting the eye and target with mouse or cursor, clicking in the same location for both over a plan or section view can sometimes create a plan perspective or section perspective.

Some software packages permit the staggering, or breaking, of a clipping plane in order to get a section perspective that more easily avoids cutting through columns or other elements that can obstruct the spatial information being communicated.

The pictorial nature of perspectives makes them useful for communicating both to oneself and to others. Although it is possible to generate images to see what "looks good," it is frequently helpful to have a conscious intent as to the purpose of the perspective before selecting an image to save or present to other individuals.

4.2.6 Three-Point Perspective

Objects, in reality, have more than just two primary vanishing points. Vertical lines vanish to a third vanishing point in angular perspectives (Fig. 4–63). The convergence of vertical lines is often referred to as

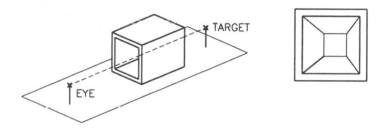

Fig. 4–61 Eye height and target height above the ground should be the same for easy one-point electronic perspective creation.

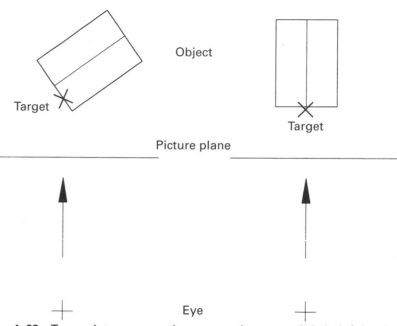

Fig. 4–62 Two-point vs. one-point perspective setup. It is helpful to look at an object or space full face—in such a way that one primary side, or face, is parallel to the picture plane and one is perpendicular. The image on the left will result in a two-point perspective, whereas the image on the right can be set up as a one-point perspective.

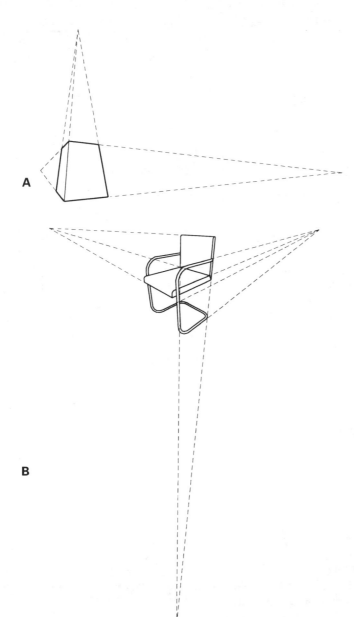

Fig. 4–63 *A,* Three-point perspective with verticals vanishing. *B,* Three-point perspective from above the object and from points near the object—a common way of seeing furniture.

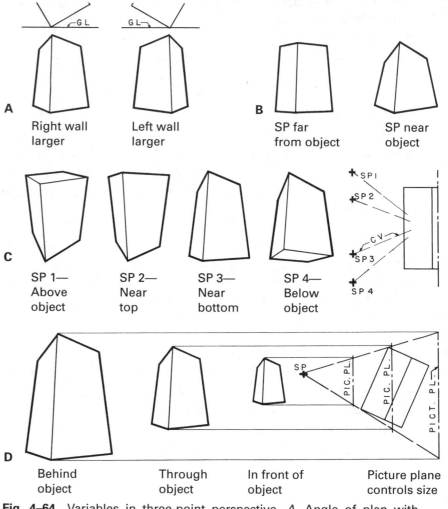

A

| Right wall larger | Left wall larger |

B

| SP far from object | SP near object |

C

| SP 1— Above object | SP 2— Near top | SP 3— Near bottom | SP 4— Below object |

D

| Behind object | Through object | In front of object | Picture plane controls size |

Fig. 4–64 Variables in three-point perspective. *A,* Angle of plan with ground line (GL). *B,* Distance of station from object. *C,* Height of station point. *D,* Position of picture plane. (*From Martin, C. L. 1968.* Design graphics. *Englewood Cliffs, N.J.: Prentice Hall, p. 147. Adapted with permission.*)

parallax distortion and is the kind that is evident when looking up at a very tall building while standing at its base. The height of the station point, however, is but one of a number of variables affecting three-point perspectives (Fig. 4–64). The creation of two-point perspectives is almost always adequate for architectural and related design uses. When laying out perspectives manually, the time and effort involved make three-point perspectives impractical. In electronic perspective creation, many computer programs automatically generate three-point perspectives. If views, targets, and eyepoints are selected with care, the distortion is minimal and there is relatively minor impact on what one sees. Furthermore, when one is inserting views of architectural models into photographs of actual sites, the perspective must approximate that found in the photograph to provide an effective previsualization tool. However, because it is possible to produce overly distorted views, care must be taken by the designer in perspective creation.

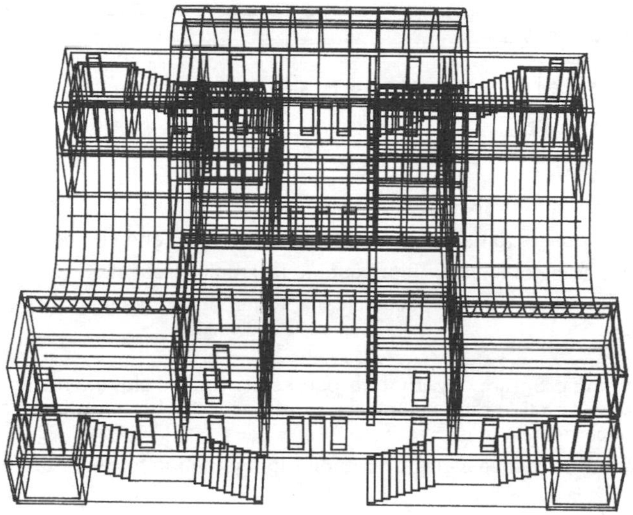

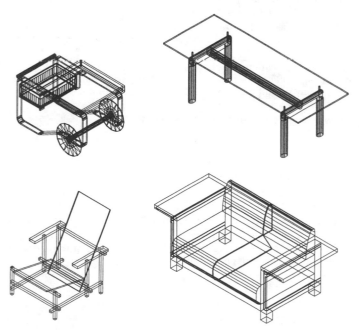

Fig. 4–65 Wireframe image. Model based on Ledoux's Director's House on the River Loue. (*Michael Hoon and James Hennesey, NJIT*)

4.3 WIREFRAME MODELS

4.3.1 "See-Through" Models

Computer graphics have provided architects and designers with a new type of image: the wireframe model. A **wireframe** image is the display of a three-dimensional

Fig. 4–66 Wireframe images. Three-dimensional models of various pieces of furniture. *Clockwise from upper left corner:* tea cart designed by Aalto, table designed by LeCorbusier, sofa designed by Wright, and chair designed by Rietveld.

WIREFRAME REPRESENTATIONS

Characteristics

- See-through or transparent model.
- Model appears to be made of only lines ("wires") and vertices.
- No hierarchy of lines or depth cueing is usually present.
- Large number of lines spaced closely together suggests, or reads as, a surface.
- Wireframe views can often be captured (either with hot keys within the modeling program or with third-party software) as either a raster line drawing or a two-dimensional vector drawing for further refinement and enhancement.
- A common "native state" or default representation for three-dimensional models.

Advantages

- Drawing and redrawing times for wireframe images are among the fastest for any image type on the computer.
- When composed well, wireframe images can be intriguing drawings that both inspire and inform and can add interest to architectural presentations.
- Unlike the case with traditional perspectives that tend to emphasize adjacent (usually planar) relationships, the transparent nature of wireframe images may permit easier study of relationships of planes and edges across space.
- Suitable as underlay for freehand sketching.

Disadvantages

- Complex wireframe images can be confusing.
- Lack of hierarchy in lines can lead to misinterpretation of intended physical characteristics of model.
- Multiple layers of information collaged without (necessarily) displaying information about depth or materials.
- Line weight usually must be added to captured views. Information about layers or materials must be color coded for display on screen.

model that appears to be created (only) out of thin lines, connected at points or vertices. It looks as if the model is created out of thin wires (Figs. 4–65, 4–66). The creation of the model is dependent on the particular software being used, and the model is usually made up of a combination of two- and three-dimensional primitives (including curved and straight surfaces), extruded elements, and lines. The model may be constructed by the computer as a solid model, a surface model (planes only), or a model consisting of corners and edges only. The wireframe is a way of displaying the model that is not, necessarily, dependent on the nature of the model itself. Any of the model types can be displayed as a vector wireframe image. (See Box 4–C.)

In its native state, the wireframe is transparent—you can see right through it. For complex models, the number and locations of lines can create a relatively dense (or cluttered) image that may not be entirely clear—especially to people who were not involved in the creation of the original model. In most cases, line weight is not part of a transparent wireframe image. Assigning different colors to different layers or to objects of different materials can help make the image more readable. Color coding according to function or area is another way to improve image legibility. Clarity can also be achieved through line density: a large number of lines spaced closely together suggests, or reads as, a surface. Although not used frequently, depth cueing, in which parts of the model closer to the observer are displayed on a monitor with brighter lines, can also improve one's ability to understand the three-dimensional characteristics of the image.

Wireframe images provide the designer with opportunities to create ambiguous and inspirational design drawings in a manner that transforms the "fuzzy" charcoal or soft pencil sketch into a new type. Because the representation is transparent, one focuses on the planes and lines in the context of complete and relatively complex architectural abstractions. The collection of lines can trigger thoughts of planar relations within spaces, as well as ideas for a variety of other opportunities for development. The visual complexity of the image can lead the designer, if open to these opportunities, to unexpected design discoveries, or it can help crystallize design concepts. The wireframe image is a computationally efficient way to display information, which, in a variety of ways, approximates some of the processes and techniques of the traditional sketch drawing on yellow trace paper.

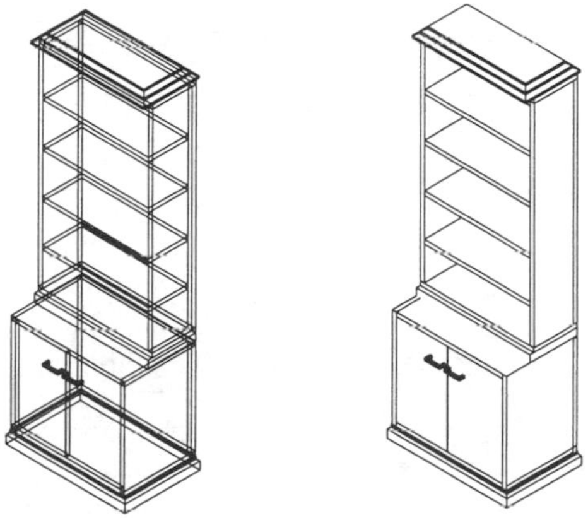

4.3.2 Hidden Line Drawings

It is possible to hide the lines in a wireframe image that would not be seen from any particular view (Figs. 4–67, 4–68). The hiding of the lines transforms the image (not the model) into the equivalent of an opaque surface model. The hidden wireframe image bears a great deal of resemblance to traditional line drawings (without shading or line weight). The hidden line drawing can be an orthographic, paraline, or perspective projection

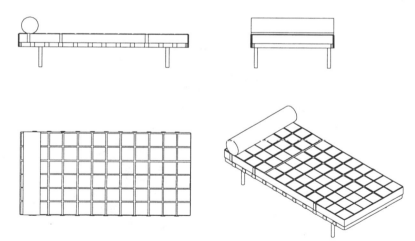

Fig. 4–67 Unhidden (*left*) and hidden (*right*) wireframe images. Three-dimensional model of Kimball bookcase and cabinet. (*Modeled by Kim DeFreitas, NJIT*)

Fig. 4–68 Hidden wireframe images. Couch by Mies van der Rohe. (*Model by Jennifer Arthur, NJIT*)

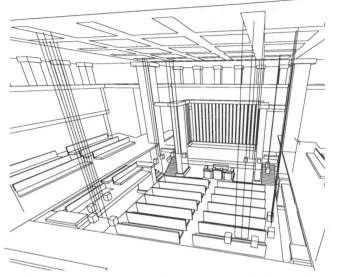

Fig. 4–69 Hidden wireframe image of Frank Lloyd Wright's Unity Temple interior (*Michael Hoon, NJIT*)

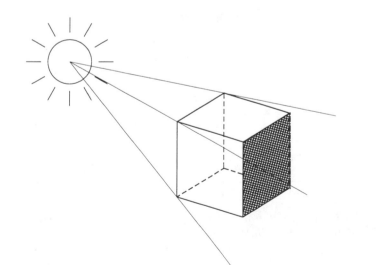

Fig. 4–70 Surfaces that receive no direct light are in shade and are usually perceived as being darker than lighted surfaces of the same color or material.

drawing. Most CAD/graphics three-dimensional software packages allow for the hiding of lines. The speed with which lines are hidden depends on the way the program was written (the algorithms used to calculate what is hidden and what is not) and the power of the computer being used. Hiding the lines removes much of the ambiguity present in unhidden images and provides a more realistic view for design evaluation (Fig. 4–69). As was the case with other image types, the hidden line drawing can be captured and used as the base for additional work.

4.4 SHADING

4.4.1 Clarity of Communication

When creating three-dimensional drawings and images, it is possible to take advantage of the fact that objects exist, and can be seen, in light. Because we see architecture (including interiors) in light, we can use the properties of light—as well as its absence—in our graphic expressions. Furthermore, because the space or building exists (or is proposed to exist) in three-dimensional space, it is usually possible to define a light source as shining on the object from a particular location. The light shining on the object causes different sides of the object to be darker (away or shielded from the light) or brighter (facing or being hit by the light). A surface of an object is in

shade when it does not have light shining on it (Fig. 4–70).

In order to shade accurately, one needs to know the direction of the light source hitting the object or within the space. The source of light (at least for exterior scenes) can be the sun. Because daylighting is a time-dependent phenomenon (it changes with date and time), one would have to either select the moment to illustrate, or create a series of images or animation illustrating the range of effects. In practice, one uses shade as much to help define a form as to illustrate a particular moment of time. However, if it is important to illustrate a building or scene under specific lighting conditions, then those conditions should be used to determine shaded surfaces. Interior light sources can be located so as to shine on that which is desired to be illuminated.

Expression of lighting on an object's surface can be added to an image to give a greater sense of depth and mass. One can draw a surface in shade by applying a tone. The variety in shades and color can be used instead of line weights to give either a paraline view or a perspective a sense of three-dimensionality. (One should be careful when applying shade to a colored surface. If the form of an object or building is to be made clear, difficult decisions must be made when a light surface is to be shown in shade and a dark surface in light.)

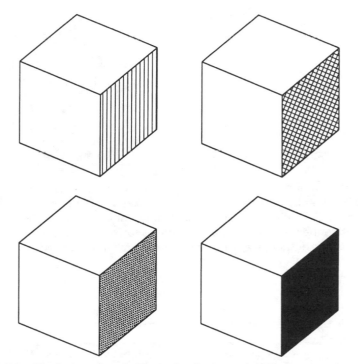

Fig. 4–71   Shaded surfaces. *Clockwise from top left:* lines, cross-hatching, continuous tone, and dot screen.

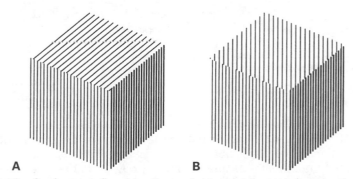

Fig. 4–72   Surfaces defined by lines. *A,* Vertical lines define vertical surfaces; horizontal lines define horizontal surfaces. *B,* Vertical lines define all surfaces. Spacing of lines varies to facilitate definition of planes.

Three-Dimensional Drawings and Models   **185**

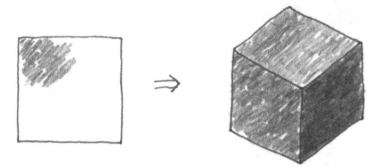

Tone used to express shaded surfaces may be made up of a pattern of discrete elements like lines, cross-hatching, or dots that, because of their value and density, give the appearance of a surface; or alternatively, the tone may be continuous as either a shade of gray or a color (Fig. 4–71). The applied tone may fall within the boundaries defined by a line drawing, or the tones themselves may define the boundaries of a form. Tones may be added to a drawing with virtually any of the media previously discussed.

Fig. 4–73 Freehand pencil strokes can be used to shade surfaces. A drawing will generally look neater when all strokes are in the same direction. Note that adjacent shaded planes have different values at adjoining edges to facilitate the visual understanding of the form. To help a viewer it may, on occasion, be necessary to have a gradient of values across a single plane.

4.4.2 Shading with Traditional Media

Shaded surfaces may be delineated with lines, dots, or continuous color. A tone created with straight lines may be applied in one of two ways (Fig. 4–72). To maximize clarity of form, vertical lines should be used on vertical surfaces and horizontal lines on horizontal surfaces. The lines should appear to lie flat on the surfaces and be parallel to the major axes. The horizontal lines, however, should all go in the same direction. Alternatively, a tone may be created with all lines going in one direction (usually vertical), with the spacing of the lines varying to emphasize differences between surfaces.

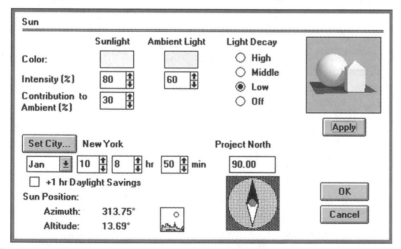

Fig. 4–74 Dialog box to set sun within a three-dimensional modeling program. Options generally include data associated with a particular city (or the ability to put in latitude and longitude), day, and time. The use of accurate sun locations to study shaded objects can provide information and feedback during the design process about the nature of the building and place being proposed. (*ArchiCAD by Graphisoft US, Inc.*)

When one is applying tone (or color) freehand with pencil, short back-and-forth strokes should be applied, all in the same direction (usually diagonal) (Fig. 4–73).

Areas can be made heavier (or darker) by going over the strokes multiple times rather than by just pressing heavily. It is important to note that adding freehand tone with strokes of widely varying lengths, or the use of strokes going in many different directions, can result in an unsatisfactory "scribble scrabble" drawing.

4.4.3 Digital Shading

A three-dimensional model can be displayed in a variety of ways. Because it can be created as a series of polygons and surfaces, the display can be defined as filled with color (or a shade of gray). Different polygons, or objects, can be defined as particular colors and, if the outline of the shapes are displayed, the ability to understand the view may be improved (depending on the colors used). *Of particular interest to the designer is the fact that most electronic three-dimensional models can be easily and quickly shown with filled and shaded polygons with relatively few commands.* The speed of the view creation makes it particularly useful during the design process. The image, once filled, can be captured and enhanced to provide additional expressive qualities needed for design exploration and presentation.

If sunlight is the means of lighting, specific data must be entered (Fig. 4–74). If the sun is not the source, one must create and "set" alternative sources. In most cases, one simply chooses (clicks on) a light to move and then selects the target or the direction in

---

Box 4–D

SETTING LIGHTS OR SHADING A MODEL

Sun or daylight
- Date, time, and location required.
- Orientation of building (north, south, etc.) required.

Alternative lights
- Create light in modeling, rendering, attributes, or editing module or component (software dependent).
- Locate light position and direction (target).
  — Usually, ambient light should be from behind the viewer or to the side (light behind the object will result in a dark model that is likely to be unclear).
  — Set individual light sources to be in actual locations of proposed light(s) and inside the building for exterior night views.
- Specify light intensity and falloff or decay.

Note: The locations of the lights usually become data associated with the three-dimensional model. However, other than accurate sunlight and specific luminaires within a building, ambient light sources may need to be changed when three-dimensional views are changed. For simple models early in the design process, the light should be changed whenever necessary in order to maintain clarity of form.

which the light is shining in much the same way that eye and target points are selected when setting up perspective views. (See Box 4–D.) In a few programs, the height of the light above the ground plane must be entered numerically. (In those few instances when the light source is not set, the computer reverts back to a default setting for lights that may not always be helpful in communicating graphic information.) Be careful in setting lights (Fig. 4–75). Lights shining directly toward a viewer can leave most of the image in shade and dark. Lights mistakenly placed inside a wall or column won't be able to illuminate anything.

Providing simple shaded models can eliminate much of the ambiguity present in wireframe images. Shading generally includes the suppression of hidden lines and may or may not include lines for the edges of the form itself. The shaded model looks like a surface or solid model but may also just be filled polygons in an edge and vertex model. *The shading is view dependent and affects the image but does not affect the three-dimensional data associated with the model.* Shaded models are excellent for the study of form and can be captured for enhancement as raster images in a paint program.

When shading with computer, there are a variety of options (algorithms) from which to choose. Each type has varying visual results and different demands on computer resources. Among the common shading algorithms used in CAD/graphics applications are **flat shading, Gouraud shading,** and **Phong shading**. There are

Fig. 4–75 Inadequate or poorly conceived light sources can obscure the form being illustrated. (*Model based on design competition entry for NJIT Student Center by Mostoller/Travisano, Architects. Model by Michael Hoon.*)

also other shading types, like **metal shading,** that are combinations of algorithms. (See Box 4–E and Fig. 4–76.) Shading programs create raster image representations of a three-dimensional model. The greater the resolution of the final image being created, the longer the rendering time.

The complexity of the model being displayed affects the shading time. Despite the inherent detail in buildings and furnishings, it is not necessary to model every component. If, for example, one expects to display a three-dimensional view of a furnished room, the bolts holding together a sofa or chair need not be modeled if they are not a significant component of the design being illustrated. They will hardly be seen and are not likely to add to the image if the furniture is a small piece of the overall scene. On the other hand, if the image is about the sofa exclusively, then more detail may be warranted.

Shading capabilities have improved the clarity of complex three-dimensional models. As computing power increases, architects and designers tend to balance speed of computation time with increased complexity in the three-dimensional model and quality of image. Photo-realistic images of proposed buildings in context provide a good way to previsualize the impact of a design proposal.

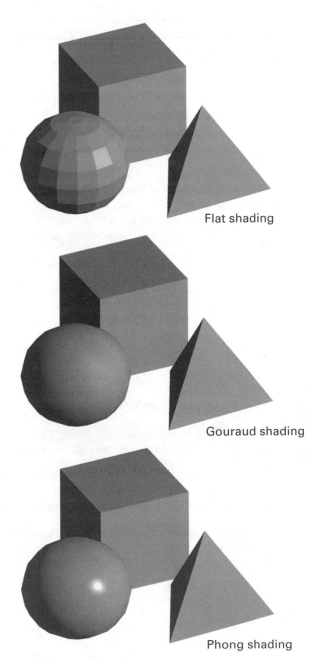

Flat shading

Gouraud shading

Phong shading

Fig. 4–76 Shading models

Box 4–E

DIGITAL SHADING

Flat shading

- Plain, continuous tone surfaces.
- Sometimes called **constant intensity** or **polygonal shading**.
- The simplest, fastest, and most common shading type available in CAD/graphics programs.
- Does not create an effective representation of curved surfaces because it emphasizes the individual polygonal facets that make up the surface.
- There is no smoothing.
- All pixels have the same value over an entire polygon.
- Large areas do not have the ability to display "hot spots" from nearby lights.
- Lighting is uniform and therefore is assumed to be somewhat diffuse and distant.
- Virtually any program that offers shading will provide flat shading—even if there are no other shading types available.
- Flat shading is most useful for quick studies of form during the design process.
- A good base from which an image can be enhanced in a paint program.

Gouraud shading

- **Bilinear shading,** most commonly called Gouraud shading after its developer, Gouraud.
- Significantly better shading than flat shading.
- A gradation of value for pixels is calculated through linear interpolation between vertices of the shaded polygon.
- Increased smoothness and shading time as compared to flat shading.
- Good for rapid-study images when the individual facets visible in flat shading become a distraction to the point of making study of the form difficult.
- Minimum shading type needed for shading domes and cylindrical elements within buildings.

Phong shading

- Improved shading over Gouraud shading.
- Rather than linearly interpolating edge and corner conditions of faces, the color values of the surface-normal vectors (i.e., lines perpendicular to the facets being shaded) are used for interpolation.
- Texts describing the algorithms used to determine Phong shading may refer to the process as **normal vector interpolation shading.**
- Phong shading represents an important option in many programs. Because it does not compute color values at each individual pixel, it is still an approximation of color values on lighted surfaces.
- Provides good, shaded, smooth-looking surfaces suitable for both design and presentation processes.
- Slower than Gouraud shading, but eliminates some of the apparent color banding ("Mach banding") that appears in digitally shaded models.

Metal shading

- Used less frequently than Phong shading. Availability tends to be limited.
- Combines algorithms to give an image that is similar to those created with Phong shading but that has greater specular (shiny) characteristics.
- A by-product of the shiny surface characteristics is the introduction of more noticeable hot spots from lights in order to simulate metal surfaces.
- Similar to Phong shading in terms of quality of image and shading time required.

4.5 ALTERNATIVE WAYS TO DISPLAY THREE-DIMENSIONAL MODELS

Beyond the ability to create flat perspectives, we can produce images, series of images, and environments that invite (or demand) an observer's participation to varying degrees. Although they are not in common use with traditional media, digital media allow for displays that can improve the simulation and understanding of proposed spaces and buildings in service to the design and presentation processes. Stereo vision (stereoscopic viewing), animation, and immersive virtual reality (VR) are all tools that can be used by design professionals (Box 4–F).

Stereo vision, usually with special glasses, gives an improved sense of three-dimensionality that can help some people get a better understanding of the qualities of a proposal.

In the creation of animations or design walk-throughs, a series of interrelated complex perspectives enables the designer to explore various sequences of movement or approaches to and through a building (both in view and design concept) (Fig. 4–77). The design emphasis is on the viewer's relative position in space and the experiential changes that occur through movement. Variety of enclosure, axis, and scale can be simulated. Movement from high to low, inside to outside, open to closed, and so on can be experienced,

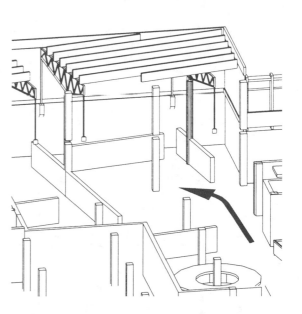

Fig. 4–77 Serial vision. Path through proposed space sets up a walk-through of the design. (*Model based on design competition entry for NJIT Student Center by Mostoller/Travisano, Architects*)

Box 4–F

ALTERNATIVE WAYS TO DISPLAY THREE-DIMENSIONAL MODELS

Stereo vision

- Stereoscopic viewing (stereo vision) takes into account that two eyes are used for seeing to provide an enhanced sense of three-dimensionality.
- Software is available that automatically splits the image into two separate, overlapping images, with slight offsets to account for the distance between the two eyes. The right and left eyes each recognize a different image.
- Special glasses allow the viewer to see a single image that appears to "jump off" the page or screen.
- Alternative types of glasses are connected by infrared signals that alternately turn the right and left lenses on and off to give the image increased three-dimensional properties.
- Looking at the image without the special glasses eliminates the special three-dimensional properties, flattens the image, and renders visible the ghosts of the overlapping images.
- Alternative multicamera or multiprojector proprietary systems with special monitors or screens permit stereo vision without glasses.

Serial vision and animation or walk-through

- Choosing a path through a design, with specific vantage and focal points, presents a proposed environment as a movement-dependent place.
- Three-dimensional views of a model can be generated at specified intervals, selecting both the eye and target for key frames. Intermediate views can be generated automatically in between the key frames that interpolate eye and target positions.
- Animations may be created with computer or with a series of traditional images (in a much more time-intensive process for comparable results), assembled in sequence, into a **flip book**.
- Automated animations may require frame-by-frame editing for improved graphic quality.
- Computer-generated animations allow for relatively quick change of viewpoints, angles of rotation, and so on.
- Resolution of animation may be tied to, and limited by, proposed output devices and their associated standards if not presented on the computer monitor.
- Sound may be added to simulate what a space might be like in order to improve the nature of the feedback to the designer about the place being proposed.

Immersive virtual reality

- Immersive virtual reality can put a viewer inside a space being designed.
- *Principal characteristics of a virtual environment are*
  — *The illusion of immersion in an environment that does not exist*
  — *The ability to interact with the environment*
- Peripheral vision must be filled (in much the way that very large screen cinemas provide quasi-immersive experiences—at least to the people sitting close enough to the screen not to see its edges).
- Although software is available to convert three-dimensional electronic models to virtual reality–compatible files, its success is also dependent on the associated hardware. Computing power required generally exceeds that needed for a typical CAD/graphics workstation.
- Tracking devices (gloves, harness, helmet, etc.) locate the participant within the model. For an immersive environment to be convincing, movement through the space must correspond to movement of the participant.
- Floor-mounted, counterweighted alternative VR devices may sacrifice mobility for improved tracking.
- Displays are generally head-mounted and stereoscopic, or projected onto large, peripheral vision–filling surfaces (like domes). Hemispheric projection can be used for group immersive experiences, requiring special and multiple projectors.
- To simulate most architectural environments, participant movement needs to be constrained so as to prevent flying through the building when one should be walking.
- If the space reacts slowly or lags behind the participant's movement, the sense of reality will be lost. Poor hand tracking breeds frustration with the lack of responsiveness and makes the environment unuseable. Poor head tracking may result in disorientation with possible side effects of motion sickness and dizziness. Very low resolution displays (used to keep the model size small enough to manipulate in real time) may induce headaches with some participants.
- There is, generally, a trade-off between speed/responsiveness and resolution or data associated with the virtual environment.

discussed, and modified. Dynamic relations of movement, path, sequence, and destination can be studied. The resulting sequence can provide a viewer with an impression of walking around or through a building and give a heightened sense of reality (including sound) to the project (Box 4–G).

Animations in which building components or construction equipment move through use of forward or inverse kinematics (the ability to control movements at joints of linked elements either upstream or downstream) can be used to help explain how a building might be put together.

Each frame in a walk-through must still be shaded, enhanced with materials and/or colors (rendered), or at least have hidden lines removed. Some software packages support distributed rendering over a network in which different frames can be rendered simultaneously on different computers. **Rendering farms** (large numbers of machines dedicated to enhancing three-dimensional models through automated processes) reduce the time needed to produce animations (Fig. 4–78).

In order for a participant (no longer just a viewer or observer) to feel immersed in an environment, there must be a sense of being surrounded by virtual (not real) objects (Fig. 4–79). Objects should be able to react to the participant (e.g., the participant should be able to open a door and decide in which direction to walk).

Box 4–G

SOUND IN ARCHITECTURAL PRESENTATION

- Ubiquitous nature of audio-capable personal computers creates client and user expectations for multimedia presentations.
- Nonobjective sound currently used in buildings themselves (background music in malls and elevators, masking sounds in open office environments, etc.) can be used in the presentation.
- Animations and walk-throughs of buildings can be accompanied by background music that expresses an architectural intent (in much the way a drawing style can express intent).
- Animations and walk-throughs of buildings can be accompanied by sounds that approximate the kind of sounds one can reasonably expect to hear in the designed spaces as a means to help communicate the nature of the total environment being designed.

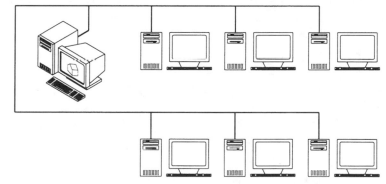

Fig. 4–78 Rendering farm. Networks provide opportunities for distributed rendering when supported by the software being used. Animations can be set up with different frames being rendered simultaneously on different computers.

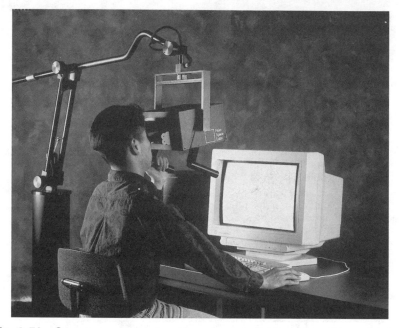

Fig. 4–79 Stereoscopic display. Floor-mounted display used to enter immersive virtual environment. (*Fakespace, Inc. 1995*)

It is important to remember that the use of alternative displays for models is a means to an end. Unlike theme park rides or music videos, the image (in whatever format it may be) is usually not the final goal of an architect, landscape architect, planner, or interior designer. Three-dimensional images and immersive environments are used in order to give information that enables professionals to create better places and to communicate the ideas to those people who are participating in the design process. The new images and displays are useful in empowering the designer to make more informed decisions by providing feedback on various aspects of a proposal. The particular image or display type used (and the media employed to create it) should be selected to accomplish a purpose: communication to ourselves and to others. Architectural design is so complex and comprehensive that the study and communication of different issues benefit from different types of graphic explorations.

REVIEW QUESTIONS

1. What are *paraline drawings?*

2. Describe the difference between *isometric* and *plan oblique* drawings.

3. Why are 30°, 45°, and 60° typical *angles of rotation* for paraline drawings?

4. Describe the role of the *plan* in the construction of a *plan oblique* drawing?

5. How does the *angle of projection* affect the emphasis of an elevation oblique drawing?

6. For what reason(s) would one draw a *cutaway axonometric?*

7. Define a *reverse axonometric.* What are its uses? What is another name for the drawing?

8. What is the *station point* in perspective? What are some other names for it?

9. What are *vanishing points?* How are they found?

10. How does moving the *horizon line* affect a perspective image?

11. How does a widening of the *cone of vision* affect a perspective image?

12. What is the impact of changing the *target* in perspective creation?

13. Explain the concept of *clipping planes.*

14. Describe a *wireframe* image.

15. What are ways in which expression of depth can be added to a drawing?

16. Explain the differences between *flat shading, Gouraud shading,* and *Phong shading.*

17. What are the requirements for a virtual environment to be *immersive?*

18. Why and how is computer hardware a necessary component of the success of an immersive virtual reality system?

19. What can *walk-throughs* of proposed designs offer that traditional discrete drawings or images cannot offer?

20. Can *sound* have any role in architectural design and presentation? If not, why? Or if so, how?

PRACTICE EXERCISES

1. Assume that a 10″ × 10″ × 10″ cube is made up of smaller 2″ × 2″ × 2″ cubes. Assume that approximately half of the little cubes are removed and create two different compositions, each with the remaining 50% (±) of the cubes and contained within the limits of the original volume. Draw a 30°-60° axonometric of one composition and a 45°-45° axonometric of the other. Be sure to apply appropriate line weights. Express each cube by using the lightest-weight line for grid lines between adjacent cubes.

2. Select one of the compositions from exercise #1 and using traditional media and methods, draw two pencil-on-vellum two-point perspectives from different viewpoints.

3. Draw a plan oblique, elevation oblique, and isometric of a chair with both traditional and digital media.

4. Draw three two-point perspectives of the chair from the previous exercise: (a) worm's-eye view, (b) eye level close to seat height, and (c) eye level at 5′-6″.

5. Draw a series of three 30°-60° axonometric 3″ cubes in ink on vellum. Shade one side of each cube with different methods: (a) freehand pencil shading, (b) pencil lines (one direction only), and (c) ink cross-hatching. Be sure to take care with the thickness of the lines and the distance between them in order to have the surface read as a tone. The spacing between the lines in (b) and (c) should be equal.

6. Draw a one-point interior perspective (line drawing only) of the kitchen in your personal residence. Include appliances, cabinets, and so on.

7. Obtain dimensional information about a house designed by a significant architect (Palladio, LeCorbusier, Neutra, Rietveld, Sert, Wright, H. H. Richardson, etc.). Draw two exterior axonometrics of the house to be created and/or printed at ¼″ or ⅛″ scale. One should be in ink on drafting film; one should be created electronically after building a three-dimensional digital model.

8. Using the 45° method, construct a section perspective of the house in exercise #7. Draw the section at either ⅜″ or ½″ scale.

9. Using the digital model created in exercise #7, create two hidden wireframe angular, or two-point, perspectives, of the house. One perspective should be an eye-level view. The other perspective may be either an aerial perspective or another eye-level view showing a different portion of the house. Be sure to show the most interesting views of the house.

10. With the sun as the light source, digitally shade one of the perspectives from exercise #9.

ENDERING

Two- and three-dimensional images can be enhanced to provide a viewer with a sense of what a place that does not exist might be like. Tone, texture, color, and representation of materials, as well as furniture, accessories, and landscaping, are all viable additions to a drawing. Materiality and the effects of light can be represented in a drawing to inform others, and ourselves, about the nature of form, order, and quality of space. The character of a place can be effectively conveyed with renderings (Fig. 5–1).

Rendering is the addition of enhancements to images or models in order to provide a more realistic and/or expressive view of an object, building, or space. (The word *rendering* is also used for the enhanced images or models themselves.)

Renderings may approach photo-realistic images and explicitly—with detail—show a designer's intent. Alternatively, rendering may be defined, in part, as an art in

Fig. 5–1 Rendered interior perspective. Pencil on vellum. (*Project: Museum of Jewish Heritage by James Stewart Polshek and Partners, Architects. Rendered by William Bricken.*)

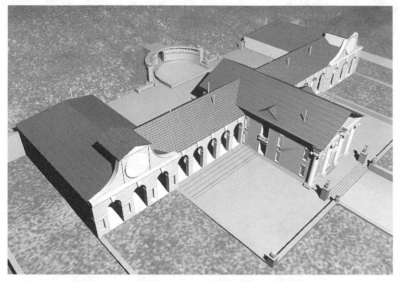

Fig. 5–2 Rendered digital model of Palladio's Villa Barbaro (*Ricardo Khan, NJIT*)

Fig. 5–3 Rendering of digital model of San Andrea del Quirinale by Bernini, focusing on rotunda (*Andrew Wai-Tat Yau, Temple University*)

which items are judiciously left out for the viewer's imagination to fill in. The type of rendering chosen is based on personal preference and style, the information one has about a proposed building or project, and the nature of the audience and message being conveyed.

Renderings can be produced with virtually any medium or combination of media, including pencil, pen, marker, airbrush, and computer (Fig. 5–2). Renderings may be line drawings, may be monochromatic shaded drawings (color or shades of gray), or may contain full-color representations of materials (either literal or abstractions), light, texture, and background.

5.1 VIEW AND IMAGE TYPE SELECTION

The particular image we choose to enhance should be selected in order to communicate *something* (Fig. 5–3). View selection is not a random process. We can generate an almost infinite number of perspectives for any project. When view creation takes little effort, as is the case with many CAD/graphics application packages, it is easy to forget that selection should be a conscious process. When one is drawing with traditional media, time constraints often dictate a careful selection of views. Sheer quantity of views does not make a project better or the presentation clearer. Reasonable candidates for presentation can include important elevations (Fig. 5–4) or plans, building or interior perspectives, and, depending on the situation, perspectives of public courtyards, axial street views, and so on, when they show unique conditions of a project. (See Box 5–A.)

Once an image type is selected, decisions about the nature of the representation must be made. If traditional media are to be employed, the particular medium (pen, pencil, marker, watercolor, etc.) must be selected. It is, of course, possible to use a combination of media: either using more than one traditional medium or combining digital and traditional. For example, one can plot a line drawing and render with color pencil, or trace over a perspective generated with computer graphics (Fig. 5–5).

It is usually wise to decide between color and monochromatic palettes. Even if color is selected, a limited palette may be most effective in communicating essential and expressive information. (Note: It is possible with image processing software to convert full-color images, either created electronically or scanned into electronic format, to grayscale monochromatic images.)

Black and white or grayscale palettes are frequently selected because of the ease with which they can be inexpensively reproduced. Monochromatic images may be used to emphasize the form of an object rather than planes of color. Finally, if the color selection has not been clearly considered, ill-chosen colors can distract the attention from other elements that need evaluation. (On the other hand, if the purpose of an image is to assist in color selection or to allow full previsualization

Fig. 5–4 Rendered airbrush elevation. Compare with Figure 1–11, an earlier, schematic version created with felt tip marker. (*Urs P. Gauchat, Gauchat Architects*)

Box 5–A

DRAWING TYPE AND PURPOSE

The selection of particular images to render or emphasize in a presentation is an important decision. Public review of work (including competition judging) often centers on those images with the greatest detail and graphic interest.

Plan	• Excellent for showing the building organization and disposition of rooms. Large-scale plans with furniture can show how individual spaces can be used. An importance space-planning tool.
Elevation	• Good for illustrating the compositional qualities of a building's facade. Effective tool for studying and showing proportional relationships within a building and between buildings along a street.
Section	• Describes the relationship between structure and space. Can illustrate the spatial experience.
Plan oblique or axonometric	• Well suited for explaining how a building goes together (especially exploded axonometrics). Can be used to emphasize the formal qualities of a construction. Cutaway axonometrics can be effective tools for looking at three-dimensional implications of plan organization.
Perspective	• Exterior perspectives can show a building in place and site. Interior perspectives can create a sense of being in a space.

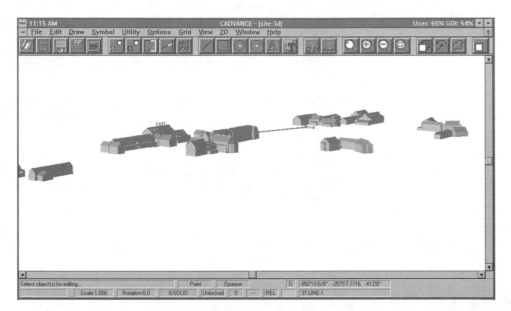

Fig. 5–5 The quickly generated three-dimensional model was used as the underlay, and a hand-rendered perspective was drawn over it. (*U.S. Fish and Wildlife Service National Education and Training Center, Keyes Condon Florance Architects*)

of a building in its site, the palette becomes a critical component.) When not all information is designed, it may be better to leave things out rather than to try to make something look finished before its time. The appearance of too much precision may invite criticism on items still to be designed and divert attention from the basic concept and intent of a project. Furthermore, at the early stages of a design project, communication of mood and character may be of primary significance.

The number of drawings to be rendered for presentation is a function of both format and time. Requirements for specific image types and sizes may be specified in competitions or academic situations. Regulatory agencies such as local planning boards or historic preservation commissions may need particular images or renderings. When requirements are not specified, the designer has to make careful decisions about which drawings should be rendered for presentation. An architect must be aware of the audience for any set of drawings and create presentations that will clearly demonstrate the nature of a project in a manner most easily understood by the intended viewer(s). Because rendered drawings are capable of attracting the most initial attention in a presentation, it is important that they be done well and illustrate an important aspect of a project (Fig. 5–6).

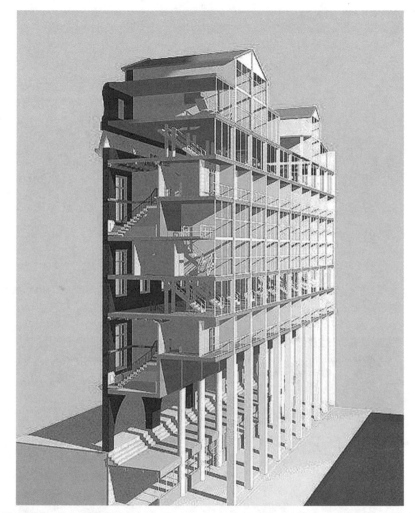

Fig. 5–6 Rendered perspective, cutaway section. View selected to illustrate the organization of internal space and structure. (*Sean McCarry, NJIT*)

Fig. 5–7 Ink rendering of dining room interior (*Francis X. Arvan, Architect*)

Fig. 5–8 Three-dimensional wireframe model captured and painted (*Eric Trepkau, NJIT*)

5.2 TRADITIONAL VS. DIGITAL RENDERING

The creation of renderings using traditional media generally relies on the building up of a drawing one element at a time. Depending on the medium, this may be a more or less complex process—and the "element" may be defined as anything from an architectural object to tone to color to a physical area on the drawing. (Airbrush renderings, for example, may be created entirely by sequentially exposing those areas of the board or paper expected to receive particular colors.) Frequently, it is most efficient to create what is considered to be the final rendering on translucent paper or film by tracing over the original (usually pencil) layout. Alternatively, the final drawing may be on an opaque surface on which an outline of the proposed image has been lightly drawn. Effective renderings can be created with almost any medium (Fig. 5–7) or combination of media, including charcoal, pencil, pen, watercolor, felt tip marker, and airbrush. Whereas some issues (especially the application of materials onto the drawing surface) may be medium specific, basic principles of representing light and shadow, sky and ground, and so on are, to a large extent, common.

Digital painting programs are used to create renderings in a manner that is analogous to that seen with traditional media. Outlines may be filled in, surfaces may have visual texture applied, and so on (Fig. 5–8). The effects of lighting can be simulated by changing hues for individual pixels.

When one is capturing a wireframe or shaded (filled polygon) representation of a model, the image can be transported to a paint program and modified pixel by pixel. (See Box 5–B.) Although, practically speaking, each pixel is not changed one at a time, the capability does exist. Entire areas may be modified, colorized, have the appearance of texture placed on them by changing hues for individual pixels, and so on.

In the past context of architectural graphics, rendering often referred to any image that was enhanced beyond the application of line weights for presentation. The term *rendering,* however, has more specific implications with digital media. There are many ways to enhance a line drawing.

Automated rendering programs, as distinct from painting programs, take the three-dimensional data and apply lighting conditions and material types while automatically calculating the values for display of the image (Fig. 5–9). Critical elements in the creation of a rendering include the way that light and reflectivity of materials will be handled, as well as how texture(s) of materials or surfaces will be displayed on the three-dimensional model. The amount of information required to be applied to a model, and the size of the model, determine the amount of space and memory needed for the creation of the image. Material characteristics, discussed in greater detail later, may be applied or assigned when rendering or, in some modeling programs, when the digital model is being created. Once assigned, the data become part of the information associated with the three-dimensional model, even if one is rendering a two-dimensional orthographic projection.

Box 5–B

PIXEL EDITING AND RENDERED IMAGES

- Images rendered to wireframe (captured hidden line images) may be painted by filling in bounded polygons. Additional enhancement may be accomplished with other brush types and on a pixel-by-pixel basis.

- Colors may be swapped or changed after rendering if the design changes or if the original rendering color is not satisfactory.

- Errors resulting from imperfect algorithms may be corrected. (One common imperfection is the failure to remove all hidden lines.)

- Details that may have been too fussy, or taken too much memory, when creating a three-dimensional model can be added on an as-needed basis that would be consistent with the screen resolution and size of the projected output. (One example is to have a model of a large building or complex contain only guidelines for exterior windows that are then added with appropriate detail in the particular view after rendering—using the initial guidelines for direction. Keeping detail down on the model reduces rendering time and makes the file more manageable.)

- Because very few materials are perfectly smooth, or perfectly clean, slight visual texture often can improve an image. Texture may be added to areas of flat color in order to eliminate large cartoonlike areas of one color. Texture may be added in a number of ways:
  - **Fat-bit editing** (zooming in to see and edit individual pixels) can allow the user to change pixel colors to whatever extent is desired.
  - Airbrush command on paint programs permits a light spraying of color on a surface. (It is usually best to use different shades of the initial color.)
  - Visual noise, or grain, may be added with single commands when supported by the paint program. Depending on the need, the texture may be added to the whole image, or only a portion may be selected for modification.
  - When supported by the software, a very fine layer of a light texture may be overlaid on the image—either over the entire image or over particular objects. (This requires the paint program to support multiple layers while working. In this technique, it is easy to have multiple options, or degrees of texture or visual noise, added.)
  - **Bump mapping,** rendering the surface with a material or color to make it appear as if the surface had imperfections (bumps) in it, results in a breaking up of the uniformity. Caution: The scale of the bump mapping should be adjusted; otherwise, the surface may not be smooth enough to convincingly represent a flat surface! (Note: Bump mapping is a rendering technique and *not* a painting modification. It is included here because it is an alternative to some of the painting techniques. Bump mapping is illustrated later in this chapter.)

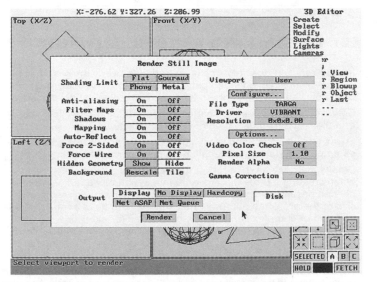

Fig. 5–9 Screen with dialog box for rendering software. Numerous variables are selectable by the user in setting up the image. (*3D Studio by Autodesk. This material has been reprinted with the permission from and under the copyright of Autodesk, Inc.*)

Fig. 5–10 Rendering of three-dimensional model: addition to Schindler's Lovell House (*Matthew Gosser, NJIT*)

Rendering systems usually create single still images from the three-dimensional vector file and create a new, two-dimensional raster image (Figs. 5–10 through 5–14). The three-dimensional model is *not* destroyed when a rendering is created. A new rendering file is created, and the model remains for future work or to be saved. For rendered three-dimensional images to be rotated without losing visible material characteristics on screen, new views must be rendered. The speed at which an image can be rendered in multiple views is dependent in part on the power of the computer (e.g., the speed with which the computer can calculate the new values for each surface under changing light conditions). In fact, when looking at an animation, one is actually viewing either the **playback** of previously rendered still images or the continuous display by the computer of three-dimensional models rendered in **realtime** (images being rendered at the same rate as their display). The rendering program works with vector data, but the rendering itself is a raster image with all of the limitations previously described.

Rendering uses automated processes to generate color and texture on a model. Properties of materials, orientation of shading type, lights, and nature of surfaces (texture, reflectivity, etc.) can sometimes be assigned to a model as associated information, or data, as part of the vector modeling program. Alternatively, there are a variety of add-on rendering packages that either operate wholly within other modeling software programs, or stand alone and accept files that are exported from the modeling software.

Fig. 5–11 Conceptual study of housing in the water (*Juan Diego Tome, NJIT*)

Fig. 5–12 Courtyard view from bridge (*Ricardo Ybarra, NJIT*)

Fig. 5–13 Rendered model of Bernard Tschumi's Folie #47 (*Oscar Mauricio Castro, University of Miami*)

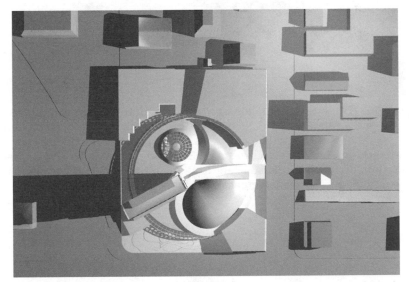

Fig. 5–14 Rendered site plan of digital model for the Korean American Museum of Art Competition (*Alastair Standing, Architect*)

Images are rendered at a user-specified resolution. The resolution may, or may not, be the same as the screen resolution. When diagonals exist (as they would in virtually any three-dimensional representation of a building or object), their raster representation may not be smooth. The stair-stepping effect, also called **jaggies** or **aliasing,** can be distracting in the image. When the stair-stepping is too pronounced, a viewer can be confused as to whether the effect is intentional or a result of low resolution and/or stark contrast between adjacent pixels along the diagonal. Many rendering programs allow for **anti-aliasing** during the rendering process, which averages pixel values along the diagonals to de-emphasize the stair-stepping (Fig. 5–15). Although the process may, on occasion, slightly soften the apparent edges in the rendering and require more rendering time, it is usually the preferable technique.

Fig. 5–15 Three representations of computer-drawn diagonal lines (enlarged and exaggerated). The top line represents a vector, resolution-independent line. The middle line represents a jagged stair-stepped raster line (black line on white background). The bottom line is an anti-aliased raster line in which pixels adjacent to the line have been given different values to reduce the visual impact of the stair-stepping.

5.3 LIGHT IN RENDERING— REPRESENTATION OF SHADE AND SHADOW

Masses and volumes are rendered in light. Material properties are expressed in light. Without light, we see nothing. Light is necessary to visually describe the three-dimensional properties of a building or space. It is used to illustrate the depth of recesses and extent of projections. The way light falls on, and is reflected by, a surface informs us about the nature of the surface. The contrast between lighted surfaces and those that do not receive light provides information about the shape and position of architectural elements.

5.3.1 Light

The fact that a building or interior space can be seen in a rendering implies that there is lighting somewhere. When the impact of light is not directly drawn on a building or scene, we nevertheless assume it is there in some undefined, perhaps diffuse manner.

Bumpy materials get their rough look from the way grazing light can skip over them. Shiny materials have hot spots because of the way light is reflected from specular (mirrorlike) surfaces.

There are many light sources available to the designer. When we render in light, we must specify (or at least assume) the type of light from a subset of the available light sources. On the exterior, there is the sun for daytime and electric lighting for night (both on the building and from the building). In an interior space, if the lighting is designed, those electric light sources may be used (along with windows) as the source of projected light into the scene.

Ambient light refers to a diffuse light that washes over an entire scene, whereas **point source** or **spotlight** generally refers to a conical-shaped beam of light aimed at a specific target (Fig. 5–16). The intensity of

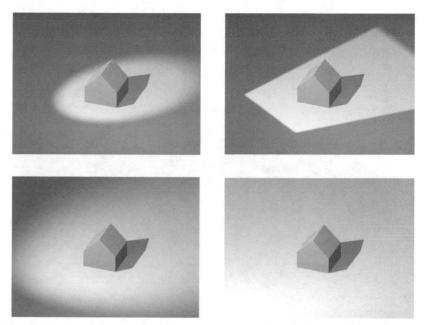

Fig. 5–16 Point source of light on an object. The aiming position and the degree to which the strength of the light dissipates are determined by the user. In some software applications, the shape, or frame, that defines the lighting cutoff may also be able to be determined by the user. (In general, this capability is most useful when one seeks to render the light distribution from particular electric light sources.)

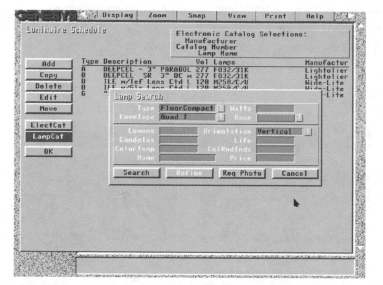

Fig. 5–17 Screen menu from lighting design and analysis software. Data and software are supplied by the manufacturer (in this case, Lightolier). (*GENESYS by the Genlyte Group*)

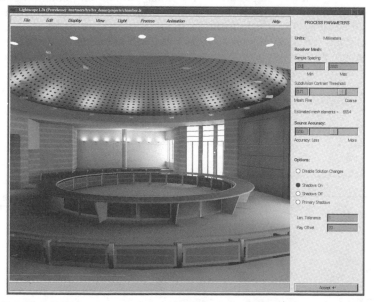

Fig. 5–18 Screen capture of rendering program that uses a variety of algorithms to create and display precise lighting effects (*Lightscape Technologies, Inc., San Jose, California*)

the light (how bright it is), the color of the light, its position in three-dimensional space, its aiming spot (target), and rate of falloff (how rapidly the light intensity diminishes) are all issues that need to be resolved when creating a rendering. The wider the beam spread and the slower the falloff, the more diffuse the light will appear on an object's surface. When a rendering is being created with traditional media, these variables can be determined precisely (either graphically or visually, or with precise photometric calculations) by the renderer. Raster paint programs allow and require the same type of control and the same degree of calculation and decision making that one would have with traditional processes. When creating the image with automated digital rendering processes, the renderer may be limited to the degree of control provided by the rendering program—but the lighting calculations are done for the renderer and their effects automatically applied.

Many common electronic rendering programs limit the lighting selection to the sun and a variety of generic electric light sources. An electronic rendering depends on the specified light in three-dimensional space to display the model. If a model is in the dark, virtually nothing is seen. *The effect of the light on the two-dimensional view used for the rendering is based on its behavior in three-dimensional space.*

There are some rendering programs (often created under the auspices of various lighting manufacturers) that enable the renderer to select a specific proprietary lamp and luminaire (Fig. 5–17). These rendering programs are most useful when a design has progressed to the point at which decisions about specific lights have been made. Others are more general with respect to the luminaire, but perform complex calculations to obtain the most accurate display possible (Fig. 5–18).

Shading type (flat, Phong, etc.) as described in the previous chapter must be selected for rendering in light. When the shading type cannot be specified, the program utilizes a default, or preselected type. In order to obtain the desired results, the individual creating the rendering should be aware of the method used in the application prior to selecting the program.

5.3.2 Conventions and Shadow Construction

As described earlier, a surface is in shade if it does not receive light. An object that is lighted can block the light from falling onto another surface. That other surface, which would be in light if it were not for the interfering object, has a shadow cast on it. The shape of the shadow is directly related to the shape of the intervening object. The shaded surface of the intervening object is the surface closest to the shadow. The shape of the shaded surface also affects the shape of the shadow.

For drawings of buildings or objects outdoors, shadows are constructed based on the direction of the sun (Fig. 5–19). As was the case with shaded elements, when one is rendering electronically, the date, time, and location can be set within the rendering program. When

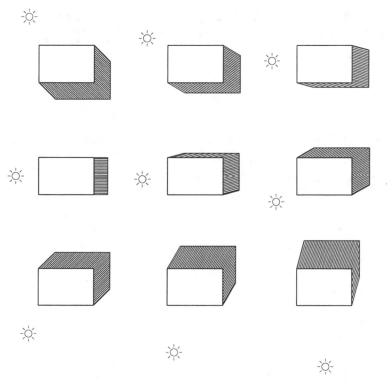

Fig. 5–19 Position of the sun and its impact on shadows. As a day progresses, the shadows cast by a stationary object change. The expression of sunlight in images introduces a time-dependent phenomenon.

Text continued on page 214.

I. SOURCE AND LOCATION OF LIGHT—DISTANCE OF SOURCE FROM OBJECT

1. Parallel Rays—Distant Light Source

   • Used to approximate the sun
   • Help to describe the nature of a form without excessive distortion

2. Nonparallel Rays—Near Light Source

   • Shadows expand as they move away from the light source
   • Form of shadow is exaggerated
   • Emphasis is placed on unusual form of the shadow rather than the object
   • Used primarily for special effects and in the entertainment industry (motion pictures, theater or live performance, theme park attractions)
   • Popular as a graphic device in Expressionist compositions

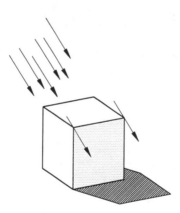

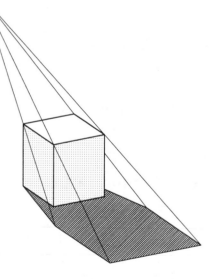

Fig. 5–20 Variables affecting shadows

Cont'd

II. THE OBJECT CASTING THE SHADOW

The diagrams below are created with the assumption that there is a horizontal and level surface and a distant parallel-ray light source. Every differently shaped object has a uniquely shaped shadow.

III. THE RECEIVING SURFACE

The nature and orientation of the surface on which a shadow falls affects the shape of the shadow.

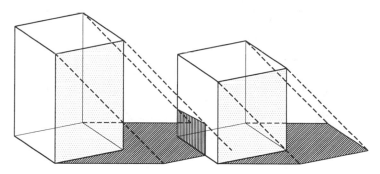

Fig. 5–20, cont'd (*The tree is a product of 3D Studio by Autodesk. It has been reprinted with the permission from and under the copyright of Autodesk, Inc. The human model is by people for people software—copyright © 1993 people for people.*)

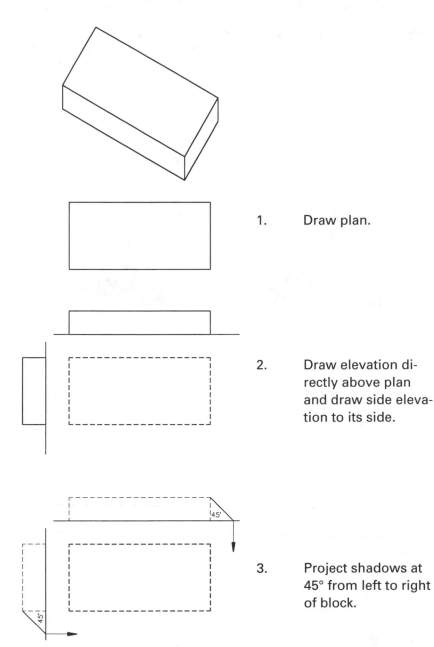

1. Draw plan.

2. Draw elevation directly above plan and draw side elevation to its side.

3. Project shadows at 45° from left to right of block.

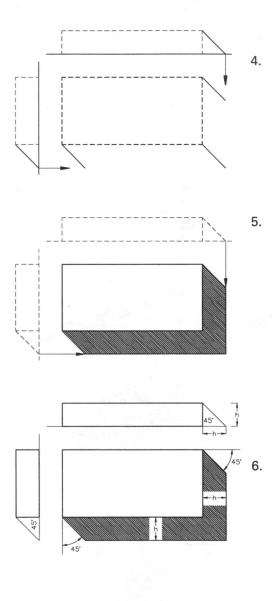

4. Project plan shadows down (or up) to the right.

5. Find intersection of shadow line projected to plan. The projection in elevation translates to the limit of the shadow in plan. Rays of light are assumed to be parallel and at 45°. Ground plane is assumed to be level (horizontal) in this example.

6. Note that when 45° rays of light are used, the nature of the geometry is such that the height equals the width of the shadow.

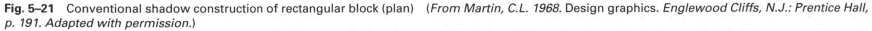

Fig. 5–21 Conventional shadow construction of rectangular block (plan) (*From Martin, C.L. 1968. Design graphics. Englewood Cliffs, N.J.: Prentice Hall, p. 191. Adapted with permission.*)

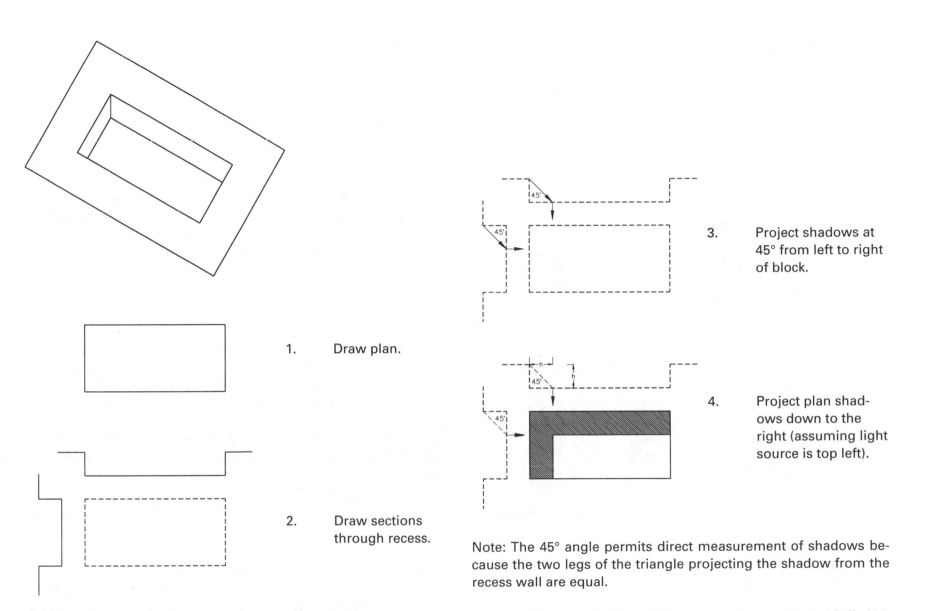

1. Draw plan.

2. Draw sections through recess.

3. Project shadows at 45° from left to right of block.

4. Project plan shadows down to the right (assuming light source is top left).

Note: The 45° angle permits direct measurement of shadows because the two legs of the triangle projecting the shadow from the recess wall are equal.

Fig. 5–22 Conventional shadow construction of rectangular recess or depression (plan) (*From Martin, C.L. 1968. Design graphics. Englewood Cliffs, N.J.: Prentice Hall, p. 191. Adapted with permission.*)

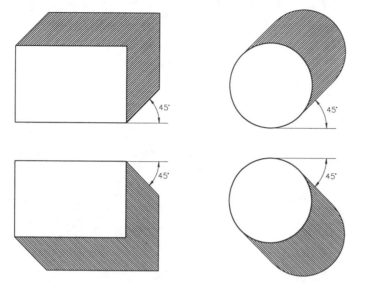

Fig. 5–23 Plan conventions. Shadows are projected at 45° up or down to the right.

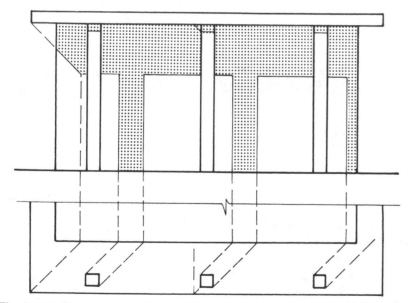

Fig. 5–24 Shadows in orthographic projections are transferred from plan to elevation with 45° conventions. (*From Muller, E., and J. Fausett. 1993. Architectural drawing and light construction. Englewood Cliffs, N.J.: Prentice Hall, p. 404. Adapted with permission.*)

creating shadows traditionally, one has to determine the location of the sun, or fall back on conventions whose purpose is to help explain the form of the building without worrying about the accuracy of sun angles (Figs. 5–21, and 5–22). When relying on architectural conventions to create shadows, one often assumes that the light comes from the left side of the drawing (Fig. 5–23). In orthographic projections, shadows are typically projected at a 45° angle (both plan and elevation) for ease of construction (Fig. 5–24). The light is assumed to be far enough away (which would be accurate when the sun is the source) that all light rays are considered to be parallel to one another. Shadow conventions were created for ease of construction and to provide delineators with artistic license that allowed them to give objects a solid visual base on a drawing that roots the objects to the page. Note: Due to the ability of CAD/graphics rendering systems to calculate shadows at any specified time, the conventions are primarily used with traditional media or when specific conditions are not known.

Casting shadows in perspective requires slightly more effort. Again, by convention, it is convenient to assume that the light rays are parallel to one another and also to the picture plane. The rays of light must be projected at the appropriate angle to the closest intersecting surface. The angle of projection, as before, is often selected to be 45° because of ease of construction. An adjustable triangle can be used to project light rays at almost any desired angle. Angles less than 45° (e.g., 30°) can be used to represent lower sun angles typically found early or late in the day and result in longer shadows. Angles greater than 45° are more typical of midday conditions and result in shorter shadows. If a specific time is not required for illustration, the renderer often selects a

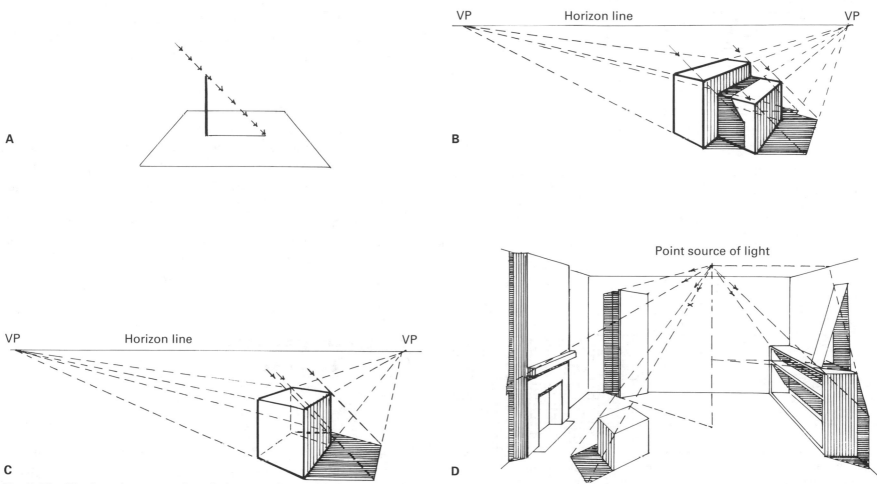

A

B

C

D

Fig. 5–25 Shadows in perspective. *A,* Assume (for convenience) a light source parallel to the picture plan for perspective shadows. *B,* Perspective shadows falling on horizontal planes. *C,* Perspective shadows falling on vertical planes. *D,* Shadows from electric light point source in interior perspective. (*From Muller, E., and J. Fausett. 1993. Architectural drawing and light construction. Englewood Cliffs, N.J.: Prentice Hall, pp. 405, 406, 409. Adapted with permission.*)

VP   Horizon line   VP

VP   Horizon line   VP

Point source of light

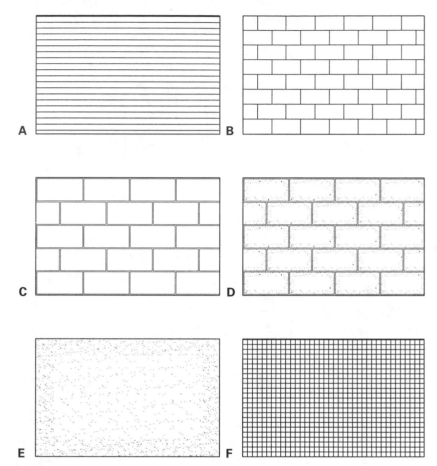

Fig. 5–26. Line drawing representation of materials. *A,* Small-scale masonry or siding. *B,* Unit masonry, large enough scale to see individual bricks or blocks. *C,* Larger masonry scale. Individual joints have thickness. *D,* Large masonry scale. Individual joints have thickness and material has texture. *E,* Stipple patterns used to represent texture. Can be used for a variety of materials—from stucco to carpet. *F,* Grid patterns used for tile in interiors and site improvements in site plans.

condition that best informs the observer of the architectural qualities of the building being shown. A variety of perspective shadow conditions is shown in Figure 5–25.

It is extremely important to remember, when relying on inaccurate conventions or estimates, that it is being done *only* to illustrate the nature of the object and *not* to show the accurate effect of the sun on the object. If the drawing is to be used to illustrate the effect of the sun and shadows on neighboring properties in a site plan, or to evaluate the effectiveness of sun control devices on a building's elevation, the time must be spent to create precise shadows based on various sun angle calculations. Precision in rendering is typically required when the consequences of design error can be politically or economically costly.

5.4 REPRESENTATION OF MATERIALS

5.4.1 Line Drawings

Materials can be rendered on drawings with black and white lines and dots expressing tone and texture. Elements of buildings have conventions that are commonly used in architectural and design graphics. The scale of the drawing also influences the selection of a technique (Fig. 5–26).

On small-scale elevations, clapboard siding and brick are rendered with closely spaced lines (Fig. 5–27). Half-timbering on Tudor elevations may be drawn to scale, and rough stone may be drawn pictorially (Fig. 5–28). Block can be shown with more widely spaced lines. At a large scale, individual bricks can be drawn. Tile patterns (interior and exterior, on floors, walkways, decks, or walls) are most often shown with a grid—in a pattern that reflects the design.

When the design of any material is not yet determined, or is meant to be a texture helping to define either the form or a separate zone or portion of a building, appropriately scaled generic square grids are often used.

Lines, when used to represent materials, are most often drawn lightly. For ink renderings, pencil lines or very thin ink lines are most often used. On pencil drawings, a hard, light pencil line may be used. Creating texture with ink on pencil drawings is likely to draw an unwanted amount of attention to the texture and overwhelm the rest of the drawing. When one is drawing with traditional media, texture in shadow or shade may be drawn darker than lighted materials in order to more clearly communicate the three-dimensional nature of the form.

Random stipple patterns (very small dots), in which the density increases near edges to help the definition of form, are used to represent a variety of materials (Fig. 5–29). Grass areas in site plans, carpet in furnished floor plans, and flat built-up roofs in plans are often shown with random stipple patterns. Stucco on walls can be shown with a stipple pattern. Extremely dense stippling can be used to represent water in both two- and three-dimensional drawings. Most often, stippling is made with the same medium as the rest of the drawing. Unless the drawing is a freehand sketch, the use of scribble-scrabble texture

Fig. 5–27 Ink line drawing with very closely spaced horizontal lines representing brick and more widely spaced vertical lines representing wood siding

Fig. 5–28 Multiple-media elevation with pencil representation of wood trim reminiscent of traditional half-timbering. The outline of the building was created in ink on drafting film. The stone is created freehand in a computer paint program after pen and pencil drawing was scanned. Varying weight of stone was determined by setting line width at 1, 2, or 3 pixels. Note that there are spaces between stones to signify mortar joints.

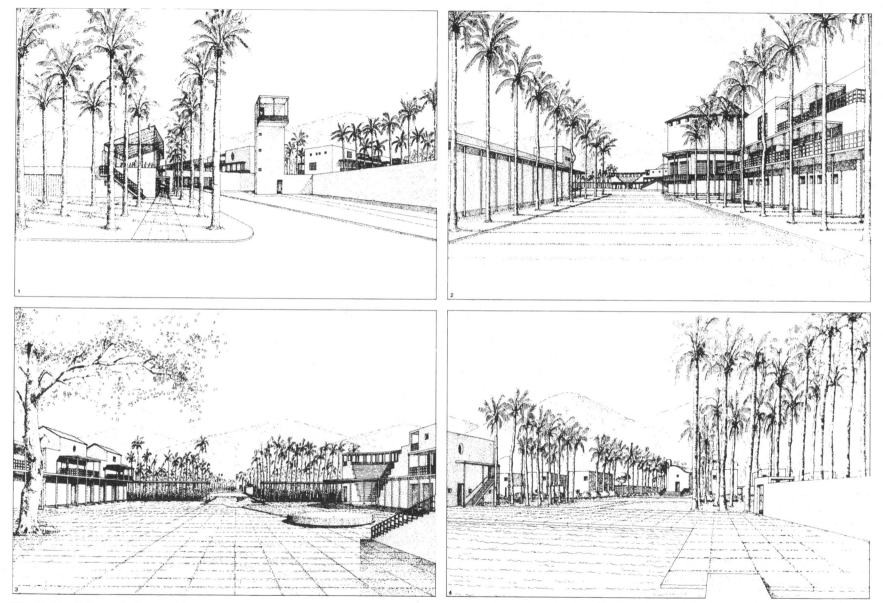

Fig. 5–29 Ink renderings with materials represented by lines, small shapes, and stipple patterns (*Las Terrenas Hotel and Resort, Francis X. Arvan, Architect*)

may result in a primitive-looking rendering if care is not taken.

When two-dimensional line drawings are created electronically, the same graphic conventions that are used with traditional media are applied. Some of the patterns must be created on an as-needed basis. Many of the textures, however, can be applied very simply as "fill" or "hatch" patterns within a defined area of the program. In vector programs, when associative hatching is supported, a change in the outline or boundary (such as a change in the shape of an elevation) can automatically result in a change in the fill pattern (Fig. 5–30). (Note: If there is a pattern that you expect to use repeatedly, and it is not included in the available selections, it may be possible to create and save the pattern for future applications.) Dots can be added either with a stipple fill pattern or, in raster programs, with an airbrush or spray paint tool that simulates the application of little drops of ink in a user-definable density.

5.4.2 Representational Sketches

Rendered images can be created that look very much like a proposed project. Materials can be rendered quite literally using almost any of the media available to the designer. Marker, pencil, watercolor, and so on can all be used to draw, or paint, images that can look like a proposed building. When one is creating a faithful reproduction, abstract conventions tend to be less

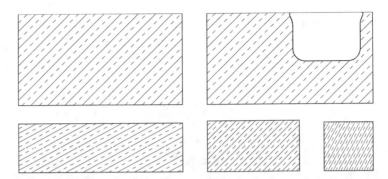

Fig. 5–30 Associative hatching. Vector software allows polygons to be filled with any texture one can create (in this case, diagonal, alternatively solid and dashed lines). Portions may be removed and polygons may be rescaled and reproportioned with the fill changing or remaining constant.

Fig. 5–31 The relationship between complex forms can be studied with monochromatic rendered massing models. *(Guardiola House by Peter Eisenman, modeled and rendered by Philip Smith, University of Miami)*

Fig. 5–32 Rendered model based on Sant' Ambrogio with expression of light and materials (*Henry A. Taylor, Jr., Temple University*)

Fig. 5–33 Photographs of materials scanned and converted to digital files for use in renderings

frequently used. Furthermore, tone or texture is less frequently used as a stand-in for a material. The actual material is rendered.

One must be careful, however, because an "overly realistic" drawing of a schematic design can both distract and detract from the intended purpose of the image: accurate communication. When a great deal of detail is placed in the representation of specific materials, much of the focus of attention on the part of the observer may be on the relation between materials, the specific nature of the rendered materials, the color (if not monochromatic), and so on. Unless the material is fairly uniform and monochromatic, issues of form and order may be overshadowed (Fig. 5–31).

If one is documenting an existing or historical artifact, or if the design has progressed to the point at which the issues of specific materials and colors are designed, a highly representational drawing—including shadows—may be appropriate (Fig. 5–32). Ultimately, a building will be built, a room furnished, or a courtyard created that will have all the properties specified by the designer. It is far more efficient to evaluate potential designs in drawn rather than built form.

5.4.3 Automated Material Selection and Texture Mapping

Depending on the software being used, color and material can be assigned by object, face, surface, group, and/or layer. Combinations of assignments may also be possible. For example, a selection of objects may be defined as concrete and then assigned the color gray.

Often, material selections may be associated with specific colors within the application and changes must be made either in a paint program after rendering, or prior to rendering. (Most rendering programs allow for the creation of materials and/or colors either within the program itself, by scanning an image, or by creating them in a paint program and importing them into the rendering program.)

In many rendering programs, photographs of materials can be scanned and applied as defined textures associated with materials (Fig. 5–33). When assigned to a three-dimensional model, the texture or material becomes associated with the object. When one is creating three dimensional models directly with architectural objects (see chapter 2), materials and colors may, on occasion, be assigned at the time the object is created.

Often, when a view is created, it is the *surface* of the model that is rendered (Fig. 5–34). The material may be defined by an algorithm, or procedure, that generates the visual texture or it may be generated from a scanned photograph or other raster image that is applied to the object's surface. In order to be an effective rendering tool, both the scale of the texture and the way in which the material wraps around or turns corners must be adjustable (Fig. 5–35). Without controls, the individual creating the rendering is at the mercy of the scale of the

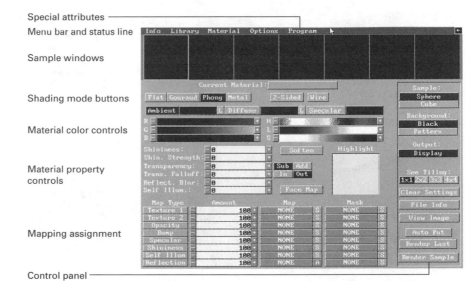

Fig. 5–34 Menu system for assignment of materials and surface properties (*3D Studio by Autodesk. This material has been reprinted with the permission from and under the copyright of Autodesk, Inc.*)

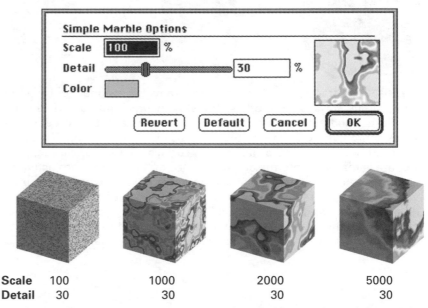

Scale	100	1000	2000	5000
Detail	30	30	30	30

Fig. 5–35 Selection of materials and variables that may be considered. In this example, marble is selected as a material, with controls over scale, level of detail, and color (*Reprinted with permission from form·Z Render-Zone manual, auto·des·sys, Inc.*)

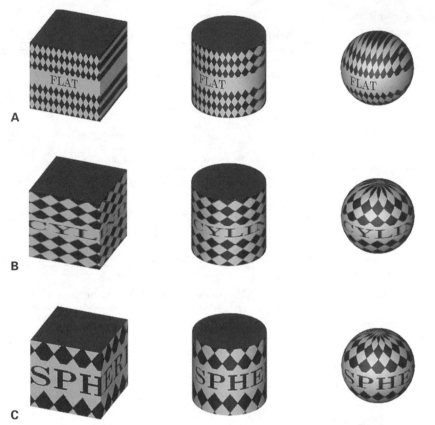

A

B

C

Fig. 5–36 Patterns, or visual texture, may be mapped onto three-dimensional surfaces of models. The way in which mapping is applied can be defined according to geometric qualities and the three-dimensional primitives on which they are based. *A,* Flat planar mapping. Texture is mapped onto a flat face or surface. *B,* Cylindrical mapping. Texture is mapped onto the curved surface of the cylinder projecting toward the central axis. *C,* Spherical mapping. Texture is mapped on the surface of a sphere projecting toward the center of the sphere. Each mapping type can be applied to objects of varying geometries. In the above illustration, each type of mapping is applied to all three objects, including their own native object used to define the map.

original photograph. A building represented at a very small scale, for example, may end up with only four or five bricks on the entire facade (which would clearly distort the perceived size, or scale, of the building). If the brick cannot be adjusted to turn the corner, with horizontal joints aligned, the elevations may look as if brick wallpaper were applied to the exterior. The three-dimensional and tactile qualities of materials would be negated.

Some materials such as wood, at large scales, have different qualities on sides and cut ends. If the wood grain is exaggerated or inappropriate, the rendering will have an artificial look to it that will detract from the overall image. In most cases, when materials are looked at so closely, the rendering is either of an important building detail or of a piece of furniture or cabinetry. Anyone involved in the design and presentation of fine furniture will need to take special care with scale and alignment of materials when rendering.

The way in which textures are mapped to surfaces can vary with the geometry of the surface. Flat or planar mapping is only one type. If software supported, textures can also be mapped spherically and cylindrically or along a path (Figs. 5–36 through 5–38).

In some rendering programs, materials may be assigned to objects, rather than just surfaces, and associated procedures may allow their representation to have appropriate corners and end conditions.

Original map

Texture tiled onto surface

Texture mirrored during mapping

Map rescaled proportionally

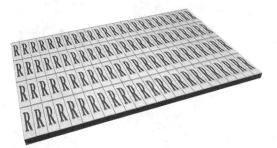

Map rescaled disproportionally

Map rotated 45°

Starting point of map adjusted

Fig. 5–37   Tiling and mapping. Textures (including text or scanned images) may be mapped onto another surface. The mapping may be modified in a variety of ways.

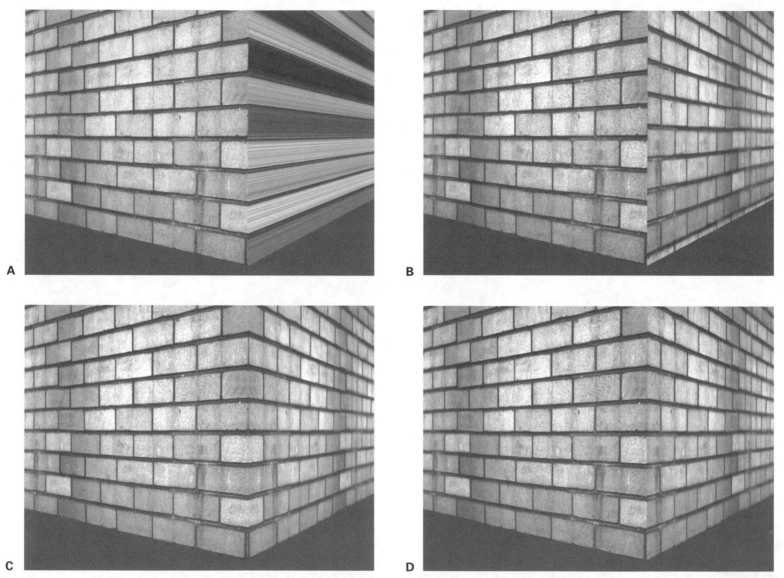

Fig. 5-38 Mapping materials. *A,* Surface mapping (one side). The planar map projects the brick back from the surface. *B,* Surface mapping (two sides). The planar map is placed on each side of the object. If the map is not applied in precisely the same way, or if the two sides have different heights, horizontal misalignment may occur. *C,* Wrapping. The appearance of symmetrically mapped brick is the result of wrapping the texture (like wallpaper) around the corner. *D,* Proper mapping. Procedural mapping, with algorithms taking into account the way a material should behave and the nature of the object, may be used to get a realistic material representation when the sides are different from the ends (e.g., with brick and wood). Note that a material like stucco does not require special care in alignment. When procedural techniques are not available, trial-and-error planar mapping can produce satisfactory results.

In addition to defining the material and color, the user may be able to set the smoothness or bumpiness. In fact, bump mapping automatically creates the appearance of a rough surface (Fig. 5–39). Bump mapping provides an alternate way to simulate materials when a particular selection is unavailable. For example, an otherwise smooth color or material, when bump mapped, may be used to simulate rough-surface materials such as stucco or concrete block. The scale, or degree of bumpiness, from coarse to fine, is generally defined by the user. The application of dents, or depressions, in a surface is the inverse of bump mapping.

It is very important to understand that the more objects (buildings, roads, plants, etc.) in a scene, the less detail that should be placed in material (unless the final output is expected to be extremely large). When looking at a close-up of a portion of a building, it is fine to see the nature of the brick. When, however, one is looking at a model of an entire housing or mixed-use development, materials should be assigned that are more general: flat colors or, perhaps, monochromatic materials (concrete, stucco, etc.). The computer makes no judgment about the appropriateness of the scale of material in an overall scene. A lot of tiny, highly rendered elements can result in a poor rendering with a disproportionate emphasis on fussy textures. Rendering with electronic media provides enormous opportunities for variety and representation. However, as is the case with traditional media, it is the person creating the rendering who must make decisions about appropriateness, scale, and emphasis.

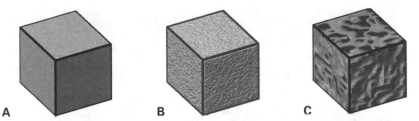

Fig. 5–39 Bump and dent mapping. *A,* Flat map. *B,* Small bumps. *C,* Large dents (negative bumps).

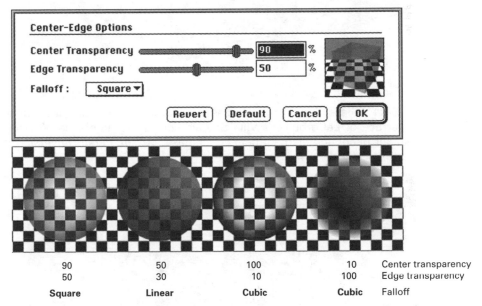

Fig. 5–40 Transparency variables. Most rendering programs allow for transparent materials and for the user to adjust the degree of transparency. On occasion, greater control is afforded to the user, who can adjust variable rates of transparency between edge and center, and the degree to which interpolation (falloff) is carried out between the two. (*Reprinted with permission from form·Z RenderZone manual, auto·des·sys, Inc.*)

Fig. 5–41 Glass digitally rendered as transparent. View looking into open-air terrace of LeCorbusier's Villa Savoye shows the difference between open-air panel and element defined as glass. (*Marc Peter, University of Miami*)

Fig. 5–42 Enlarged detail of rendering with glass delineated as transparent. Rendering shown in Figure 5–43. (*Rendered by William Bricken*)

Transparency is another variable that is generally user selectable (Fig. 5–40). The levels of transparency, opacity, and reflectivity impact the way light bounces off and passes through objects. For example, a ray traced rendering of a highly reflective element can cause the element to take on the color or patterns of nearby objects. Depending on the shading method selected, partially transparent or reflective objects can significantly increase the rendering time required by the computer. (Reflective glass block is one of the most time-intensive materials that one can render.) Furthermore, each time a view is changed, the ray trace calculations are redone.

5.4.4 Transparency and Reflectivity

The depiction of *glass* is a special case in rendering. In general, glass should either be transparent (Figs. 5–41, 5–42) or reflective (Fig. 5–43). When a window is transparent, lightly draw whatever would be seen through it. Edit out extra lines so that the scene visible through the window does not overpower the image of the building. When seen from inside, the framed views through windows are often important, but again, they should be drawn with lines more lightly applied than those of the room itself. When creating digital renderings, adjust the transparency of the glass material to obtain an appropriate effect. When glass is reflective, the image of the reflected element can be drawn lightly. The technique of rendering glass as black, or darkly shaded, in line drawing perspective

Fig. 5-43 Pencil-on-vellum rendering with transparent glass at the corner and reflective glass on the side elevation (which is delineated as being hit by the sun). The large tree is casting a shadow indicating the direction of the sun that reinforces the expectation of seeing reflections in the glass. (*Project: Mandel School for Social Science at Case Western by James Stewart Polshek and Partners, Architects. Rendered by William Bricken*)

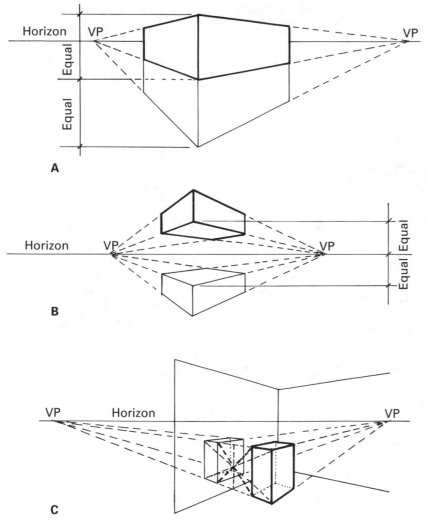

Fig. 5-44 Reflections. *A,* Object on reflecting surface. *B,* Object above reflecting surface. *C,* Object adjacent to reflecting surface.

renderings is best used only when there is a need to emphasize the figure-ground relationship between the openings and the wall. Deeply recessed shaded openings or glass may, at times, also be rendered as dark because the contrast between the light and dark might make it difficult to see through.

Reflections exist in renderings when there is a shiny surface (water, mirror, specular metal, plastic, etc.) capable of reflecting a nearby object or surface. The nature of the reflection depends on the surface and lighting. Rough surfaces reflect less than smooth ones. **Grazing light** (i.e., light that tends to skim along a surface and is created or defined in some software programs by increasing the angle of incidence—the angle between the perpendicular to the surface and the ray defining the light direction) is more likely to result in one material being reflected in another than is a light source at 90° to the lighted surface. Furthermore, reflections are actually attenuated by the angle of light and surface properties as they relate to one another under physical conditions. When creating renderings electronically, it is important to understand the degree of control one has over surfaces and lighting in order to best illustrate a project.

The image of the reflected object appears to be the same distance from the reflecting surface as the object itself. The reflection is equal and opposite but vanishes to the same vanishing points (Fig. 5-44). The result is a reflection that the eye perceives to be the same size as the object because it conforms to the same perspective requirements. Traditional construction of reflections requires the knowledge of traditional perspective

Fig. 5–45 Reflections in still water   (*Sean McCarry, NJIT*)

Fig. 5–46 Rendered model of atrium. Radiosity algorithms were used to model effects of lighting on nonspecular surfaces. (*Copyright © 1994 A. J. Diamond, Donald Schmitt and Company [Toronto, Canada]. Rendered with the Lightscape Visualization System, Lightscape Technologies, San Jose, Calif.*)

Box 5–C

RENDERING METHODS USED FOR MODELING LIGHT, SHADOWS, AND REFLECTIONS

Radiosity

- Algorithms model diffuse and secondary lighting on objects (taking into account the interaction of radiant energy between surfaces in a model).
- High in quality but initial rendering long in computation time.
- Inefficient model for displaying reflections from specular surfaces.
- Light and inter-reflections are considered as part of an object's surface—independent of view.
- Lighting effects are calculated based on surface materials and the relationship of one object to another in the three-dimensional model. View independency allows for relatively rapid re-creation of scenes with diffuse reflections even when viewpoint is changed.
- Calculates direct light on objects and also adds in values attributable to light being scattered from other diffuse objects in the model. (The light calculated as coming from a surface may be either generated or reflected [diffusely] by the surface.)
- The inclusion of ambient light in calculating the effect on different faces assists in providing a more photo-realistic image than that of most shading or rendering algorithms.

Ray tracing

- Provides the most time-intensive and highest-quality shaded images *commonly* used in CAD/graphics programs.
- "Rays of light" are sent from the point of view to each pixel. Each ray is then reversed and describes the path of light coming from each pixel in the image, considering surface characteristics including geometry and position in the scene, color, absorption or transparency, relation to light sources, and so on.
- The quality of light bouncing from surface to surface is scene dependent (based on the particular point of view). If elements are changed in a scene, or the point of view is changed, the image must be rendered again.
- Provides high-quality photo-realistic images.
- Certain properties (like light shining on reflective glass block), or very complex scenes with multiple light sources, can require comparatively long rendering times.
- Long image creation times often limit ray tracing to use for presentation images and images used for intermediate, periodic review of design work.
- Software that combines radiosity for diffuse reflections and ray tracing for specular ones is often successful in modeling realistic scenes.

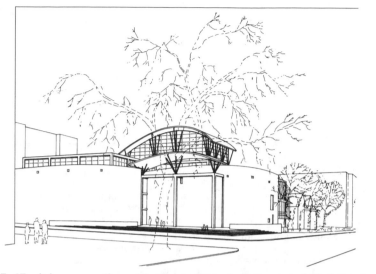

Fig. 5–47 Ink perspective with ghosted tree in foreground. Building is unobscured, and landscaping is still present for information and to provide character to the image. (*Evanston Public Library, Francis X. Arvan, Architect*)

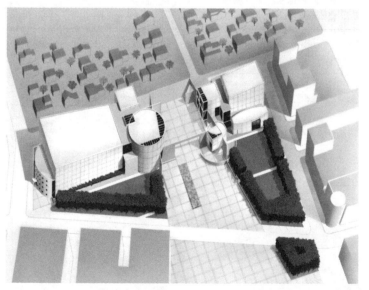

Fig. 5–48 Airbrush site rendering showing context as plain block buildings with detail only on proposal. The observer's attention is focused on the proposal. (*NARA Convention Center, Francis X. Arvan, Architect. Rendered by John Arvan*)

construction techniques. Typical examples in architectural rendering include buildings along waterfronts (Fig. 5–45), mirrors on walls (including reflective glass buildings), and mirrors on ceilings.

Photo-realistic renderings must include proper reflections in order to be convincing. Even when the intent of the rendering is to be photo-realistic, however, one should recognize that it is virtually impossible to capture the precise subtleties of a real place including atmospheric qualities, inter-reflections of surfaces, dirt and dust, and so on. The closest one can often get is to be like a photograph of an actual place.

5.4.5 Digitally Rendered Material in Light

In addition to the shading types previously mentioned, there are rendering algorithms that take into account both light and the nature of materials (Box 5–C, Fig. 5–46). These include shade and shadows, as well as inter-reflections (the reflections of one material into another).

5.5 LEVELS OF ABSTRACTION— FROM PERSONAL STYLES TO PHOTO-REALISM

The purpose of a rendering should dictate the degree to which there are consistent levels of abstraction and resolution within the image—regardless of the media employed.

When there are differing levels of abstraction, attention is usually focused on that part of the image containing the highest level of detail. If, for example, the intent of the image is to communicate landscaping proposals, it may be reasonable for the buildings to be shown in a relatively simple manner, and the plantings to be rendered in detail. If however, one is studying the front elevation of a building, the level of detail in the landscaping should either be consistent with that of the building (so as not to detract from or overwhelm it) or developed in less detail. It is possible to "ghost" in an outline of foreground vegetation (place simple outlines in the front of a three-dimensional perspective image) that would set the scene but not detract from the central element (Fig. 5–47). It is also possible to render a building or a piece of a building and have its context in less detail in order to focus on the new proposal (Fig. 5–48). Blocklike, preliminary massing studies of a building do not (usually) look good with finely rendered grass and trees, or in front of scanned images of sky and clouds.

When using computer-generated quick shading techniques, one should be aware that the diagrammatic nature of buildings represented by the large areas of flat color common in filled polygon images tends to look very crude when placed in finely rendered sites—or when superimposed over scanned site photographs. *This in no way diminishes the importance of looking at schematic models in site during the design process.* The "quick and crude" images are often suitable for schematic design evaluations—as long as the technique does not interfere with one's ability to evaluate

Fig. 5–49 Model of Palladio's Villa Emo with homogeneous texture on walls and arches in top image. Level of resolution appears consistent. In the bottom image, the horizontal banding is emphasized against the uniform untextured shading of the arches. (*Robert A. Mayo, University of Miami*)

SUMMARY OF ISSUES TO BE RESOLVED, AND STEPS TO TAKE, IN DIGITAL RENDERING

- Select view for rendering from three-dimensional model.
- Assign materials or colors to objects or surfaces if not already assigned. Adjust scale of materials to be appropriate for scale of rendered image.
- Assign mapping type to materials and objects.
- Determine surface characteristics of various elements, including specularity (shininess), transparency, smoothness or bumpiness, and so on.
- Decide on shading and rendering algorithm(s) (flat, Phong, Gouraud, ray tracing, radiosity, etc.). At some point, use fast shading techniques to create a quick test rendering to see if variables need adjustment.
- Determine background color (above and below horizon—sky and ground in most cases).
- Assign lights, and if daylight is present, enter required data for sun.
- Determine the path to which the new raster image will be sent: usually any combination of screen, hard disk, diskette (if the image is small enough), and printer. (If the rendering is for personal evaluation only, or for a discussion, with an observer at the workstation, rendering to screen only is usually the fastest alternative.)
- Post-process as needed with raster painting and editing software (focus or sharpen, color, touch up, etc.). Add entourage that was not part of the three-dimensional model as needed.
- Save final rendering in digital format for printing and future use.

Note: Some variables have only default values available to renderers because not all are user determined in all software packages. The sequence that users must follow in setting up a rendering is not consistent in every software program. Furthermore, different programs allow different degrees of user control and different numbers of options for the renderer. Nevertheless, the issues listed above must be accommodated, either by default or by choice.

the relevant design issues. Presentation renderings, however, should be created so as not to force the viewer to compensate for awkward visual relationships.

When it is desired, diagrammatic elements in a computer-generated rendering can be given *the appearance of greater detail* by adding texture, dots of color, or visual "noise" in paint or image processing programs. The applied texture can create an apparent consistency of abstraction and resolution.

Problems resulting from overly large diagrammatic elements are not as common in renderings created with traditional media because there is no automatic default on which a presenter may rely—all decisions are more likely to be specific choices. A rendering of a schematic proposal is generally created in a sketch format (often freehand, or freehand over hard-line layout) or is drawn at a small size appropriate for the level of resolution of the design.

Particular details of a building may be rendered with greater information than the rest of the building in order to call attention to a specific element—either because of its importance in the design or because it is the element that most requires discussion and evaluation at a particular stage of the design process (Fig. 5–49).

Finally, one should note that choices may have to be made between accuracy and clarity. Double lines, for example, may be needed to communicate the edges of a flat roof, or a section cut through glass. Yet, to scale, only one line would be drawn. The double line improves the clarity of *expression* of the material. Care must be taken with digital rendering wherein the minimum expression is a resolution-dependent pixel. Modification may have to be made in a raster editing program after the rendering is produced. A summary of the steps taken when creating renderings with digital media is shown in Box 5–D.

5.6 GIVING DRAWINGS LIFE— ADDING THE ENTOURAGE

Buildings exist in a context. All of the "stuff" that we know exists around them helps give our buildings and their representations a sense of reality and scale. Although many architectural elements—like doors and windows—give clues to how big the building is, scale is often best given by those things around the building whose size cannot be manipulated by the architect. In a rendering, the extra elements of context, including trees, grass, streets and cars, people, and furniture, are referred to collectively as the **entourage.**

As always, the intent of the rendering must be clear in the designer's mind. When the responsibility of the designer is the furniture selection and design for a pre-existing interior space, accessories are primary elements and not really part of the entourage.

5.6.1 Landscaping
Landscaping is often one of the first and most prominent elements added to a rendering (Figs. 5–50, 5–51).

Fig. 5–50 Rendering of housing on a forested hill. The trees form the context within which the buildings sit. Black Prismacolor pencil on drafting film. (*Project: Headlands at Plymouth, housing in Plymouth, Mass., by Sert, Jackson and Associates, Architects. Rendered by William Bricken*)

Fig. 5–51 Details of rendered trees

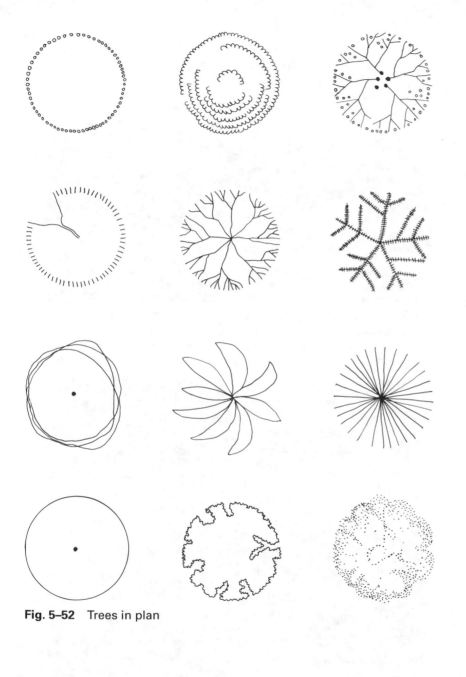

Fig. 5–52 Trees in plan

Isolated buildings look far more dreary without trees. Trees and other plantings can be used as architectural elements in the definition of space and sequence. There are different types of trees that must be considered when creating a landscape design. Trees introduce time-dependent and location-specific elements into a rendering. Deciduous trees look different in summer than in winter. Young trees are smaller than mature ones.

When one is drawing with traditional media, freehand sketches testing different landscaping material may be created to help compose the design and image. With digital media, many rendering programs include a number of three-dimensional trees (with variety in both type and age) that can be added to the model when rendering. One warning, however: digital three-dimensional trees, complete with leaves and branches, can consume enormous amounts of memory that may use up all of the available storage for a model and/or significantly increase the computer's rendering time. Some paint and image processing applications, however, have two-dimensional photo-realistic symbols (in plan and elevation) of various trees that can be added to a raster image after rendering.

Trees are very important to add to large-scale plans and site plans. They may be created with traditional media and with raster and two-dimensional vector software as reuseable symbols (Fig. 5–52). Three-dimensional trees in plan represent top views of the actual model rather than reflecting the standard architectural conventions. Trees are also important in elevation and three-dimensional images (Fig. 5–53).

Fig. 5–53 Trees. *A,* Three-dimensional trees available within modeling and rendering software. Shown here as orthographic projections in shaded and wireframe representations. (A, *3D Studio by Autodesk. This material has been reprinted with the permission from and under the copyright of Autodesk, Inc.*) *B,* Trees and shrubs in elevation. *C,* Trees and shrubs in axonometric.

Willow

Deciduous (Maple)

A   Tropical

B

C

Fig. 5–54 Rendered building in front of photo-realistic sky (*Gabriel Seijas, NJIT*)

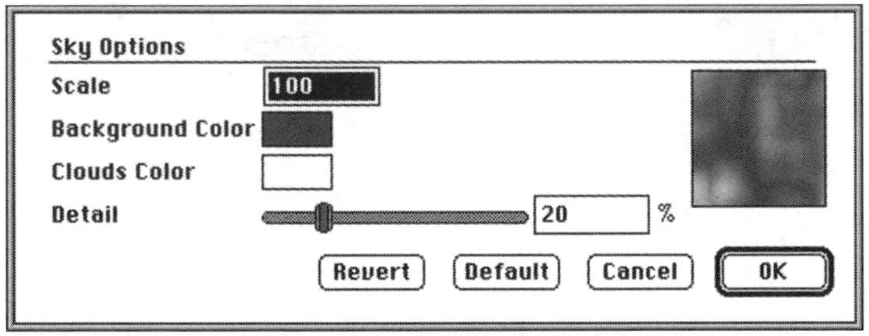

Fig. 5–55 Automated cloud generation may be selected within some rendering programs. Increased detail generates denser cloud cover. (*Reprinted with permission from form·Z RenderZone manual, auto·des·sys, Inc.*)

Software applications that create specific three-dimensional trees are available as add-ons to common modeling programs. Generic trees can also be created using software that contains algorithms that define branch growth and leaf patterns. The type of tree, its age, and the season are all user selectable. It is, in fact, relatively easy to render the same building in different seasons to show how landscaping and lighting change the perception of it over time.

As is the case with trees, ground cover and shrubs can be specifically selected or generic.

5.6.2 Sky

Eye-level exterior perspective renderings often have an overhead sky (Fig. 5–54). Even in renderings of dense urban settings, there are breaks in the street wall or distant views that show sky.

Just as in real life, sky can be clear blue, gray, partly cloudy, or heavily clouded. Many rendering programs have integrated cloud makers, with the density defined by the user (Fig. 5–55). It is important to experiment with various densities of cloud cover to see what best emphasizes the building. There should be some contrast between the sky and the structure being rendered to best delineate the building's form. Whether one is using digital or traditional media, the size of individual clouds should be consistent in scale with the rest of the image.

Clouds can also be added to the raster image after rendering. The airbrush tool found in most paint programs (as well as traditional airbrushes or careful application of watercolor) generally works well in creating wispy clouds.

Night and sunset skies can sometimes be used as a contrast to the building's form and to create a dramatic image. Gradients of color or tone can work effectively in creating various effects (Fig. 5–56).

5.6.3 Ground

The ground plane in a rendering can be used to lead the viewer into the scene. Ground cover (often shown as leaves without branches), grass (stipples or lines), and pavement (streets with a stipple texture, courtyards with paving grid, etc.) can all be used as types of rendered ground planes (Fig. 5–57). For most architectural applications, it would be rare to render the ground plane in greater detail than the building. In part, the function of the ground plane in a rendering is to provide sufficient graphic weight so as to act as a visual base on which the building(s) sit and to draw the observer's eye toward the focus of the image.

Fig. 5–56 Night sky can be used to show a building under different lighting conditions. Light emanating from the building emphasizes its openings. In this example, the contrast between the open and solid portions of the building is emphasized. (*Ricardo Khan, NJIT*)

Fig. 5–57 Ground plane rendered with a variety of materials including grass, trees, and concrete pavers (*Elli Shani, NJIT*)

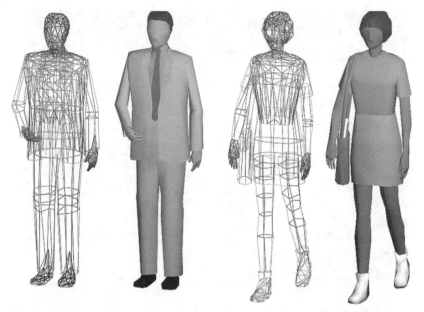

Fig. 5–58 People can be added to electronic images with digital two-dimensional clip art and three-dimensional models. (*Human models by people for people software—copyright © 1993 people for people.*)

Fig. 5–59 Image puts three-dimensional people in the model for scale clues. The size of the people gives viewers an idea of the size of the space. (*Elli Shani, NJIT*)

5.6.4 People and Cars

People and cars have value in a drawing in providing scale and for exploring, in drawing form, what a place might be like when used. People and cars can help give a sense of life to the place being rendered. Buildings and spaces can have very different qualities when filled with activity than when empty.

When one is drawing with traditional media, the people and automobiles should be drawn and constructed as any other element. Breaking down the object or person into smaller geometric components (rectangular blocks, spheres, etc.) and then subdividing it into as many elements as needed to add detail provides an efficient way of drawing the entourage. Provide only as much detail as needed to enhance the drawing. In addition to drawing original figures, people (and pets and cars) can be added to traditional renderings by tracing photographs and by collage (cut and paste).

When one is drawing electronically, cars and people can be created in much the same way that one constructs any three-dimensional model. After a few cars or people are constructed, they can be repeated and modified slightly in order to increase their density. Newly constructed elements can be saved as separate files and reused in other models at a later date. A number of programs have premade symbols of cars and people that can be placed directly into the model (Fig. 5–58). Three-dimensional models of specific cars and different people can also be purchased from companies that specialize in creating digital elements of entourage in file formats that are readable by most application programs. Care must always be taken to avoid overloading a model with additional elements that can result in too large a file to reasonably manipulate or render.

When it is not desirable or possible to add cars or people directly to the model before rendering, two-dimensional people and cars can be added to the raster image by using paint programs to create the image, or by scanning and superimposing the desired pictures (Fig. 5–59).

All renderings benefit from careful planning and thought. The composition of the rendering must work with the subject matter, media used, and drawing style when creating a rendering (Box 5–E). Eventually, architects and designers develop a drawing or rendering style with which they are comfortable. Whether renderings are created with one medium or multiple media, the potential for variety and personal expression while creating images that communicate is limitless.

Box 5–E

ENTOURAGE AND COMPOSITIONAL ELEMENTS

- Drawings can often be divided into foreground, midground, and background for compositional development. The focal point, or object that commands the most visual attention, is generally found in the midground area.

- Careful placement of the main object(s) is important in order to direct attention to the desired location. Typical placement may be just below or above the middle of the sheet or screen, or very high or very low for purposeful contrast. (Note that these are only rough guidelines and may be changed at any time for expressive purposes and to better communicate the intended message of the designer.) Care should be taken so that foreground elements do not unintentionally obscure important objects in the midground.

- Elements in renderings, especially in the foreground, can be used to visually lead an observer into a scene. Often, an image can be successful in engaging the viewer when the observer is led into it from the lower left corner.

- Entourage can give visual interest to objects in particular, and entire drawings in general. Because entourage often consists of elements of familiar size (such as people), it can give scale to a drawing.

- Framing devices that either start in, or are found entirely within the foreground (trees and shrubs, people, sides of buildings or rooms, etc.), on the right and left can balance a composition and focus attention on the important part of the drawing. Framing devices can also have a way of making an observer feel part of a scene, as if one is standing at a place and looking toward a building.

- Depth cues may be given with line weight and tonal value. When the background is further away, lighter values in line weight or shading may be used. When rendering digitally, some programs allow the placement of "fog" or "haze," which, if judiciously employed, can simulate depth as well as provide atmosphere or mood.

REVIEW QUESTIONS

1. What are *renderings* and why are they created?

2. What are the purposes of drawing an *elevation* for presentation?

3. Describe *anti-aliasing*.

4. Under what conditions would landscape be *ghosted* in a rendering?

5. What are the variables that affect *shadows?*

6. How can *materials* be represented in a rendering without photo-realistic color?

7. In what ways can *glass* be rendered?

8. What is *bump mapping?*

9. What types of materials are best rendered with *radiosity;* with *ray tracing?*

10. Why does the presence of *people* often help a rendering?

PRACTICE EXERCISES

1. Draw two rendered site plans of the building in which you live. The first should be black and white in ink on drafting film. The second rendering should be in color and approach photo-realism. The site plan should show surrounding materials and landscaping.

2. Construct and draw shadows for the building in the site plan in exercise #1.

3. Draw a representation of an 8' cube. Render an eye-level perspective of the cube (in sunlight) as (a) brick, (b) covered with wood clapboard siding, and (c) stucco.

4. Render two of the perspectives drawn of the house for the earlier exercises. The first rendering should be in black and white only and the second in color.

5. Capture a hidden wireframe image of the house (interior or exterior) and create a painted image with paint software.

6 IMAGE PROCESSING AND PRESENTATION

The post-processing of images and their components is an important step in creating coherent and compelling presentations. Parts of images can be combined to make new images, and entire images can be combined to make presentations in any medium (Fig. 6–1). Images and presentations themselves can be modified, or processed, in order to improve their effectiveness in communication.

Image processing in the context of CAD/graphics is the changing of a raster, or bit-mapped, image by applying a variety of operations and filters to the image, which may include tone and value, brightness and contrast, sharpness and softness, color balance modification, and so on. Image processing software operates on raster images and creates new raster images.

Fig. 6–1 Two rendered images of a model taken from approximately the same viewpoint are combined in a presentation to illustrate a before-and-after scenario with a proposed addition. (*Original house designed by Fernau and Hartman. Model and proposed addition by Kim DeFreitas, NJIT.*)

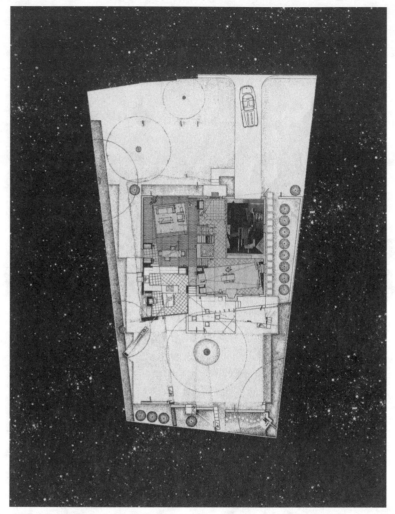

Fig. 6–2 Building plan and collage. Image is collaged onto plan, which is, in turn, collaged onto its background.   (*Jeffrey Hildner, Architect*)

Image processing can be applied to either painted or rendered files. Furthermore, after filters are applied, painting operations can be then applied (or applied again) to the processed image. (Raster files, once created, cannot be transferred back to the model for rendering.) Image processing software is also frequently used to prepare bit-mapped images for printing or other output.

6.1 CUT AND PASTE

The principle of cutting something out from one place, and pasting or inserting it into another, is used in both traditional and digital media to edit and enhance drawings. Errors can be corrected with cut and paste. Elements can be duplicated with cut and paste. Collages, by definition, are created by pasting together pieces created independently and/or found elsewhere.

6.1.1 Traditional Cut and Paste

Scissors and Glue

The process of cutting and pasting can be performed as simply as the words imply. Scissors or art knives (X-Acto® knives) can be used to cut portions of images, which can then be glued to another drawing (Fig. 6–2). Depending on the media employed, and taking into account possible interaction with inks, various adhesives are used (Box 6–A). Available are temporary and repositioning adhesives that may be used when composition needs to accommodate changes.

Care should be taken with the application of glues. Too much glue can leave bubbles in the paper being glued. Excess glue can leak out of the sides of a pasted drawing and compromise the overall appearance. Insufficient glue can result in portions of the image falling off or corners lifting and being bent during handling.

When paste-up originals are being created for the purpose of photocopying, it may be acceptable to be very light with the adhesive if one can be sure that care will be taken with the originals. The brightness-darkness controls on a photocopy machine must be adjusted to minimize the printing of the unwanted edges of a cut piece. Collaged originals usually are unsuitable for automatic document feed copiers and should be handled one at a time.

Multiple Drawings or Images

Small drawings or prints are often arranged and glued onto stiff boards for presentation to public groups and for submission to design competitions.

Pieces of images may be composed in a variety of ways, including the superimposition of small images over larger ones, to add interest to a presentation and to graphically convey a message. The larger image can function as a piece of graphic art that helps to express the designer's intent, and it can also serve as a unifying

---

Box 6–A

ADHESIVES FOR CUT AND PASTE

Rubber cement
- Effective for mounting opaque images onto board or paper.
- Excess glue cleaned with rubber cement pickup.
- Excess glue can damage some inks and the face of photographs.
- Pressure sensitive.
- Light application can allow for some repositioning.
- Very strong long-term adhesive can be gotten by placing light applications of cement on each surface, allowing to dry until tacky, and pressing together carefully.
- Rubber cement thinner can be used to thin cement to desired consistency and to release the bond of rubber cement.

Glue sticks
- Dry adhesive suitable for short-term mounting of photographs or paper.
- Color or clear—both dry clear. The visibility of the color adhesive helps in positioning the paper.
- Repositionable.

Spray adhesive contact cement
- Aerosol spray. Area of application should be ventilated. *Pay attention to directions and warning labels on can.*
- Good for adhering photos or prints to presentation board. Application of glue is smooth.
- Very sticky. Nonrepositionable glue adheres permanently on contact. Cannot remove without damaging original artwork. Even repositionable glue is sticky and requires very light application.
- Can be difficult to control during application. Surrounding area should be protected from damage!
- Can be flammable and must be used with caution.

White craft glue
- Suitable for cardboard models but *not* for paper or photographs. (Paper can become wrinkled.)
- Shrinks when drying.
- Cleans up with water when wet.

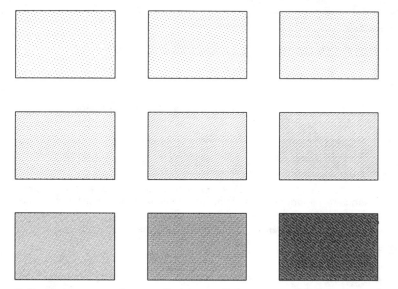

Fig. 6–3 Dot screens for applied tone. Screens are made up purely of black and white (often used for ease of reproduction) rather than continuous tones.

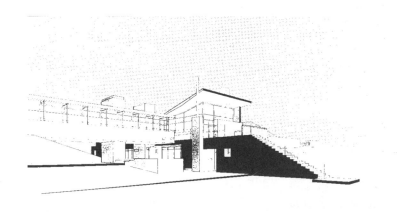

Fig. 6–4 Dot screen tone applied to line drawing perspective (*Buckingham residence, Resolution: 4 Architecture. Joseph Tanney, Gary Shoemaker, Robert Luntz; Partners.*)

technique. Another example of useful large-and-small juxtaposition is to superimpose details drawn at a large scale on top of something drawn at a smaller scale. The two different scales can illustrate the relation between the detail and the overall project.

Adhesive-Backed Appliqué

Images, patterns, and tone (grayscale, single color, and color gradient) can be applied to drawings with adhesive-backed appliqué. Dot screens at various densities, and patterns made up of lines, hatching, or shapes can be added to any printed composition (Figs. 6–3, 6–4). Many patterns and screens are commercially available on the appliqué. It is also very easy to create one's own supply of patterns and screens with a drawing program and laser printer. Blank sheets of appliqué are available that are suitable for the high heat applications of both photocopiers and printers.

6.1.2 Digital Cut and Paste

Selection and Placement

There are a number of processes for dragging images or parts of images from one file to another. When one is combining two separate images, it may be easiest to start a new file, select each image one at a time, copy it, and paste it into the new files. (This process maintains both the original image and the new one as independent entities; otherwise, the original file is replaced.) Alternatively, if software supported, one can select (with any of the methods previously mentioned) a portion of the image with the mouse, and literally drag the piece from one window into another. The ability to drag pieces as an automatic copy ("clone") and drag, rather than cut and drag, is user definable in some applications. Although the copying and dragging is, in theory, applicable to any type of software program, it is most common with image processing and word processing software. (Three-dimensional models generally have more parameters involved and require selecting and merging while keeping track of size, orientation, and origin.)

When dragging one part of an image onto another, the selected element can be modified prior to final pasting onto the original. When one is dealing with single-layer raster applications, the new composite image becomes that which can be modified. Parts of images may also be cut and moved within the limits of the original image (Fig. 6–5).

Layers

In some instances, raster applications support layers. There are two common ways for layers to be created and manipulated (Box 6–B). Although the resulting final image is independent of the way layers are created, the data structure may affect the ability of some systems to efficiently handle information and it can affect the extent to which an image may be modified.

Fig. 6–5 Painting of digital model moved and skewed to represent a paste-up of facades in order to communicate the distinction between new facades and ghosted buildings behind. Each piece of the image was individually selected by drawing an outline around it with a selection tool and then moved and/or cut out. (*Michael Buldo, NJIT*)

Box 6–B

LAYERS IN RASTER IMAGES—TWO TYPES

- Each layer represents an entire image at the specified resolution. In those instances in which nothing is drawn, the pixels are defined as transparent. File sizes are relatively large and may require an extensive amount of RAM for image manipulation.

- The program maintains information about objects rather than entire planes of color. When the history of the object being created is maintained, it may be possible to go back to any specific point in the image creation process to modify the object. Because data are stored on an object-by-object basis, file size can be significantly smaller than that of other file structures.

Fig. 6–6 Image sampling. Two images made up completely of pieces of the same scanned images taken from various sources. The buildings and sites are both examples of image sampling. There is *no* three-dimensional model or associated data. (*Lori Ryder and Ana Aznar, NJIT*)

Once saved as a generic painted raster image, however, the objects and layers may be collapsed to a standard bit-mapped image and lose all associated data that would allow a return to a multilayered, or multi-object, state.

The names of objects or selected elements vary with each application. Some packages require the saving of the selected elements as separate files or *clippings*. Other packages do not require the saving of discrete elements at all and allow them to be dragged from one window to another.

Image Sampling

Scanners provide designers with a virtually infinite palette of pieces of images to manipulate (Boxes 6–C, 6–D). "Analogous to music sampling, in which sounds from the environment are recorded, distorted, and used in unique ways to create music, 'image sampling' is the visual equivalent of a sound bite used to create new visual forms, textures, patterns, and types of architecture."* The digital scanning process reduces everything to dots of color, equally editable by the designer. It is, in fact, possible to combine and distort pieces of great architecture and other fragments and recombine them into new buildings, or textures out of which new expressions can be developed (Fig. 6–6). When designers use this technique in the design process, they can collage or sample building types to see if a particular design direction is worth exploring in depth.

*Goldman, G., and M. S. Zdepski. 1990. Image sampling. In J. P. Jordan (ed.), Proceedings of the Association for Computer Aided Design in Architecure 10th Annual Conference: From Research to Practice, pp. 21-28.

Box 6–C

TIPS FOR SCANNING

- Use the best original glossy photograph possible for scanning. A clear, crisp original will scan best. (Scratches, folds, and dirt all show up on scans.)

- Select appropriate resolution for scans—know the purpose of the image. Screen resolutions are generally less than 100 dots per inch. Laser printers will print 60 to 100 lines per inch, and scanning at 150 dpi is usually sufficient. Rule of thumb is to scan at a resolution twice that required by the output path. (Note: Although printers are described in dots-per-inch resolution, the actual printing can be measured in line frequency per inch, and the scanning rule of thumb is based on that number.)
  - Scanning at too low a resolution, or at a size too small, will result in poor image quality with visible pixelization.
  - Scanning at too high a resolution will result in overly large files that will take longer to manipulate and require extra memory to print. Images on screen may not display all of the information in the file, which makes modification less precise unless zooming in.

- High resolution is important when scanning line drawings (like existing architectural drawings) that will be converted to vector files. The smoother the lines, the more likely the accurate translation, and the closer the bit-mapped image will look like the original.

- Scans used as a base for additional CAD/graphics work can be scanned at screen resolution if that is consistent with the intended model and rendering resolutions.

- Images scanned as halftones (black and white pixels only, grouped in order to give the appearance of gray) have smaller files than images scanned as grayscale photographs. Halftone images, however, cannot be modified with many of the filters and effects available with image processing software.

- Scanning halftones (like newspaper photos) can result in moiré patterns on the scan. "Remove moiré" commands in some scanning software reduce—but rarely eliminate—the problem. Post-scanning work will be required to make the image acceptable for printing.

Box 6–D

TIPS FOR CREATING PHOTO COMPOSITES

Photo composites can be useful in creating background images over which architectural proposals (either sketches or rendered three-dimensional models) can be placed in order to previsualize a design in context. Images (photographs or a combination of photographs and original artwork) may also be combined into a collage as part of a project presentation or graphic composition. Photo composites are particularly useful in stitching together photographs for a panoramic site view.

1. Scan and adjust (focus, color balance, brightness and contrast, tone, etc.) photographs as necessary. Save each scan as a separate file for archival purposes.

2. Import scanned images into a drawing or illustration program capable of maintaining bit-mapped layers.

3. Carefully reposition photographs to their desired positions. Take care to match seams of position-critical elements as closely as possible. Make sure the layers are in the correct order, front to back, for the final image. (If the image looks right on screen, then the layers are in an acceptable order.)

4. As a backup, save the image in the program's native (program-specific) file format that will preserve the layers.

5. Depending on the program, either export or save as a single-layer raster file that does not contain layers and is not program specific (e.g., TGA, TIF, PCX, or PICT). This new file is a single raster image with the photos in the right location and matched appropriately.

6. Open the new file in a paint program that allows individual pixel editing to eliminate undesired seams or matchlines. After adjustment, the new composite image should be saved as a new file so that it can be reused with different superimposed alternative proposals.

7. A copy of the new image may be used within the paint program—or it may be used as a single layer within the original illustration program, with new proposals being treated as new layers.

One of the most common uses of digital cut and paste in architectural imaging is the insertion of a three-dimensional model of a building into a site photograph (Fig. 6–7). Once the model is rendered at an appropriate perspective view, it can be saved and then superimposed—just like any other raster image or object—onto a scanned photograph of a site.

Image processing in architectural drawing is particularly important in superimposing proposed buildings onto scanned photographs of existing sites. Image processing can be used to adjust the relative clarity of background and superimposed objects in order to maintain a consistent level of abstraction of the image, thereby focusing attention on the subject of the image rather than on the image itself. The ability to previsualize a project in a photo-realistic manner may prevent architectural mistakes from being built.

Because almost anything is visually possible, the burden of evaluation is heavy on the designer. Unbuildable concepts can be made to appear photo-realistic. Sites that do not exist can be made to appear as if they do (Fig. 6–8). Textures that are based on almost any source can become the inspiration for new buildings. Nevertheless, if one is not conscious of the process, it may be easy to lose sight of what is logical, or what makes sense, and get lost in the image.

Fig. 6–7 Building superimposed onto site photograph. Shadows added in paint program. (*Michael Hoon, NJIT*)

Fig. 6–8 Image processing in action. Studies of focal point, site, and scale are made with a scanned photograph of the village of Silwan and image processing software. (*Amado Batour, NJIT*)

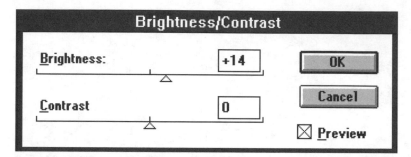

Fig. 6–9 Slider controls adjusting percentages for brightness and contrast. Previews are full size on image. (*Adobe Photoshop by Adobe Systems, Inc.*)

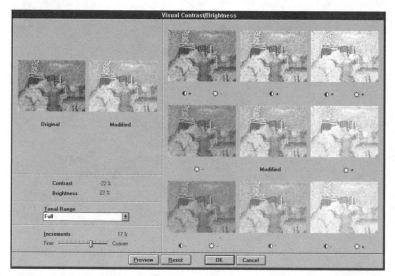

Fig. 6–10 Visual controls showing relative options for brightness (sun icon) and contrast (split black and white circle). Increment slider determines how big the jump is between options. (*Picture Publisher by Micrografx*)

6.2 IMAGE FILTERING

One of the fastest methods of changing a digital image is by filtering it. Digital filters change the appearance of an image in much the way that photographic filters do. One applies an effect (mosaics, swirls, blurs, bumps, and lumps, to name a few) when filtering an image. Unlike physical filters, which are used to purify or cleanse a substance by acting as a strainer and removing material, a digital filter can add to, as well as take away from, an image. Filters can be applied globally (to an entire image), or to a user-selected area. Images created by automatic rendering processes can be improved dramatically with the application of various filters. *One should not assume that a rendering is complete based solely on the original assignment of light and materials.* Clarity of image and fidelity of color often can be improved with additional work. Although many filters can be used (only) to provide visual interest to a presentation, there are some that, due to the nature of the images architects and designers create, are extremely important and used repeatedly.

6.2.1 Brightness and Contrast

Brightness and contrast can be adjusted in painting and image processing software by numeric percentage and/or interactively with slider bars or arrows, visual thumbnail previews, and so on (Figs. 6–9 through 6–12).

Brightness

Brightness adjustment is often used for three different purposes in the architectural design and presentation processes. First, brightness is increased to compensate for poor or low-quality scans. In addition to having faulty color balance, scanned images are sometimes darker than the originals. Second, brightness can be applied as a filter to lighten or darken a composition and is used as one of the graphic tools available to the designer. Third, depending on the output device, brightness may have to be adjusted prior to color printing. When the monitor and output device are not precisely calibrated to conform to one another, test prints often show that the level of brightness is out of alignment with the image on the screen. In laboratory, design studio, and/or network situations with more than one color output device (as well as work being done on different computers), complete synchronization can be very difficult to maintain. Brightness may need to be adjusted prior to printing. Color wax thermal printers, in particular, may occasionally print darker than one expects.

It may be helpful to remember that screen images generally look brighter than printed images because the monitor is light *emitting*, whereas a printed image is visible because it is light *absorbing* and *reflecting*.

In those instances in which brightness is adjusted for printing, the adjusted file should be saved only if one expects to print more copies from the same printer. Furthermore, the file should be saved as a new file while

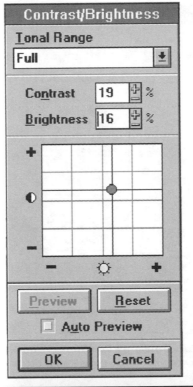

Fig. 6–11 Additional interfaces used to adjust contrast and brightness. Joystick (*on left*) is moved by mouse to adjust numeric values. (*Picture Publisher by Micrografx*)

Fig. 6–12 "What if" scenarios are played out with this interface, used as a plug-in filter with image processing programs. (*KPT Convolver™ by MetaTools, Inc.*)

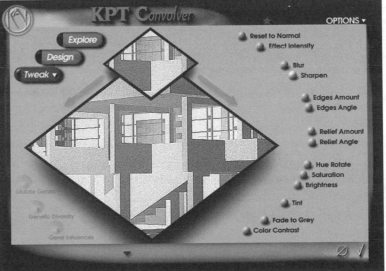

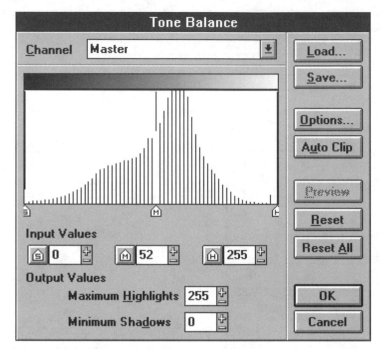

Fig. 6–13 Tone adjustment graph (*Picture Publisher by Micrografx*)

Images in *Figure 6–14* represent the subtle adjustments required to improve a rendering. The top image is raw—fresh from the rendering software. The bottom image is modified in the following ways:

- Wires at the top of the image added after they were lost during rendering

- Tone adjusted to include more white

- Highlights increased 10% in brightness
  Midtones increased 5% in brightness
  Shadows decreased 5% in brightness
  Overall brightness increased 10%
  Overall contrast increased 5%

- Unsharp mask applied (see section 6.2.2)

maintaining the original, base image. If the brightness adjustment is for the one-time printing application, it may not need to be retained.

Image processing applications may allow separate brightness adjustment of the darkest range of pixels ("shadows"), the lightest range of pixels ("highlights"), and the middle level ("midtones").

Borrowing from photography, some paint and image processing applications also provide **dodge** and **burn** tools. Used like a pencil or brush applied with mouse or cursor, the dodge command progressively lightens an area and the burn command darkens it. The brightness command usually functions as a filter and is applied over an entire selected area.

Tone

Correction of tone provides another method by which one can modify the apparent lightness of an image through adjustment of the pixel range of values toward black or white (Fig. 6–13). In other words, if the image is too dark (i.e., has too many dark tones), its range of values can be reset to include more white. Conversely, if the range has too much white (or not enough black), the image may appear cloudy. The result of tone modification should be an image that seems to be correctly exposed rather than one that is underexposed or overexposed. Tonal correction is used not only on scanned photographs but also on rendered images to further enhance the detail available (Fig. 6–14). Note that automatic tonal correction commands may not always give the most favorable results. The degree to which tone may be corrected is software specific. When tone is modified, it should be visually evaluated after each change to determine if the image has been improved or not.

Contrast

Contrast controls are usually found within the same menu or command group as brightness controls. Increase of contrast can make an image look sharper and more dramatic, but it may also remove some of the more subtle details that have been rendered. Very light tones may get washed out to white when the contrast is too high. Conversely, when the contrast is reduced too much, detail can also be lost if the entire image takes on a muddy or cloudy look. A common mistake is to increase contrast to the same degree as brightness when adjusting an image. The wide variety of images architects create makes it virtually impossible to establish an effective rule of thumb for the relation between brightness and contrast. As with most filters, contrast adjustment should be made in small increments, with each step being judged.

Fig. 6–14 Images before (*top*) and after (*bottom*) post-rendering processes (*Original model by David Boyle, NJIT*)

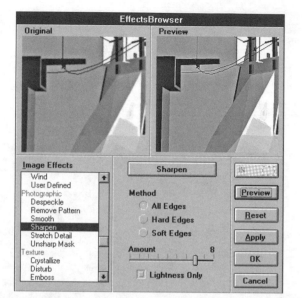

Fig. 6–15   Interface for sharpening filter   (*Picture Publisher by Micrografx*)

Fig. 6–16   Image after sharpening has been applied. Notice the effect of excessive sharpening on thin lines.

Gamma

Modification of gamma levels changes the apparent brightness level of the middle range of an image. Its effect is influenced by the overall tonal range of pixels. The impact of gamma adjustment may be similar to that of tonal modification or brightness adjustment. When available, the command is often found in the same subset of menus as brightness and contrast.

There is often overlap between different commands, and similar end results on an image can frequently be achieved through a variety of paths.

6.2.2 Focusing

Focusing an image involves the sharpening or softening of an image's appearance.

Sharpening

Sharpening filters are most commonly used for enhancing images created by automatic rendering programs (Fig. 6–15). Although fully ray traced images can be sharp, not all renderings utilize ray tracing. When the shading method used does not create crisp edges or shadows, the image may be able to be improved with sharpening. The sharpen command creates a greater definition of, and contrast between, the edges of forms, and a greater contrast between areas of different color. Sharpening can also be used to improve poor scans or the scans of slightly out of focus originals. Excessive sharpening can create a harsh image with too much contrast between pixels that can distort the image and distract the observer to the point that the original design message is overshadowed (Fig. 6–16). In scanned images, excessive sharpening can also highlight stray pixels that were not immediately obvious from poor-quality scans or scans of dirty originals. In most cases, **edge enhancement** sharpens an image only along edges where there are distinct color changes, resulting in clearer (albeit harsher) definition. Some software accomplishes edge enhancement by increasing contrast between those pixels found along edges; in some programs, this process is activated by an "unsharpen mask" command. This filter is particularly useful after rendering a model because it can leave some of the more subtle tones alone while giving greater clarity to the architectural form.

Softening

Softening and blur commands reduce the contrast at edges and between colors or shades of gray. The commands can be used to improve scans of printed photographs and to correct overly harsh images.

Softening and blurring of an image can be used to create special effects. **Motion blur** or **wind** can be used to simulate the movement of an object (Fig. 6–17). Although this is relatively important in many applications of graphic design, it is less so in architecture or interior design. Most buildings (other than windmills) do

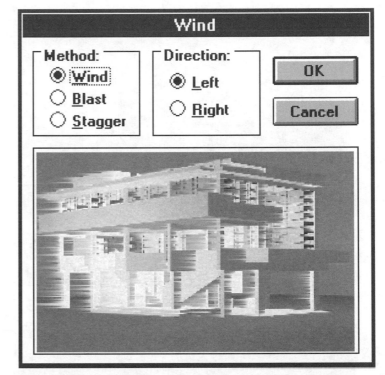

Fig. 6–17 Wind or motion blur can be applied to any image. Although an important filter when simulating movement—especially rapid movement—its use is greatly limited in an architectural context. (*Adobe Photoshop by Adobe Systems, Inc.*)

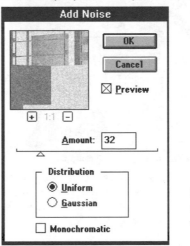

Fig. 6–18 Interface used to add noise to any image (*Adobe Photoshop by Adobe Systems, Inc.*)

257

Fig. 6–19 Addition of noise applied (to the entire image).

Fig. 6–20 Mosaic filter. Although many filters are available, it is not always clear that they should be applied. Special effects useful to graphic artists may or may not be appropriate in an architectural context. *(Filter from Adobe Gallery Effects by Adobe Systems, Inc.)*

not move perceptibly to the extent that we want to exaggerate it in an image. Motion blur may be useful to enhance part of the entourage in a rendering—as long as it does not overpower the message of the image. Motion blur is most useful in an architectural context when creating an animation.

6.2.3 Texturing or Graining

The addition of **visual texture** (sometimes called **noise** or **film grain**—because of its important use in photocompositing in the film and motion picture industry) adds visual noise to the image (Figs. 6–18, 6–19). As stated in chapter 5, the addition of noise is sometimes a good way to equalize the levels of abstraction within an image composed of areas with varying detail and is therefore used frequently in architectural rendering. When adding noise, the application randomly creates pixels of different colors (or levels of gray). The total amount of noise, the degree to which any pixel may vary from its original color, and the distribution of the noise are often user defined. The addition of noise can result in an image with the appearance of greater detail than is actually present.

The texture of an image can also be changed by using **pixelization** and **mosaic** filters (Fig. 6–20). Both filters result in more blocklike images. Pixels are combined into blocks of like color or value within a user-determined tolerance range. The value of these filters is primarily graphic.

Posterization of an image reduces the number of colors or levels of gray in that image to a user-specified number (Figs. 6–21, 6–22). When an image (especially one from the schematic design phase) appears to have more detail than a designer wants, posterization can be used to reduce a full-color, photo-realistic image to one that is more abstract. It can be used to make an image look more stark, or dramatic. Because architects may use output devices with fewer colors than are available on their computer, posterization may be used to see how a full-color image could appear if printed with fewer colors.

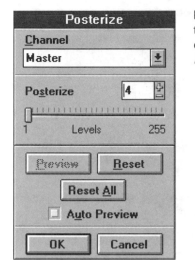

Fig. 6–21 Slide control interface for posterization. Number of levels may be entered directly or through slider bar. (*Adobe Photoshop by Adobe Systems, Inc.*)

6.2.4 Washing, Tinting, and Color Balance

Washing or tinting with traditional media usually means either to go over an existing drawing with another transparent color (typically with watercolor) or to overlay a transparent colored sheet of adhesive-backed appliqué cut to size.

Digitally, it is possible to change the color of an image with only one or two commands. A "wash" or "stain" command functions exactly as its traditional counterpart. Color and level of transparency are user determined. (Note: In order to preserve traditionally created originals, it is sometimes efficient to scan a drawing or rendering and then adjust its color after the image has been translated into digital format rather than to actually apply the appliqué.)

Fig. 6–22 Posterized image reduced from 256 levels of gray to 6. A common application is to reduce millions of colors to lower numbers to accommodate printers and/or older graphics cards, as well as to generate special effects.

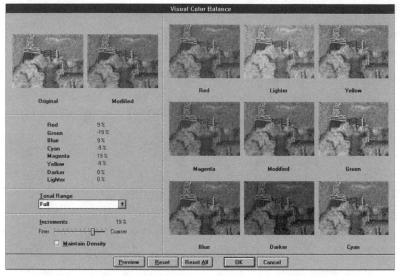

Fig. 6–23 Color balance interface (*Picture Publisher by Micrografx*)

Fig. 6–24 Digital simulation of watercolor (*Michael Buldo, NJIT*)

Most image processing applications allow for a change in the color balance (Fig. 6–23). Although the user interface may vary, the essence is the same. One can split a color image into its three components (red, green, and blue channels) and adjust each one independently and interactively. Alternatively, one can simply shift the entire selected area with all three channels simultaneously by picking the color toward which the shift must be made. For example, it is not uncommon for some slide scanners to impart a blue-green tint to the image. By changing the color balance toward red-orange, the user can adjust the image to more accurately reflect the original.

Color balance can be adjusted to make a scanned photo better than the original. Site photographs taken in inclement weather can be modified to reflect more pleasant conditions that might better describe the nature of an architectural proposal. Again, however, care should be taken to avoid deliberate misrepresentation and not to distort reality and present a situation that would not occur.

6.3 FAKING IT

Computers are extraordinarily useful as tools for making something look as if it had been created with another medium (Fig. 6–24) or by another artist. Images created with computer need not all look alike. Although there are clearly some image types—like the wireframe—that imply that they were developed on a computer, the possibilities for variety are almost endless. (Note that it is also a relatively simple task to create a wireframe drawing with pen or pencil.)

It is worthwhile to ask *why* one would want to simulate one medium with another rather than create an original with whatever medium is desired. Time, money, and flexibility are reasons often cited for medium selection and simulation. When an investment is made in developing expertise in a particular medium, or when there are capital expenses in purchasing supplies or equipment, it is logical to get as much use as possible from the investment. When a particular look or style is desired in a presentation—for whatever reason—it is nice to have options for the way in which the image is created and at what point in the design process the selection is made (Figs. 6–25 through 6–27).

6.3.1 Simulating Alternate Media with Computers

Computers are valuable for simulation of alternate media. The variety of editing and modification tools provides a breadth of flexibility not easily found elsewhere. It may be helpful, for example, to create an image that *looks* like an ink drawing and yet to be able to adjust contrast or brightness, add color, twist the image, modify the texture of the "paper" on which the drawing appears to have been drawn, and so on without destroying the original drawing or model. The decision to use a particular presentation style or medium may be made after a model is created. Although this may remove

Fig. 6–25 Graphic pen filter is effective at giving a hand-drawn look (although the precision with which the strokes align is fairly mechanical). The processing can provide an image that communicates the nature of the building without being photo-realistic (and without time being spent assigning particular materials, mapping types, and so on). Of particular interest to architects and designers is the fact that an effective rendering is created that is completely black and white (no gray) and that is easy to reproduce with many inexpensive and common techniques.

Fig. 6–26 Graphic pen options with stroke direction and density changed (*Images generated with Adobe Gallery Effects by Adobe Systems, Inc.*)

Fig. 6–27 Two computer-drawn elevations. The bottom image is modified to simulate freehand pen drawing. The degree of waviness is selected by the user. The freehand look can provide a more informal drawing, or simply a personal touch. As noted earlier, a freehand look may be useful when one wants to focus attention on the overall character of a proposal, or when one does not want to convey the impression that the project is completely finished. (*Created by Richard Jones, NJIT, with AutoCAD by Autodesk, Inc. and Squiggle™ by Insight Development Corporation*)

some of the beneficial influences and limitations a medium may have on its image and associated design, it frees the designer from having to always make sequential decisions during the design and presentation processes. More options may be kept open for longer periods.

Physical Models

Chipboard and foamcore are used by architects to create physical, three-dimensional study models of architectural proposals. The ability to look inside a model and test ideas in physical form is invaluable. Mock-ups of buildings, landscape, and furniture can all be built.

There are times, however, when a digital three-dimensional model may serve a designer's purpose (Figs. 6–28, 6–29). The contours of a site can be created digitally in a manner that mimics cardboard or cork (as shown in Example 2–3). Buildings, interiors, and landscape material can all be on separate layers or created as individual objects to facilitate shading and rendering. A plain gray-brown color or material can be assigned to the entire model prior to rendering. If the model has both existing and new construction on it, the existing buildings can be rendered in the same chipboard color, with the new one(s) rendered in white (Fig. 6–30). The rendered image will look like a chipboard model.

If desired, one can assign various materials or colors to a schematic model in anticipation of future design

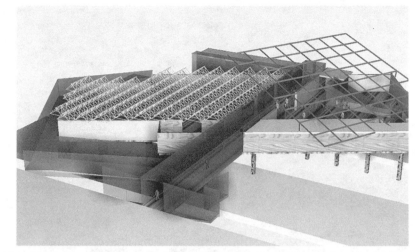

Fig. 6–28 Digitally simulated model with elements rendered at a large scale (*Jeff Brockmeyer, NJIT*)

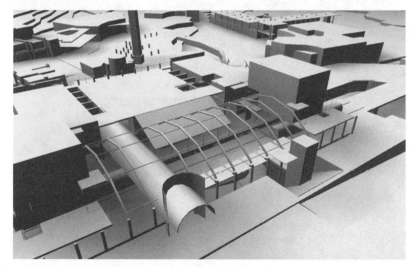

Fig. 6–29 Simulated cardboard model with all components at the same level of resolution and detail. Material can be rendered in a flat cardboard color, or if in color (default colors or otherwise selected), it may be converted to grayscale and then converted back to full color. After the two conversions, one has a gray model that is capable of being rendered in color. By either staining or washing the image with a sepia color, or by globally adjusting the color balance, a cardboard color can be applied to the model. (*Elli Shani, NJIT*)

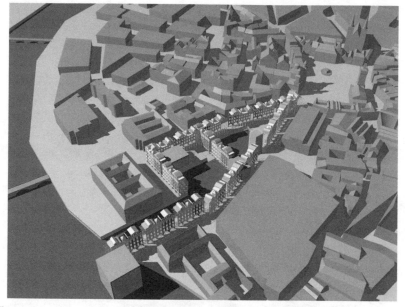

Fig. 6–30 Site model rendered monochromatically with design proposal rendered in greater detail than the simulated cardboard model (*Sean McCarry, NJIT*)

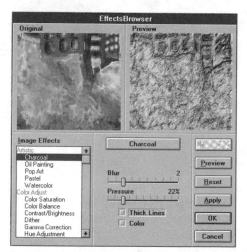

Fig. 6–31 Artistic effects, or those created by other media (in this case, charcoal), can be globally applied with filters. (*Picture Publisher by Micrografx*)

development. If desired, a full-color rendering of an interim design model can be modified with image processing software to simulate both color and level of detail of a cardboard model. The monochromatic model can be used when one wants to communicate information about form and organization rather than material or color.

The creation of the electronic model allows easy modification and "cutting" while maintaining the integrity of the original. Rather than cutting up and rebuilding a physical model, the same level of abstraction (at least from a "distance") can be achieved with multiple digital originals. The ability to easily manipulate contours electronically can remove some of the inhibition a designer may have in manipulating the ground plane during the design process. The fact that the model can be made to look like a traditional physical one reinforces a familiar level of abstraction that can remove the focus from either the detail of the model or the medium with which it was made.

Two-Dimensional Traditional Media

Many different traditional media can be simulated by paint and image processing software. In one instance, rendered models or paintings can be filtered with a particular medium in mind. For example, a rendering can be "converted" to a charcoal image (Fig. 6–31). Variables such as stroke length, angle, paper type, and color are all user selected prior to filter application.

Additional filters available include stained glass, color pencil, chalk, and crayon (Fig. 6–32). Alternatively, global filters may be applied *after* the rendering has been completed and enhanced.

Prior to rendering, one can create painted images using a computer to simulate alternate media (Fig. 6–33). One can either start from scratch or grab a wireframe image of a model as the guide for painting. Software painting packages are available that allow the mouse or cursor to paint in a manner that mimics oil, watercolor, crayon, color pencil, and so on. The creation of a simulation is exactly analogous to the creation of a traditional image. Depending on the medium being simulated, brush size and shape, color and transparency of media, paper grain and type, and so on are all adjustable. (It may even be possible to set the amount of material a "brush" can hold, and how quickly it will run out of paint on the digital paper.) Although a mouse can bc used to create these images, a pressure-sensitive stylus and pad may be easier (especially for artists trained in traditional media), and they more directly correlate to traditional methods. Speed of application and pressure of pen result in changes in density and size of an applied stroke.

6.3.2 Simulating Alternate Styles with Computers

Simulation of styles is not new in fine arts, industrial design, or architecture. It is possible, for example, to create oil paintings in the style of the great impressionists or other styles found within traditional media.

Fig. 6–32 Image processed with a charcoal and crayon filter

Fig. 6–33 Various strokes simulating chalk and pen (including calligraphic pen and leaky pen). Raster images are created directly with the brushes and simulated media.

VARIABLES IN BRUSH SELECTION IN DIGITAL PAINTING AND MEDIA SIMULATION

Media
- The selection of medium to simulate with each stroke. Common media available include charcoal, watercolor, crayon, chalk, pencil, felt tip marker, and oil.

Brush size
- The size of the applicator of color. The selection may be based on the number of pixels high and the number wide and/or by visual slider (with a relative scale rather than an absolute number of pixels).

Brush shape
- The geometric configuration of the brush. Circular brushes are universally available, but pointed brushes, flat brushes, diamond brushes, and so on are all useful and result in different strokes when combined with various angles.

Brush angle
- The implied angle of a brush during application of paint. Angle is particularly important when dealing with calligraphic pens and felt tip markers to simulate variable-sized strokes.

Spacing
- Spacing between application, or dabs, of paint along a line. Relative spacing is determined as a percentage of brush size; absolute spacing is determined directly by the number of pixels.

Opacity or transparency
- The degree to which paint is applied as a solid color (expressed as percentage of either opaque or transparent).

Bleed
- Controls the degree to which one color mixes into another color already applied. Especially important when simulating media like watercolor.

Texture or underlying grain
- The degree to which brush strokes reflect the assigned texture, or pattern, of the canvas or paper.

Smoothness
- The toggling on or off of filter that suppresses the harshness between adjacent pixels of different colors when strokes are applied. Automatic anti-aliasing as lines are applied.

Sensitivity
- Controls the degree to which speed and pressure influence the application of paint when using pressure-sensitive tablet and stylus.

Just as one can create one piece of art in the style of another, it is possible, within any electronic paint application that supports media simulation, to create an image that looks as if it were created in another style. To be successful, one must understand the way in which the digital brush can be manipulated (Box 6–E) and carefully study the style that is intended for simulation. The variables listed in Box 6–E may not be available in all software programs, and not all variables are listed. They are, however, useful variables when attempting to use computers to create images that mimic another medium or combination of media.

Pointillist style is, in some ways, one that has a direct correlation with digital media. The creation of images with dots of color is similar to the pixelization process. Zooming in and applying paint pixel by pixel, together with the careful use of airbrush or spray commands and the addition of noise, is a technique that can be used to create pointillist compositions.

It should be noted that there are application packages that will simulate brush strokes that mimic those of individual styles. Pointillist strokes are created of visually discrete multicolored dots. Impressionist strokes translate the continuous movement of the cursor to create the equivalent of shorter strokes of color. The styles may, in some applications, be named after important artists who painted in the particular style, such as Monet for impressionism or Seurat for pointillism.

A nonliteral, or "artistic," painting of an architectural proposal can be used as a method to help inspire or generate ideas during the design process, and/or to convey an architectural intent of the quality of a place that one hopes to achieve.

6.4 PRESENTATIONS

An important purpose of an architectural presentation is to clearly communicate ideas to people other than the designer (Box 6–F). The ideas must be presented in a clear graphic format that reflects the intent of the designer, as well as the thought and care that went into the project. In most cases, presentations should move from the general to the specific: starting from concept diagrams, moving to site plans, and all the way to detailed interiors. The presentation should illustrate how a project works and what it will be like.

6.4.1 Posted or Mounted Presentations

Drawings and images, whether created digitally or traditionally, often must be displayed or posted on walls or easels for presentation and evaluation. The posting of all drawings simultaneously allows an observer to make connections between different images and facilitates a more holistic evaluation of a project.

Composition of Individual Sheets

Borders on single-sheet presentations are discretionary and depend on the overall format of the presentation. When a single image appears on the sheet, a border helps frame the view in full size; but it may be distracting when photographically reduced for display, publication, or portfolio. Borders are useful in providing unity

---

Box 6–F

TIPS FOR ORGANIZING PRESENTATIONS

- Individual drawings, as well as groups of drawings, generally are read in the same direction as the language of the area in which the presentation is made (left to right in English-speaking countries). On occasion, presentations may be organized in other ways (including concentrically from the center out) that rely on the relative visual weights of the components of the drawings to make the intent clear.

- Attention can be diverted to the most detailed or most colorful portion of a presentation. When there is a graphic disparity within a presentation, it is critical that the center of attention be an important component. (If the graphic center of attention is not important, much of the accompanying verbal presentation may be spent trying to refocus the viewers.)

- Unless there are reasons otherwise, presentations often are organized from the most general (large-scale site plans) to the most specific (details, interior spaces, etc.).

- Diagrams explaining the organization of the project are often best placed at the beginning of a presentation. They set the framework for critics and observers to more easily understand the issues being presented. (The only drawback occurs in those instances in which the diagrams and project don't match. The focus may be diverted to discussing discrepancies.)

- Drawings should be labeled either with text or with small key plans to make clear to the viewer the exact context of a particular drawing or image.

- The project should always be shown in context: the building in its site, the space in its plan, and so on.

- Plans should be oriented in the same direction. One graphic convention dictates that north (or the side closest to north, called **project north**) should be at the top of the page. Alternatively, the entry to the space or building can be at the bottom. (Putting the entrance at the bottom allows the observer to visually enter the space and become engaged in the project, whereas putting the entry at the top leaves viewers feeling as if they are looking down from above.)

- Elevations may all be either oriented horizontally, or shown projected from, and around, the associated plan. (The method of projection works when dealing with interior elevations associated with a single floor plan. The projection method of presentation is less successful when showing an elevation that refers to multiple floors.)

- Although presentations may be made to people familiar with a project, it is usually wise to assume that there will be viewers who are not familiar with it. Graphic presentations often are accompanied by verbal ones, but there is rarely any disadvantage to having the visual presentation be self-explanatory and clear.

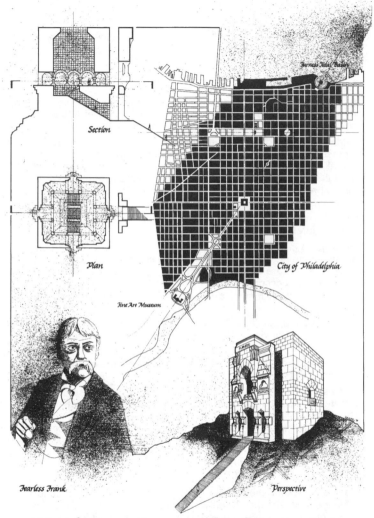

Section

Plan

Fine Art Museum

City of Philadelphia

Furness Tidal Basin

Fearless Frank

Perspective

Frank Furness Commemorative Monument

Fig. 6–34 Single-sheet composition (ink on drafting film). Implied border—including text on the bottom—bounds the composition. Building plan and section align. Image of architect aligns with primary axis of site plan labeled "City of Philadelphia." (*Kevin Havens, Iowa State University*)

if the image is to become part of a larger collection of separate drawings.

As with sequential presentations, all plans should be oriented in the same direction. (The two most common conventions are to orient plans with [1] the project north at the top of the page or [2] the entrance at the bottom so that observers feel as if they are entering the space, rather than looking "over the shoulder" from a distance.) Varying orientation within a presentation can confuse an observer unfamiliar with the project—especially if there is no accompanying verbal presentation.

There are two common ways of placing more than one drawing or image on a single sheet. The selection of the particular method is based on personal style and preference, as well as the media used. In the first way, there is no separation between the background sheet or mounting surface and the background of an image. This includes drawings created directly on the background surface (board, vellum, drafting film, etc.). Depending on the scale, one may compose a sheet of plans and elevations, paraline drawings, perspective views, and so on (Figs. 6–34, 6–35). Under certain circumstances, juxtaposition of details on a background of a more general image may be used as a method of organization for the presentation. The composition is governed by design intent, format, and clarity.

Visibly discrete images can also be placed on a mounting surface with a clear separation between the image and its background. Images created or printed

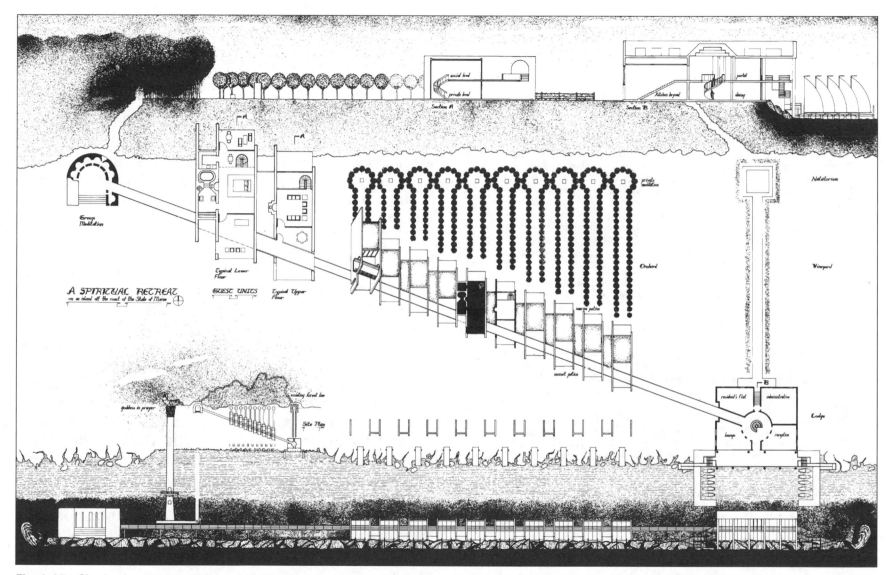

Fig. 6–35 Single-sheet composition relating sections, plans, and elevations. Horizontal elements define top and bottom, with diagonal areas in the middle, visually anchored at ends. (*Dale Gienapp, Iowa State University*)

TIPS FOR MULTIPLE-SHEET PRESENTATIONS

- All sheets or boards should be the same size and shape, and oriented in the same direction. Different shapes or sizes can distract from the actual work on the boards and focus attention on the shapes themselves.

- There should be some measure of consistency in the style of drawings or images. This does *not* mean that all drawings should be created in an identical style. On the contrary, one or two images of contrasting style(s) can be used to draw attention to important aspects of the presentation. Plans and paraline images may, for example, be executed as line drawings, with a series of rendered perspectives illustrating some of the qualitative elements of a proposal. However, there should be a limited palette of styles to be effective. If each image is in a different style, the presentation runs the risk of lacking any visual hierarchy. If every image type is different, the presentation will emphasize the difference in media or styles rather than the design intent of the project.

- An element of continuity (format, style, medium, borders, etc.) across multiple boards may be helpful.

- Organizing elements in a presentation may be orientation, shape of images, zones of color, background, color palettes, and so on.

- Text and titles can add continuity.

- Grids (implied or explicit) can be used to give cohesion and graphic organization.

- When a presentation is composed of sparse line drawings, printing the negative (white lines on black background) can be an effective technique to provide a sense of unity. (Negative prints can also be used in presentations meant to evoke the historical sense of traditional blueprints.)

- In order to maintain the clarity of the architectural message, the color of mounting boards should usually be neutral and not the focal point. Specific colors, however, may be selected when coordinated with the type and content of the presentation. For example, when producing a sample board (the overmounting of samples of materials and/or colors for a space or building) or creating a traditional drawing directly on illustration boards, the background color may be used to complement and enhance the palette selected. Nevertheless, when mounting discrete images onto a board, black *or* white is often the best choice.

There are always exceptions to rules. However, when violating the above guidelines, it is important to do so with intent—and not by accident—and to understand the possible consequences. The purpose(s) of the presentation must always be clear in order to organize it.

on a background of the same color as the mounting surface, when boxed with borders to emphasize separation, are still visibly discrete elements. The composition of the elements on the board becomes an important factor in the design of the presentation.

A large board composed of smaller digitally created images is a common example of the application of discrete elements on a background. A variety of prints, whose size and type may be governed by availability of output devices and cost, often has to be placed on larger mounting surfaces.

Discrete images should not be pasted randomly on a board. When there is high contrast between discrete elements and the background on which they are mounted, the spacing should be sufficiently small so that there is no ambiguity in the figure-ground relationship between image and blank background. Although the images should be individually legible, they must also "hold together" graphically as a group. There should be a limited number of sizes of visibly discrete pieces that are mounted on a board. When multiple drawings are made directly on a sheet, a balanced composition should be created without sacrificing clarity. Checkerboard organizations (which include alternating line and shaded images, color and black and white, or image and blank space) are difficult compositions for the eye to focus on and should generally be avoided.

Composition of Multiple Sheets

There are a few guidelines that can be used to help organize multiple-sheet presentations (Box 6–G). It is important to have some degree of continuity across boards or sheets, and there are many ways that presentations can be organized. The images may be organized by shape and size across an entire presentation. Top and bottom borders, and/or horizontal divider lines, can organize a horizontal presentation. Zones of color or tone can also help to organize a presentation across boards. Grids, annotation, drawing style, and so on are among the variables available to the person designing the presentation (Fig. 6–36).

It may not always be within the architect's or designer's ability to guarantee that a presentation will be displayed in a certain way. Design competitions rarely afford the entrant an opportunity to control the way in which a project will be viewed. Although it is sometimes difficult to avoid images that must span across separate boards, the problem should be specifically avoided if it will be difficult to control the mounting of the presentation. Presentations that do not require a connected horizontal or vertical organization can be created as compositions of discrete boards. The cohesion of the presentation will occur at the level of style, format, and background. Although not a standard shape of board, squares are nondirectional (implying neither horizontal nor vertical composition) and can be an effective shape for a presentation that must be sufficiently flexible for mounting.

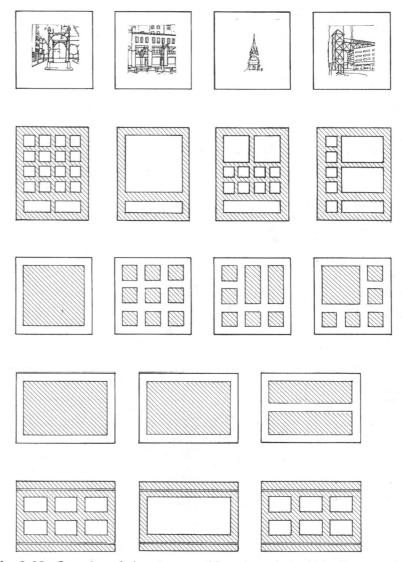

Fig. 6–36 Samples of sheet compositions based on grids. Top row has single image per square sheet.

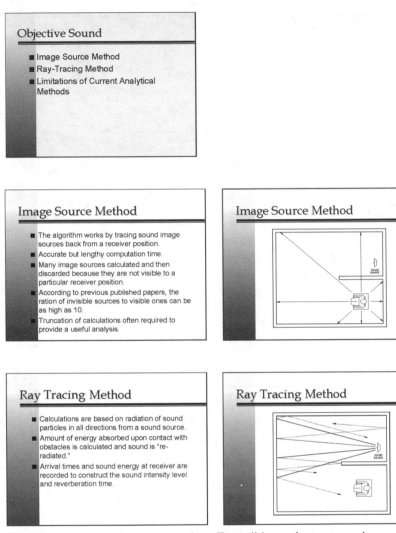

Fig. 6–37 Sequential presentation. Two slide projectors can be used to make presentations. After initial outline is presented, individual points are illustrated. Left and right slides always relate. Viewer in English-speaking regions will look at the slides from left to right. Similar organization may be applied with building designs, with orientation slide on left and detail slide on right. (*Presentation created with Microsoft PowerPoint. Screen shots reprinted with permission from Microsoft Corporation. The presentation illustrated above is from the ACADIA '94 presentation of "Digital Design in Architecture: First Light, Then Motion, and Now Sound."*)

6.4.2 Time-Dependent, Sequential Presentations

When the presentation is one utilizing multimedia, it should be organized in a sequence that leads the viewer through a project. Linear presentations must be particularly clear, because information is not usually visible long enough to allow detailed study. The presentation may consist of slides shown either by projecting traditional transparencies or by projecting an electronic slide presentation from a computer. In either case, going back and forth between images can disrupt the flow of the presentation and tends to create confusion—even when the individual images are clear (Fig. 6–37).

Each image or slide should be limited in the number of points being communicated. Diagrams preceding detailed drawings help the viewer understand proposed concepts. In dual-screen presentations, pieces of drawings may be shown on one side while the overall drawing may be projected (and held) on the other.

All plans of the project should be oriented in the same way. When plans are viewed for limited amounts of time, changes in orientation force viewers to constantly readjust their viewpoint and leave less opportunity to study the images.

Video or animation may be included in the presentation. In general, however, it should be placed appropriately. If at the beginning, it is used to "whet the appetite" of the viewer prior to giving more information. If in the middle, it can be used to illustrate specific points supported by images (either diagrams or architectural drawings) when they occur. If the animation is at the end of the presentation, it is used as a summary or conclusion providing a wrap-up of the information shown. Ending with a walk-through of an architectural project is an effective way of showing what a place may be like, after the presentation of orthographic projections and paraline drawings that show how the place is organized. Depending on the size of the audience, the animation may be shown with a projector or directly on screen.

It bears repeating that, ultimately, the presentations designers create have a purpose: communication. They must be clear, comprehensive, and compelling to be effective.

REVIEW QUESTIONS

1. What is *image processing*?

2. How can image processing help improve digital renderings created with automated processes?

3. What is the difference between a *dot screen* and *continuous tone*?

4. Describe *image sampling*.

5. What are some of the problems associated with scanning at either too low or too high a resolution for the intended purpose?

6. What are *dodge* and *burn* tools in image processing software? From what field did the names of the two commands come?

7. Increasing *contrast* can make an image look sharper. What can be lost?

8. What is the difference between *edge enhancement* and a global *sharpening* filter?

9. What is the importance of *image orientation* in a presentation?

10. Describe at least two ways a *multiple-sheet presentation* can be organized.

PRACTICE EXERCISES

1. Scan a photograph of an urban environment to modify. Create three new cityscape images reflecting the following:
   a. Increase or decrease of scale of the image or cityscape
   b. Introduction of a new focal point or change of focal point
   c. Depiction of a humorous or absurd situation or event (in a technically precise, photo-realistic manner)

2. Scan a rendering (or a photo of a rendering) created with traditional media and enhance and modify with digital media. Recreate the rendering, simulating a different medium such as charcoal, graphic or technical pen, and/or watercolor.

3. Using a rendering of the house created in the practice exercises for chapter 5, electronically transfer the building to another site. Use painting and image processing software only. Revise the image and *not* the model in order to create a new image. Strive for a visually seamless integration of the disparate components of the building and site to make the building look like it belongs on site.

4. Organize the various images and drawings created for the house used in previous exercises into a coherent presentation on boards.

IMAGE GALLERY

This image gallery contains color plates of digitally created images.

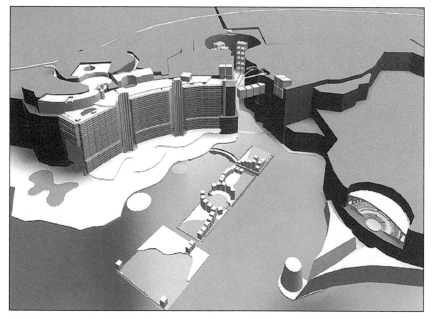

Hotel. *(Elli Shani, NJIT)*

Housing. *(Andrew Guzik, NJIT)*

Parlor. *(Copyright ©1994 A.J. Diamond, Donald Schmitt and Company, Toronto, Canada. Rendered with the Lightscape Visualization System, Lightscape Technologies, San Jose, CA.)*

Housing. *(Juan Diego Tome, NJIT)*

Housing. *(Ricardo Khan, NJIT)*

Museum. *(Paul DeStio, NJIT)*

Rendered model of Frank Lloyd Wright's Unity Temple. *(Copyright ©1994 Lightscape Technologies, Inc. Rendered with the Lightscape Visualization System, Lightscape Technologies, San Jose, CA.)*

Housing. *(Michael Buldo, NJIT)*

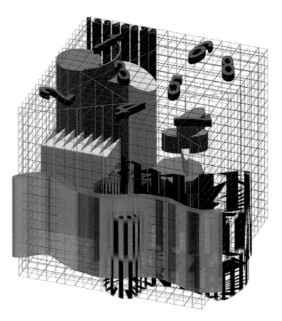

Grid composition. *(Christopher E. Perez, NJIT)*

Hotel. *(Eric Trepkau, NJIT)*

Housing. *(Marc W. Young, NJIT)*

278

Town Center. *(Mark Fernandez, NJIT)*

Painted (without scanning) facsimile and adaptation of *Landscape after a Poem by Tu Fu* by Tung Ch'i-ch'ang. *(Melanie Pakingan, NJIT)*

Set design for a proposed remake of *The Cabinet of Dr. Caligari. (Juan Diego Tome, NJIT)*

Painted (without scanning) facsimile of *The Arrival of the Normandy Train at the Gare Saint-Lazarre* (1877) by Claude Monet. *(Paul DeStio, NJIT)*

Set design for a proposed sequel to *Prospero's Books. (Kristen Brett Malak, NJIT)*

280

Hotel lobby. *(Copyright ©1995 Design Vision, Inc., Toronto, Canada. Rendered with the Lightscape Visualization System, Lightscape Technologies, Inc., San Jose, CA.)*

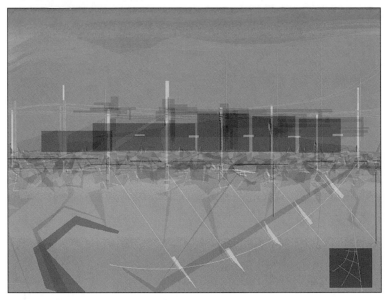

Collage. *(Amado Batour, NJIT)*

Model based on the Giovannitti House by Richard Meier. *(Clive Lonstein, University of Miami)*

Transportation terminal. *(Ricardo Khan, NJIT)*

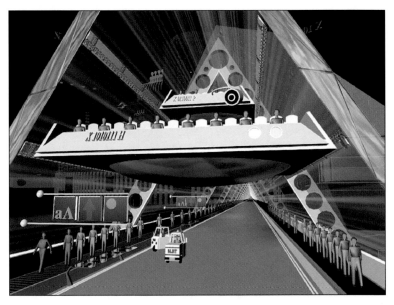

Set design for a proposed remake of *Metropolis. (Elli Shani, NJIT)*

GLOSSARY

The following list of terms is an eclectic and limited list. There are many other words and phrases that are relevant to design graphics. Words included here tend to have particular relevance to the subject of this book and/or have meanings in architectural graphics that are different from those expected by common use in English.

Adhesive-backed appliqué (*246*)—A thin film with an adhesive on one side for application onto a drawing. The appliqué may be patterned (grids, dots, etc.) on otherwise transparent film, or it may be solid with color or tone. Adhesive-backed appliqué may also be blank, suitable for use with copy machines and laser printers.

Aliasing (*206*)—Stair-step effect, or jaggies, seen in diagonal lines on monitors or raster output resulting from the orthogonal relationship of one pixel to another.

Anti-aliasing (*206*)—The averaging of adjacent pixel values along diagonal lines to blur the stair-step effect evident on monitors and raster output that results from the orthogonal relationship of one pixel to another.

Architectural object building (79)—The use of architecture-specific elements (doors, windows, walls, etc.) as primitives in the creation of three-dimensional models.

Array (command) (*85*)—The command that allows the creation of multiple copies of a shape or object at prescribed intervals.

Aspect ratio (image)—The proportion of horizontal length to vertical length of an image. Aspect ratios may refer either to actual length or to number of pixels in raster images.

Axonometric (*136*)—Paraline drawing with horizontal planes represented in scale without angular distortion. Also called plan oblique drawing.

Axonometric (Choisy or reverse) (*146*)—Axonometric drawing that looks at the object or space from underneath and projects vertical elements upwards. Named after August Choisy.

Barrel distortion (monitor) (*27*)—The bowing out of an image across the horizontal center of the monitor (geometrically similar to an old wooden barrel). The opposite of *pincushion* distortion.

Bézier curve (*59*)—A curve made up of multiple segments containing control points for modification. The curves are named after mathematician Pierre Bézier and may be nonuniform.

Bit (*26*)—Binary information (1 or 0, on or off, presence or lack of presence of a signal) that is the smallest unit of storage in a computer.

Boolean operation (*78*)—Software operation that allows for subtractive design (removing one element from another, resulting in openings or holes) based on a branch of mathematics developed by George Boole.

Brush pen (*9*)—Technical pen nib made like a brush to allow for easy creation of wide solid ink lines.

Burn (*254*)—A command used to darken an area of an image (term used by painting and image processing software that is borrowed from photography).

Butt cap (*62*)—End of a thick line segment that has square corners and whose outside edge is flush with the end of the defining segment.

Byte (*26*)—Eight bits of information. The standard of measurement for digital storage.

CAAD (*32*)—Acronym for computer-aided architectural design or computer-assisted architectural design.

CAD (*32*)—Acronym for computer-aided drafting, computer-aided design, or computer-assisted design.

CADD (*32*)—Acronym for computer-aided drafting and design or computer-assisted drafting and design.

CAE—Acronym for computer-aided engineering or computer-assisted engineering.

CAM—Acronym for computer-aided manufacturing or computer-assisted manufacturing.

Central processing unit (CPU) (*25*)—The principal chip(s) of the computer that, in part, determine(s) the speed and capabilities of the machine—it is responsible for much of the sorting of instructions and calculations (the "computing") in the computer.

Clipboard (*85*)—A predefined temporary file area used to store information while working on an application in order to recall the information later, and/or to facilitate transfer to another application capable of addressing the clipboard. Also commonly called a notebook.

Clipping plane (*169*)—A plane (usually parallel to the picture plane) that cuts off, or slices, information from a model and excludes it from an image.

Command line—The line on which keyboard input to an application may be made to enter either instructions (commands) or data.

Compass (*19*)—An instrument used for drawing circles or parts of circles with pen or pencil.

Contrast (*252*)—The degree to which relative values of tones (or pixels) in an image differ.

Digitizing tablet (*31*)—A pad connected to a computer that is configured, according to a particular set of instructions, so that contact at specific points on the tablet corresponds to instructions and/or places on the screen.

Distortion (monitor) (*27*)—The skewing or irregular display of an image such that geometry is not accurately displayed. Distortion types include *pincushion, barrel, skew,* and *trapezoid.*

Dithering—The creation of intermediate colors or shades of gray between two colors or shades that simulates a smooth transition of one color or shade to another in a raster image. Dithering algorithms are used extensively in creating files for printing when an image must be scaled down or up. Different algorithms are best suited for printing different images based on the printer, as well as the specific colors and patterns in an image (number of thin lines, sizes of polygons with flat colors, etc.).

Dodge (*254*)—A command used to lighten an area of an image (term used by painting and image processing software that is borrowed from photography).

Drafting film (*45*)—A dimensionally stable translucent material with at least one matte, nonglare side that is suitable for pen or pencil.

Edit (menu subgroup) (*84*)—A group of commands in a menu system that allows for image modification within the application.

Elevation (*111*)—(1) An image representing a vertical slice through the ground in front of, and looking at, the subject. Building elevations are flat views of the building face, or facade. Interior elevations are flat views of walls or other vertical surfaces inside a space. (2) Height above a defined horizontal base in a three-dimensional Cartesian coordinate system. The elevation may be relative (distance above the base or selected plane) or absolute (distance above a defined zero point).

Erasing shield (*15*)—Thin metal plate with holes of varying sizes that are used to expose portions of drawings that are to be erased, or removed, while protecting the rest.

Filter (*252*)—(1) An overlay that allows the application of various effects onto an image, either in whole or in part (term borrowed from photography and used to refer to digital effects in image processing and painting software). (2) A process that modifies a digital file and transforms, or translates, the file into a different format capable of being read by another application.

French curve (*21*)—Plastic or metal guide for irregular curves drawn by hand.

Full-bleed—Image printed on a page extending to the edges of the paper without any margins.

Gigabyte (*26*)—Abbreviated GB, 1 gigabyte = 1024 megabytes = 2^{30} bytes = 1,073,741,824 bytes (sometimes approximated as one thousand megabytes or one billion bytes).

Hot keys (*168*)—Keys, or buttons, on a keyboard that when struck (either individually or in a predefined sequence) activate a command within an application. The hot keys provide rapid shortcuts that often allow a bypass of an extensive menu system. The assignment of functions to any particular key is program specific.

Illustration board (*45*)—Thick board (frequently 1/16" or 3/32") with 100% rag facing suitable for both pencil and pen and used for presentation purposes.

Image sampling (*248*)—The use and combination of existing images, or fragments of images, to create new visual compositions, textures, patterns, and/or types of architecture.

Isometric (*140*)—Paraline drawing similar to plan oblique or axonometric with horizontal planes drawn to scale but without angular accuracy.

Kerning (*98*)—The spacing between letters that takes into account different widths of letters.

Kilobyte (*29*)—Abbreviated KB, 1 kilobyte = 2^{10} bytes = 1024 bytes (sometimes approximated as one thousand bytes).

Kinematics—The linking of objects around joints, or connection points, for the purpose of simulating motion in animation. Forward kinematics causes movement in downstream (child) components when an initial (parent) component is moved. Inverse kinematics moves the upstream component on a defined chain or path when a downstream component is moved.

Layer (*128*)—A primary subgroup of information defined, collected, and modifiable together within a CAD/graphics program. Layers management is an important component in organizing information when creating electronic drawings and models.

Leading (*98*)—The spacing, measured in points, between lines of text.

Line (*56*)—A one-dimensional element connecting two or more points.

Loft (*76*)—The process of extruding a shape along a defined path to create a three-dimensional model.

Mapping (*221*)—The application of a predefined texture or image onto a three-dimensional surface.

Megabyte (*29*)—Abbreviated MB, 1 megabyte = 1024 kilobytes = 2^{20} bytes = 1,048,576 bytes (sometimes approximated as one million bytes).

Menu (*41*)—A list of operations, visible on screen, from which a user can select a desired command.

Mesh (*77*)—Objects that are made up of common interconnected edges and vertices with polygonal (frequently triangular) faces.

Mirror (*87*)—A modifying command that creates a new element defined as the geometric reflection of the original image, model, or component about a user-selected axis.

Morphing (*96*)—The incremental transformation of one element into another.

Mouse (*31*)—A hand-held input device that is a central component of a graphic user interface (GUI) and that controls the cursor on screen. The mouse is operated (mechanically and/or optically) by moving it with the hand across a level surface.

Noise, visual (*258*)—The random addition of pixels with a different color or shade to a full-color or grayscale raster image.

Nonphoto blue leads (*8*)—Pencil leads whose marks do not show up on photographs of a drawing. Nonphoto blue leads are frequently used for layout of drawings on paper and drafting film.

Nonprint leads (*8*)—Pencil leads whose marks do not show up on diazo prints of a drawing. Nonprint leads are frequently used for layout of drawings on paper and drafting film.

Notebook (*85*)—A predefined temporary file area used to store information while working on an application in order to recall the information later, and/or to facilitate transfer to another application capable of addressing the notebook. Also commonly called a clipboard.

Oblique, elevation (*139*)—Paraline drawing in which a selected vertical face is drawn to scale with both measured and angular accuracy.

Oblique, plan (*136*)—Paraline drawing with horizontal planes represented in scale without angular distortion. Also commonly called axonometric drawing.

Orthographic projection (*110*)—Two-dimensional representation of three-dimensional objects in which the viewer's line of sight is perpendicular to the drawing plane, and representations of lines parallel to the drawing plane are shown without distortion—and are capable of being accurately measured.

Painting (*33*)—The use of raster, or bit-mapped, software applications to create two-dimensional images in which each pixel is given a color or shade of gray.

Pan (*88*)—To visually move across an image, to recenter the image on the screen.

Paraline drawings (*136*)—Drawings in which parallel lines in a space or object are drawn as parallel in the image itself, and in which vertical lines are drawn as verti-

cal. Lines parallel to the x, y, and/or z axes (in a Cartesian coordinate system) are created in accurate scale.

Parallel rule (*15*)—Straightedge held to a drawing board with guide wires that facilitates the manual drawing of horizontal straight lines parallel to the top or bottom of the paper, film, or board.

Pen, technical (*9*)—Device used in traditional drafting for applying ink to paper, film, or board with precise line thickness.

Perspective (*149*)—A two-dimensional representation (image) of a three-dimensional model that accurately reflects an observer's specific viewpoint and placement in relation to the space or object being described.

Pincushion distortion (monitor) (*27*)—The squeezing in of an image across the horizontal center of the monitor. The opposite of *barrel* distortion.

Pixel (*28*)—Picture element; individual dots of color that make up a raster image or display.

Plan (*116*)—A representation of a horizontal slice through a building and/or space.

Plan, furnished (*119*)—A floor plan including pictorial representations or conventions of furniture within the space.

Plan, reflected ceiling (*119*)—A plan showing the reflection of a ceiling created by having an imaginary mirror on the floor.

Plan, roof (*118*)—Orthographic projection of the top of a building. The horizontal slice used to define a plan is taken above and outside the building being represented.

Plan, site (*118*)—Orthographic projection of the top of a building and its surrounding area. The horizontal slice used to define a plan is taken above and outside the buildings being represented. Similar to roof plan but generally covers a larger area.

Poché (*124*)—The hatch pattern, or infill, of a line representing solid elements that have been cut through for the purpose of the drawing or image. (In architectural design, poché can also refer to those solid elements—either inaccessible or dedicated to service spaces—that exist in a three-dimensional design that define, or set off, primary volumes or spaces.)

Point (*56*) (*98*)—(1) A location in space that can be defined by three coordinates (x, y, and z) in a Cartesian coordinate system. (2) The size of a letter of text determined by measuring the maximum extension from the lowest letter to the highest letter in the alphabet. 72 points = 1″.

Posterization (*259*)—A graphic filter that reduces the number of colors or levels of gray in an image to a user-specified number.

Primitive (*65*)—Predefined shape or volume used as a building block for composite images in CAD/graphics applications.

Projecting square cap (*62*)—End of a thick line segment that has square corners and whose outside edge extends beyond the end of the defining segment.

Random access memory (RAM) (*25*)—Short-term operating storage and memory for running computer software. Memory is used for both application and files during operation. All information in RAM disappears when the power to the computer is turned off.

Raster image (*23*)—An image defined solely as a series of dots or pixels. The color and location of each pixel represent the only data associated with the image.

Rendering (*197*)—(1) An image enhanced with color, texture, tone, and/or shadow that expresses the nature of a proposed place or building. (2) An automated digital process that takes three-dimensional models and applies user-defined enhancements (either in color or shades of gray) to provide a more realistic view that may include representations of light, texture, materials (either literal or abstractions), and background.

Rescale (*88*)—To stretch (enlarge) or shrink (reduce) an element or image.

Rotation (*86*)—The turning of an element in an image or model (or an entire image or model) around a specified axis or axes.

Round cap (*62*)—Semicircular end of a thick line segment whose outermost point extends beyond the end of the defining segment.

Save (command) (*82*)—The command that stores the information currently being worked on in the active open file, overwriting the previously stored version.

Save as (command) (*82*)—The command that stores the information currently being worked on in a file on a specified medium (often, internal hard disk or other removable storage) in a user-defined location (drive). The command does not overwrite the current active file, which retains information present the last time it was saved. The command does overwrite an existing file with the same name and location as specified during the "save as" process.

Scale (*21*)—(1) When describing architecture, the representation of how big something is, or seems to be, in relation to something else—usually a known element like a person. (2) The proportional enlargement or reduction of an object or space for representation in drawing, image, or model form. (3) A drawing tool marked with precise graduations used for proportional representation.

Scanner (*30*)—A peripheral device used with a computer that takes pictures of items and converts them to two-dimensional electronic images on a pixel-by-pixel basis.

Section (*111*)—A representation of a vertical slice through an object, building, and/or space.

Serif (*99*)—Little tails on the ends of letters that improve the readability of the letters, in part by implying horizontal continuity.

Shade (surface) (*184*)—The absence of light on a surface of an object.

Shading (algorithm types) (*188*)—The processes by which a computer applies tones to represent light falling on and being absent from various surfaces of three-dimensional models.

Shape, irregular (*68*)—Noncircular closed curve or polygon whose sides or angles are not all equal. Irregular shapes include ellipses, rectangles, and trapezoids, as well as those shapes in which no two sides are equal or parallel.

Shape, regular (*64*)—Circle or polygon in which the defining line segments are all the same length, and the angles formed by the meeting segments (vertices) are all equal.

Skew (*87*)—To twist an element without regard to its principal axes.

Skew distortion (monitor)—The rotation of an image such that the sides of a rectangular image do not align with the outer edges of a rectangular monitor.

Snap (*60*)—A command that locks the cursor onto the nearest grid point, or other defined element, in order to place the exact location of the start or end of a drawing object.

Station point (*152*)—The height and location of the viewer's eye in perspective creation. It corresponds to *sight point*, *eye location*, and *camera location*.

Stereo vision (*191*)—Stereoscopic, or three-dimensional, views of a space or object that take into account the distance between the two eyes of an observer.

Stylus (*31*)—An input device that looks and feels much like a ballpoint pen.

Symbols (*41*)—Predesigned shapes or elements for repetitive use in drawings

T square (*15*)—Straightedge held to a drawing board with physical pressure (hand or arm) from the drafter that facilitates the manual drawing of horizontal straight lines parallel to the top or bottom of the paper, film, or board.

Template (*19*)—Stencil of predetermined shapes of objects that can be used to add the selected element to a drawing or image.

Terabyte—One terabyte = 1024 gigabytes = 2^{40} bytes = 1,099,511,627,776 bytes (sometimes approximated as one trillion bytes).

Trackball (*31*)—An input device that is conceptually an inverted mouse. Movement of the cursor on screen is accomplished by manually moving the ball.

Trapezoid distortion (monitor)—The pinching in of an image at either the top or bottom such that rectangular images do not appear to have the same horizontal lengths. (Rectangular or square images appear to have the geometric shape of a trapezoid.)

Triangle (*17*)—A three-sided closed geometric shape usually made of plastic that acts as a rule for vertical and angled lines in traditional drafting.

Triangle, adjustable (*17*)—A drafting triangle with a moveable leg that can be used as a guide for lines of any angle with the horizontal or vertical.

Tweaking (*95*)—Linear and incremental sequence of image or model modification.

Tweening (*95*)—The process of creating intermediate images at user-defined intervals between two extremes. Derived from the word *between*.

Twiddling (*94*)—Random application of commands or modifications to an image or model.

Vanishing point (*154*)—The location at which parallel lines give the appearance of convergence as they recede into the distance.

Vector image (*36*)—Image in which the lines, planes, and volumes are created and stored according to mathematical formulae that refer to coordinates in space (either two- or three-dimensional), and that is independent of the graphic resolution of the display device used for viewing.

Vellum (*45*)—White translucent paper suitable for use with pencil or pen, as well as some plotters and engineering copiers.

Wireframe (*181*)—The display of a three-dimensional model that appears to be created (only) out of thin lines, connected at points or vertices.

Zoom (*29*)—To reduce (*zoom out*) or enlarge (*zoom in*) the display of an image on screen.

BIBLIOGRAPHY

Albers, Josef. 1975. *Interaction of color.* New Haven, Conn.: Yale University Press.

Bacon, Edmund N. 1976. *Design of cities.* New York: Penguin Books.

Day, Jerry B. 1993. *Super scanning techniques: The Hewlett-Packard guide to black and white imaging.* New York: Random Books.

Duncan, Robert. 1986. *Architectural graphics and communication.* Dubuque, Iowa: Kendall/Hunt Publishing Company.

Goldman, Glenn, and Michael Hoon. 1994. Digital design in architecture: First light, then motion, and now sound. In *Reconnecting: Proceedings of the Association for Computer-Aided Design in Architecture Fourteenth Annual Conference,* eds. Anton Harfmann and Michael Fraser, 27–37. Cincinnati: ACADIA.

Goldman, Glenn, and M. Stephen Zdepski. 1990. Image sampling. In *Proceedings of the Association for Computer-Aided Design in Architecture Tenth Annual Conference: From Research to Practice,* ed. J. Peter Jordan, 21–28. Cincinnati: ACADIA.

Goldman, Glenn, and M. Stephen Zdepski. 1990. Twiddling, tweaking, and tweening: Automatic architecture. In *Proceedings of the Association of Collegiate Schools of Architecture Annual Conference: The Architecture of the In-between,* 98–107. Washington, D.C.: ACSA.

Goldman, Glenn, and M. Stephen Zdepski. 1988. Abstraction and representation: Computer graphics and architectural design. In *Proceedings of the Association for Computer-Aided Design in Architecture Eighth Annual Conference: Computing in Design Education,* ed. Pamela Hill, 205–215. Cincinnati: ACADIA.

Goldman, Glenn, and M. Stephen Zdepski. 1987. Form, color and movement. In *Proceedings of the Association for Computer-Aided Design in Architecture Seventh Annual Conference: Integrating Computers into the Architectural Curriculum,* ed. B.J. Novitski, 39–50. Cincinnati: ACADIA.

Hearn, Donald, and M. Pauline Baker. 1994. *Computer graphics.* Englewood Cliffs, N.J.: Prentice Hall.

Hegemann, Werner, and Elbert Peets. 1922. *The American Vitruvius: An architects' handbook of civil art.* New York: Architectural Book Publishing Co. (Reprinted with new prefatory matter in 1988 by Princeton Architectural Press in New York.)

Itten, Johannes. 1970. *The elements of color.* New York: Van Nostrand Reinhold.

Kerlow, Isaac Victor, and Judson Rosebush. 1994. *Computer graphics for designers and artists.* New York: Van Nostrand Reinhold.

Kliment, Stephen. 1984. *Architectural sketching and rendering: Techniques for designers and artists.* New York: Whitney Library of Design.

Martin, C. Leslie. 1968. *Design graphics.* New York: Macmillan Company.

McGarry, Richard, and Greg Madsen. 1993. *Magic marker: The rendering problem solver for designers.* New York: Van Nostrand Reinhold.

Mitchell, William J., Robin S. Liggett, and Thomas Kvan. 1987. *The art of computer graphics programming.* New York: Van Nostrand Reinhold.

Muller, Edward J., and James G. Fausett. 1993. *Architectural drawing and light construction.* Englewood Cliffs, N.J.: Prentice Hall.

Norman, Richard B. 1990. *Electronic color: The art of color applied to graphic computing.* New York: Van Nostrand Reinhold.

Porter, Tom. 1990. *Architectural drawing.* New York: Van Nostrand Reinhold.

Porter, Tom, and Sue Goodman. 1983. *Manual of graphic techniques.* New York: Charles Scribner's Sons.

Simmons, Gary. 1992. *The technical pen.* New York: Watson-Guptill Publications.

Manuals from the following software programs:

AccuRender™ by Robert McNeel and Associates
ArchiCAD® by Graphisoft® US, Inc.
AutoCAD® and *3D Studio*® by Autodesk®, Inc.
Canvas™ by Deneba Software
form•Z™ and *form•Z RenderZone*™ by auto•des•sys, Inc.
MegaMODEL by MegaCADD™, a division of Design Futures, Inc.
Fractal Design Painter® by Fractal Design Corporation
PhotoFinish® by Softkey International, Inc.
Adobe Photoshop™ and *PhotoStyler*® by Adobe Systems, Inc.
Picture Publisher® by Micrografx®, Inc.
upFRONT™ by SketchTech, Inc.
Visio® by Visio Corporation

TRADEMARKS AND ADDITIONAL CREDITS

Microsoft, Windows, Windows NT, and the Windows logo are either registered trademarks or trademarks of Microsoft Corporation in the United States and/or other countries. Apple and Macintosh are registered trademarks of Apple Computer, Inc. form•Z is a trademark of auto•des•sys, Inc. Autodesk, AutoCAD and 3D Studio are registered trademarks and DXF is a trademark of Autodesk, Inc. Lightscape and the Lightscape Visualization System are trademarks of Lightscape Technologies, Inc. KPT Convolver is a trademark and KPT is a registered trademark of MetaTools, Inc. Adobe is a registered trademark and Adobe Photoshop and Type Twister are trademarks of Adobe Systems, Inc. ArchiCAD and Graphisoft are registered trademarks of Graphisoft. Picture Publisher and Micrografx are registered trademarks of Micrografx, Inc. Fractal Design Painter is a registered trademark of Fractal Design Corporation. upFRONT is a trademark of SketchTech, Inc. Diazit is a registered trademark of Diazit Co., Inc. Lasergraphics is a trademark of Lasergraphics, Inc. Koh-I-Noor and radidograph are registered trademarks of Koh-I-Noor, Inc. Helvetica, Times Roman, and Univers are registered trademarks of Linotype-Hell AG and/or its subsidiaries. Monotype is a trademark of Monotype Typography Ltd. which may be registered in certain jurisdictions. Times New Roman is a trademark of The Monotype Corporation which may be registered in certain jurisdictions. Courier New is a trademark of The Monotype Corporation.

All trademarks, marked and not marked (including those listed above), as well as all product names and logos, are the property of their respective owners.

Screen shots of Microsoft Windows applications are reprinted with permission from Microsoft Corporation. Material in section 2.5 was adapted with permission from "Twiddling, Tweaking, and Tweening: Automatic Architecture," an article previously published by the Association of Collegiate Schools of Architecture.

INDEX